Reproduced by permission of The Sphere

The storming of the Tanga Pass, 7th January, 1898.
The 1st Battalion gaining the top.

THE QUEEN'S OWN ROYAL WEST KENT REGIMENT
1881 — 1914

By

Lieutenant-Colonel
H. D. CHAPLIN

THE REGIMENTAL HISTORY COMMITTEE

Published by

The Queen's Own
Regimental History Committee,
The Barracks,
Maidstone,
1959.

To the everlasting memory of the two hundred and nineteen members of The Queen's Own Royal West Kent Regiment who gave their lives on Active Service during the years 1881 — 1913.

FOREWORD

THIS part of the history of The Queen's Own follows in chronological order "The History of The 50th or The Queen's Own Regiment," by Colonel A. E. Fyler. It fills the gap between that history and Captain C. T. Atkinson's "The Queen's Own Royal West Kent Regiment, 1914 — 1919," which recorded the exploits of the Regiment in the first World War. This volume has been written by Lieutenant-Colonel H. D. Chaplin, whose history of the Regiment between 1920 and 1950 brought our story up to date. The Regiment is therefore very much in his debt.

The present book takes us back to the days when British County Regiments were formed, to the time when the Infantry was first given fixed Depots and definite Recruiting Areas. It opens with a description of how The 50th Foot, The 97th Foot, the West Kent Light Infantry Militia and three corps of Kent Volunteers were united to form The Queen's Own Royal West Kent Regiment. It goes on to show how the Regiment was constructed, was modernised, and was made ready for battle in the greatest war which till then had been fought.

During this period The Queen's Own fought in Egypt in 1882, on the Punjab Frontier in 1897—1898, and in South Africa from 1900 till 1902. It also took part in two military expeditions, the one to rescue General Gordon from Khartoum and the other in the hinterland of the Aden Protectorate. A number of individuals also fought in East and West Africa. In these campaigns 219 members of the Regiment lost their lives. Of these, 22 were killed in action or died of wounds, and the deaths of 12 were caused by accident. The remainder succumbed to disease. The names of those who fell on active service have been inscribed on memorials and plaques in All Saints' Church, Maidstone.

Perhaps the most pleasing features of this part of the story of The Queen's Own are the commendable way in which The 50th and The

97th accepted amalgamation, the speed with which the Regulars and the Auxiliaries merged into a homogeneous organisation, the important part played by the Volunteers in the life of the Regiment, and the close comradeship that existed among all ranks and all battalions.

Today we face another change, a further amalgamation. Our forebears set a fine example in such matters, as in many others. We can do no better than follow their example.

Lieutenant-General.
Colonel The Queen's Own Royal West Kent Regiment.

October, 1958.

PREFACE

BRITISH County Regiments were formed in 1881. Yet their story really begins in 1873, when the Infantry of the Line was "localised." By this scheme the British Isles were divided into infantry sub-districts, to each of which were assigned either two single-battalion regiments or one regiment of two battalions. Normally these military areas corresponded to the existing counties. Exceptionally, as in Kent and Surrey, Lancashire and Yorkshire, counties were divided into two or more sub-districts. In this way Regimental Recruiting Areas were for the first time clearly defined. The most far-reaching part of the scheme was the establishment of Depot centres — one to each sub-district. These gave regiments a fixed Home, which till then they had lacked.

Kent was divided into two areas, known as Nos. 45 and 46 Sub-districts. The boundary between them was not the River Medway, which separates East from West Kent, but an arbitrary line some distance east of it. Thus the Men of Kent who lived in such places as Tunbridge Wells, Sutton Valence and Hollingbourne, found themselves militarily in the camp of the Kentish Men.

The Depot of No. 46 (West Kent) Sub-district was established in the barracks which stood on the verge of the River Medway at Maidstone. In 1881 this Depot became the Home of The Queen's Own (Royal West Kent Regiment). As time went by the Old Colours of the Regiment and the Regimental Memorials were placed within the walls of the neighbouring Church of All Saints. This Shrine is a permanent link with the Past.

The recruiting area of The Queen's Own (Royal West Kent Regiment) included several of the boroughs of South-East London. At first some people may have doubted whether the Londoners would blend with the Kentish Men. There need have been no concern. From the start all ranks set out resolutely to establish honourable traditions for their Regiment. That they succeeded will be manifest as their story unfolds.

The frame of the story has been constructed from the Orderly Room Records of the Line battalions of the Regiment. The picture has been painted with details gleaned from the pages of the Regimental Journal, "The Queen's Own Gazette." Further details have been gathered from the dwindling number of survivors who witnessed the events described. The historical background was obtained from the books listed under "Acknowledgments."

In order to save space, initials have as a ule been given in the text only to distinguish individuals with the same name. They can be found, if required, in the Personal Index at the end of the volume. Battles and other important events can be readily traced by reference to the chapter summaries in the table of Contents.

During my research, I have found some errors in other works concerning the history of the Regiment. The necessary amendments are in Appendix F.

H. D. CHAPLIN.

ACKNOWLEDGMENTS

IN order to obtain the background for this history I have consulted the following works, to the authors and publishers of which I am indebted: —

The Egyptian Campaign, 1882 — 1885, by Charles Royle (Hurst and Blackett).

The Campaign of 1882 in Egypt, by Colonel J. F. Maurice (H.M.S.O.).

History of The Sudan Campaign, by Colonel H. E. Colvile (H.M.S.O.).

With The Camel Corps Up The Nile, by Count Gleichen (Chapman and Hall Ltd.).

The Royal Engineers in Egypt and The Sudan, by Lieutenant-Colonel E. W. C. Sandes (Institution of Royal Engineers).

The Malakand Field Force, 1897, by Winston L. Spencer Churchill (Longmans, Green and Co.).

The Operations of The Malakand Field Force and The Buner Field Force, 1897 — 98, by Captain H. F. Walters (Government Central Printing Office, Simla).

A Frontier Campaign, by P. C. Eliott-Lockhart and Fincastle (Methuen and Co.).

History of The War in South Africa, 1899 — 1902, by Major-General Sir Frederick Maurice and Captain M. H. Grant (Hurst and Blackett).

The Great Boer War, by Arthur Conan Doyle (Thomas Nelson and Sons).

With 8th Division in South Africa, by E. C. Moffett (Knapp, Drewett and Sons).

The Development of The British Army, 1899 — 1914, by Colonel J. K. Dunlop (Methuen and Co.).

His Majesty's Territorial Army, by Walter Richards (Virtue and Co.).

The Mutiny at The Curragh, by A. P. Ryan (Macmillan).

I desire to record my thanks to the Staff of the War Office Library, in particular to Mr. C. A. Potts, for kind and courteous assistance during my research; and to the Director of Military Survey for reproducing the maps.

Finally, I would like to express my gratitude to all those members of The Queen's Own Past and Present Association who have given me information and help. Of these I would especially mention Major-General R. A. Riddell, C.B.E., who criticised the first draft of this work and did much of the research for Appendix B; and Lieutenant-Colonel H. N. Edwards, M.B.E., D.L., to whose Medal Rolls I referred while compiling Appendices C and D and the Roll of Honour.

CONTENTS

CHAPTER   PAGE

1. THE ORIGINS OF THE REGIMENT, 1756 — 1881.   1
    The Localisation of the Forces in 1873: No. 46 (West Kent) Sub-district: Depot Established at Maidstone. — *The 50th Foot*: Its Association with West Kent: Its Campaigns: Becomes a Royal Regiment: At Colchester in 1881. — *The 97th Foot*: Its Campaigns: Joins the Natal Field Force in 1881. — *The West Kent Light Infantry Militia*: Headquarters Transferred to No. 46 Sub-district Depot: Augmentation: Presentation of Colours to its 2nd Battalion. — *The Rifle Volunteers*: Lay-out of the Corps in West Kent.

2. CONSTRUCTION, 1881 — 1886.   8
    The Formation of The Queen's Own (Royal West Kent Regiment): Badges, Devices and Facings: The Colours: Battle Honours: Regimental Marches: The Colonel of The Regiment: " The Queen's Own Gazette ": Colours for Games: 50th Regimental District: The Regimental Depot. — *1st Battalion* at Aldershot: The Royal Review: Mobilization: Inspection by Queen Victoria: Sails for Egypt. — *2nd Battalion* at Dublin: Civil Unrest: Moves to the Curragh: The Mounted Infantry Contingent: Moves to Chatham. — *3rd and 4th Battalions (Militia)*: Annual Training: The Honorary Colonel. — *The Volunteer Battalions*: Organisation: Compulsory Drills: Camps. — *Laying-up of Colours* (50th and 97th Foot).

3. EGYPT AND THE SUDAN, August 1882 — June 1886.   20
    1ST BATTALION AND A CONTINGENT FROM THE 2ND
    The Situation in Egypt: The Expeditionary Force: The Feint at Aboukir; The Landing at Ismailia: Occupation of Nefisha: Advance to Qassassin: The Battle of Tel-el-Kebir: The Army of Occupation: Cyprus: The Gordon Relief

Expedition: The Journey up the Nile: Arrival at Korti: The Desert Column Rides to Mettemmeh: Gordon's Death: The Desert Column Reinforced: Withdrawal to Korti: Summer Quarters: Return of the Expedition: The Sudan Frontier Force: Ambigol Wells: The Battle of Ginnis: Alexandria: Departure from Egypt.

4. DEVELOPMENT, 1886 — 1899.   42

Battle Honours: Esprit de Corps: 1882-86 Memorial: General Fowler Burton: "The Queen's Own Gazette": The Lee-Metford Magazine Rifle: The Punjab Frontier Memorial: Successes at Sport. — *1st Battalion* arrives at Gibraltar: Presentation of Medals: Officers' Ball: Sails to Malta: Quarters: Training and Recreation: Sails to India: Meerut and Chakrata: Training: Moves to Peshawar: Ordered on Active Service. — *2nd Battalion* at Chatham: Military Life in Kent: Entrains for Portland: Sport in Dorsetshire: Moves to Shorncliffe: Presentation of New Colours; Moves to Northern Ireland: Enniskillen, Londonderry and Belturbet: Wins the Army Football Cup: Entrains for Dublin: Ceremonial Occasions: Range Courses at Kilbride: Manoeuvres in England: Chatham Again: A Recruiting March: Ordered Overseas. — *The Militia Battalions:* Annual Training at Shorncliffe, Lydd and Chattenden: Queen Victoria's Diamond Jubilee: Amalgamation. — *The Volunteer Battalions:* Annual Camps and Inspections: Week-End Exercises: A Drill Hall Opened at Woolwich: Re-organisation.

5. THE FIRST BATTALION IN THE PUNJAB FRONTIER CAMPAIGN AND THE ADEN EXPEDITION, July 1897 — November 1902.   56

The Rising of the Hill Tribes: Assembly of The Malakand Field Force: The Action at Landakai: Pacification of the Swat Valley: The Expedition against the Mohmands: The Engagement at Agrah and Ghat: The Skirmish at Badalai: Submission of the Tribesmen: The Buner Field Force: The Capture of the Tanga Pass: The Pacification of the Bunerwals: The Battalion Moves to Dum Dum: Presentation of Medals: Sails from Calcutta to Rangoon: Ordered to Aden: Crater Camp and Steamer Point: Fever and Plague: The Ad Daraijah Expedition: Sails to Malta: Nine Months on the Island: Departs for England.

6. THE WAR IN SOUTH AFRICA, September 1899 — November 1902.   73

      2ND BATTALION AND THE 1ST, 2ND AND 3RD
         VOLUNTEER ACTIVE SERVICE COMPANIES

The 2nd Battalion at Alexandria: Ordered Home to

Mobilize: Sails to South Africa: Joins Rundle's Division: In Action at Wakkerstroom: Thaba'nchu: The Battle of Biddulphs Berg: Hammonia and Ficksburg: The Boers Encircled: De Wet Escapes: Prinsloo's Surrender: "Rundle's Greyhounds": A Respite at Harrismith: The Defence of Frankfort: Raids: Enteric Fever: The Evacuation of Frankfort: Heilbron: Colonel William's Column: Railway Protection Duties: The M.I. Company Joins Western's Column: The Hunt for Louis Botha: The Heilbron — Tafel Kop Blockhouse Line: "Drives" to Round-up De Wet: End of the War: The 2nd Battalion Sails to Ceylon: Medals and Clasps: Operations of the M.I. Company.

7. THE HOME FRONT IN ENGLAND AND MALTA, October 1899 — November 1902.　　　　　　　　　　102

A Surge of Patriotism: Difficulties at the Depot: Comforts for the Troops: Death of Queen Victoria: Coronation of Edward VII: The Details at Shorncliffe. — *3rd Battalion* embodied: Sails to Malta: Training: Celebrations: Trooping the Colour: The Queen's Birthday Ceremony: An M.I. Contingent Embarks: The Return to England: Presentation of Medals. — *Volunteer Battalions:* Expansion and Training: The 1st Active Service Company Leaves for South Africa: Departure of the 2nd and 3rd Active Service Companies: Return of the Active Service Companies: Presentation of Medals: The Formation of the 4th Volunteer Battalion.

8. MODERNISATION, November 1902 — December 1908.　　111

Memorials for the South African War: Battle Honours: The Short Lee-Enfield Rifle: Adoption of Service Dress: Re-organisation of the Army: The Regimental Compassionate Fund: The Association of Sergeants: General Leach: Successes at Sport. — *The Regimental Depot:* Grouped Regimental Districts: Depot Commanders Appointed: Welfare and Recreation. — *The Details at Dover.* — *1st Battalion* at Shorncliffe: Liaison with Auxiliaries: Moves to Malta: Quartered at Floriana: Training: Boxing: Memorial: Returns to England: Grand Shaft Barracks, Dover: Ceremonial Occasions: Training and Sport. — *2nd Battalion* in Ceylon: Diyatalawa, Trincomalee and Kandy: Echelon Barracks, Colombo: Presentation of Medals: Shooting Trophies: Moves to China: Peking, Tientsin and Hong Kong: Sails to Singapore: Tanglin Barracks: Training: Officers v. Sergeants: Sails for India. — *3rd Battalion (Militia):* Its Last Years: Becomes The 3rd Battalion (Reserve). — *The Volunteer Battalions:* The West Kent Volunteer Brigade: A Drill Hall at Chatham: Formation of The Territorial Force: The End of the 2nd Volunteer Battalion.

9. ON THE VERGE, January 1909 — August 1914. 126
Laying-up of Old Colours: Death of King Edward VII: Coronation of King George V: The Old Comrades' Association: Alliance with The 1st (Canterbury) Regiment: Issue of Web Equipment: War Declared: Successes at Sport. — *The Regimental Depot* amalgamated with the 3rd Battalion (Reserve): Numerous Recruits. — *1st Battalion* at Dover: Presentation of Colours: Moves to Bordon: Training in the Aldershot Command: Memorial to Queen Victoria: The Royal Drives through London: The Railway Strike: Moves to Dublin: Richmond Barracks: Labour Unrest: Re-organisation: Boxing: Leaves for Active Service. — *2nd Battalion* disembarks at Calcutta: Goes to Lebong: Detachment at Barrackpore: Two Visits to Calcutta: Unites at Peshawar: Roberts' Barracks: Cherat: Wins the Delhi Durbar Boxing Cup: Moves to Multan: Dalhousie: Outbreak of War. — *3rd Battalion (Reserve):* Annual Training: Presentation of Colours: Laying-up of Militia Colours: Mobilization. — *Territorial Battalions:* Their Organisation: 6th (Cyclist) Battalion Leaves the Regiment: Presentation of Colours: Drill Halls at Tonbridge and Maidstone: 1914 Manoeuvres: Embodiment. — *Conclusion.*

ROLL OF HONOUR 141

BIBLIOGRAPHY 150

APPENDICES
A. Badges and Devices Adopted in 1881. 151
B. Roll of Colonels and Commanding Officers. 152
C. Lists of Officers in Campaigns. 157
CC. Officers With the 3rd Battalion in Malta. 161
D. Honours and Awards. 162
E. Presentation of Colours to The 20th London. 167
F. Errata in Other Works Concerning the Regiment. 168

INDEX 170

MAPS AND SKETCHES

KENT	*facing page*	2
LOWER EGYPT		21
THE NILE		31
THE NILE, Wadi Halfa to Khartoum		33
THE PUNJAB FRONTIER		57
THE ACTION AT AGRAH		61
THE ACTION AT AD DARAIJAH		69
THE ORANGE RIVER COLONY		75
THE SOUTHERN TRANSVAAL		85
THE EASTERN TRANSVAAL		93

CHAPTER 1

THE ORIGINS OF THE REGIMENT
1756—1881

1. The Localization of the Forces in 1873

THE localization of the military forces of Great Britain and Ireland took place on April 1, 1873. The British Isles were divided into 66 Infantry and 12 Artillery Sub-districts. To each Infantry Sub-district were assigned two battalions of Infantry of the Line. These battalions were linked together for the purposes of enlistment and service, but, if they belonged to different regiments, retained their distinctive number and uniform. They functioned as one corps, in three separate bodies: one battalion abroad; one battalion for Home service; and a Depot centre[1]. The essence of the scheme was the establishment of Depot Centres, which set up a machinery for the enlistment and training of recruits in their own locality. They also provided a connection between the Regular and Auxiliary forces in the Sub-districts.

The Depot Centre, the Militia and the Volunteer Corps in each Sub-district constituted a brigade. This was under the supervision of a lieutenant-colonel or brevet-colonel. The duties of this officer embraced the training and inspection of the Auxiliary and Reserve forces in his brigade; the superintendence of recruiting both for the Line and the Militia; and the charge of the arms and stores at the Depot Centre.

Kent was divided into two Infantry Sub-districts: No. 45 (East Kent) and No. 46 (West Kent). To the West Kent Sub-district were assigned The 50th or The Queen's Own Regiment and The 97th or Earl of Ulster's Regiment, both of which, at that time, were single-battalion

[1] This was known as "The Cardwell System" because Lord Cardwell, then Secretary of State for War, was its originator. The Foot Guards, the 60th Rifles and the Rifle Brigade were outside this organisation.

regiments. The Auxiliary forces in 46th Sub-district were the West Kent Light Infantry Militia and the 1st, 2nd and 3rd Administrative Battalions of Kent Rifle Volunteers.

46th Brigade Depot was established at Maidstone on August 1, 1874. On that date the Depot Companies — I and K — of both The 50th and The 97th moved there from Colchester, where The 50th was then stationed. The barracks occupied by 46th Brigade Depot were known as the Cavalry Barracks. They had been completed in 1797. The first occupants were The 7th Light Dragoons, by whom the trees round the square, which are grouped in sevens, were planted. These barracks had later been used as a Cavalry Depot. In order to make them suitable for Infantry, the stables were converted into married quarters and the riding school (built in 1861) into a drill-shed.

2. *The 50th or The Queen's Own Regiment*

The 50th Foot had been formed in notable circumstances. In December 1755 the threat of French domination caused the standing army of the United Kingdom to be increased by 10 Regiments of the Line. The first of these additional units was The 52nd Foot, which was raised under a Royal Warrant dated January 7, 1756. In December of the same year The 50th and 51st Regiments were disbanded, whereupon The 52nd was re-numbered The 50th.

The first campaign of The 50th Foot was in Germany during the Seven Years' War. In 1778 it fought as Marines in the action against the French off Ushant. The practice of piping the men of the Regiment to dinners is probably a link with this naval event.

While The 50th was encamped at Rame, near Plymouth, in August 1782, the Colonel of the Regiment received from the War Office a letter which stated that His Majesty King George III was "pleased to order that The 50th Regiment of Foot, which you command, should take the county name of The 50th or West Kent Regiment, and be looked upon as attached to that division of the county . . ." At that time the Colonel of the Regiment was Lieutenant-General Sir Thomas Spencer Wilson, Bart., whose seat was Charlton Court, near Woolwich. It was because of this that the association with West Kent appears to have originated.

The 50th or West Kent Regiment was with the expedition which expelled the French from the island of Corsica in 1794. During this campaign a combined force, the naval part of which was commanded by Captain (later Admiral Lord) Horatio Nelson, captured Calvi after a siege of some six weeks. The 50th was thus one of the few regiments which served with the great admiral on land.

The next enterprise of The 50th was in 1801, when it served with Sir Ralph Abercrombie's expedition to Egypt. The casualties in battle were few. But so many of the Regiment suffered from ophthalmia, a disease which caused temporary or even permanent loss of sight, that it was given the nickname "The Blind Half-Hundred."

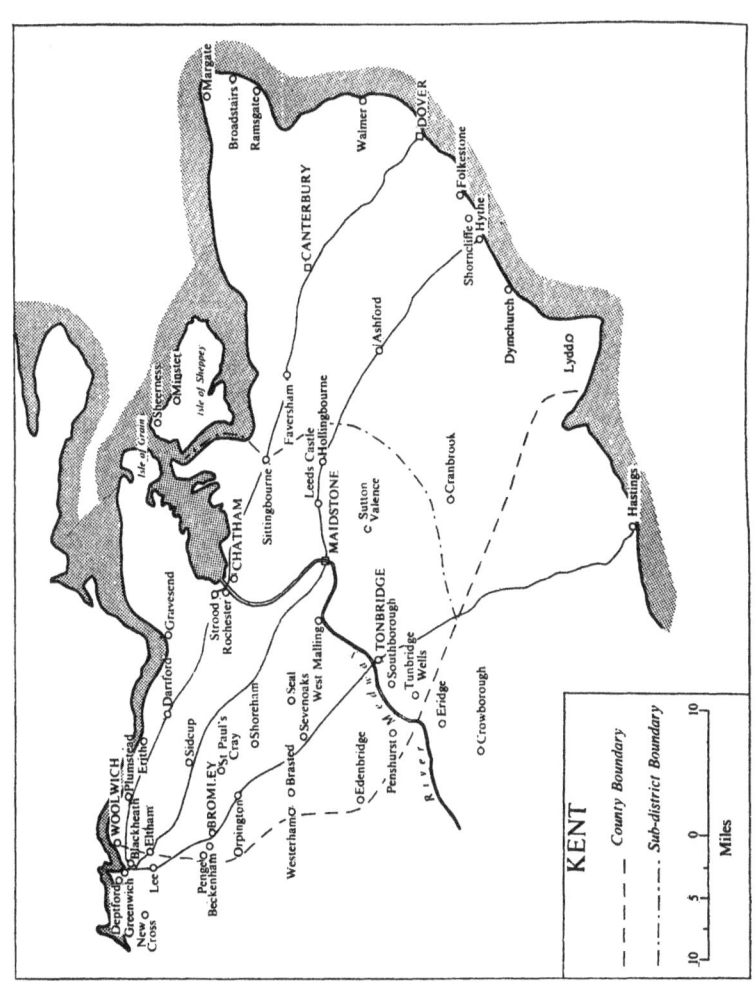

During the Peninsular War the Regiment fought in many of the great battles, the most notable being Vimiera, Corunna, Vittoria and St. Pierre. At Corunna The 50th advanced and recaptured the village of Elvina. Riding behind them, Sir John Moore exclaimed "Well done, 50th ! Well done, my Majors ! " The officers he referred to were Major (later General Sir Charles) Napier and Major Stanhope, who led the counter-attack. To commemorate this event it became the custom of the officers of the Regiment to toast " The Corunna Majors ! " on the anniversary of the battle. The nickname " The Dirty Half-Hundred " was given to The 50th during this war, probably because the dye came off the black cuffs of the troops when they wiped their faces in " sweating times." When recalling the Battle of Vimiera, The Duke of Wellington is reputed to have said " The enemy were first met by The 50th, not a good-looking Regiment but devilish steady . . ."

In 1827, soon after The 50th or West Kent Regiment had been presented with new Colours by The Duke of Clarence, the title was changed to The 50th or Duke of Clarence's Regiment. This designation was short-lived, for when the Duke had come to the throne as King William IV, the following letter was addressed to the Commanding Officer by the Adjutant-General: —

"Horse Guards, 22nd January, 1831.

Sir,

I have the honour to acquaint you by direction of the General Commanding-in-Chief that His Majesty has been pleased to command that the 50th Regiment shall in future be styled The 50th or " The Queen's Own " instead of " Duke of Clarence's " Regiment, and that the facings of the Regiment be accordingly changed from black to blue."

The facings were changed from black to blue because The 50th had now become a Royal Regiment. By special permission the officers were authorised to retain velvet as the cloth for their facings.

The 50th or The Queen's Own Regiment arrived in India in 1841. During its tour of duty in that country it took part in the Gwalior and Sutlej Campaigns. Then, after a few years at Home, it fought in the Crimea, where it was present at all the major battles except Balaclava. Its last campaign was in New Zealand from 1863 to 1866.

When the localization of the forces took place The 50th was stationed at Colchester. On November 4, 1873, the Depot Companies of The 97th arrived for attachment. Having sent these, together with its own I and K Companies, to Maidstone, the Regiment embarked at Tilbury on August 4, 1874, for passage to Ireland. The first batch of recruits from 46th Brigade Depot was received in March 1875. Drafts of trained men were sent to The 97th, which was then overseas, from October 1876 onwards. " Before many years," observed a correspondent in the Regimental Journal, " The 97th will be entirely composed of men who have passed through our ranks, and, in time, we shall learn to look upon it as our Second Battalion."

The 50th or The Queen's Own Regiment moved from Ireland to Edinburgh in February 1878, and from there to Colchester in March 1880. It was during this second tour at Colchester that The 50th and The 97th did in fact become battalions of the same regiment.

3. The 97th or Earl of Ulster's Regiment

The 97th Regiment, with which we are concerned, was placed upon the establishment of the Army from March 25, 1824, inclusive. The personnel assembled at Winchester. In September 1826 King George IV approved of the title The 97th or Earl of Ulster's Regiment. In the following month the Regiment was given permission to bear the motto *Quo Fas et Gloria Ducunt.* Owing to its sky blue facings The 97th was nicknamed " The Celestials."

The first campaign of The 97th was in the Crimea. It landed at Balaclava in November 1854 and took a prominent part in the Siege of Sevastopol. During the recapture of a sap, Sergeant John Coleman won the Victoria Cross for bringing in an officer who had been wounded. In the final assault on the Great Redan, Captain Charles Henry Lumley gained a Victoria Cross for outstanding leadership. A memorial to those of the Regiment who were killed in this war is in Winchester Cathedral.

During the Indian Mutiny The 97th marched with a Field Force from Benares in January 1858. Having driven some rebels from a strong position at Sultanpore, the Column joined the army of Sir Colin Campbell before Lucknow and assisted in the recapture of that city.

When The 97th or Earl of Ulster's Regiment became linked with The 50th, it was stationed in Dublin. In November 1873, a few days after I and K Companies had been sent for attachment to The 50th, the bulk of the Regiment embarked for the West Indies. The first draft from 46th Brigade Depot joined in Bermuda early in 1876. Thereafter, drafts of replacements came from The 50th.

The 97th left the West Indies in December 1876 for a tour of four years at Halifax, Nova Scotia. It arrived at Gibraltar on December 12, 1880. Within a week the Regiment was placed under orders for active service in South Africa. It sailed on December 27 and disembarked at Durban on February 4, 1881. From Durban The 97th proceeded inland to Newcastle to join the Natal Field Force. On March 7, before the Regiment could go into action, an armistice was signed with the Boers.

Four months later The 97th or Earl of Ulster's Regiment, as such, ceased to exist.

4. The West Kent Light Infantry Militia

The origin of the Militia as an organised national force dates back to Saxon days. The conditions of service varied from time to time, but the general principle was that the men were raised by ballot, each county providing a specified quota. After the Waterloo Campaign the significance of the force lapsed, and the staffs were greatly reduced.

The Militia was modernised and placed on a voluntary basis in 1852. The new regulations stated that the force could be embodied for service in the United Kingdom whenever a state of war existed or at any time of great national emergency. The men were to enlist for six years and might re-engage for another six. Commissions were to be granted to officers in the same manner as if they were Regulars. Training was to be carried out annually for 21 days. The pay during training or embodiment was to be the same as for the Regular Army. The uniform was to be similar to that of the Line, but silver lace was substituted for gold.

The quota fixed for the West Kent Militia was 1,000 privates. These were obtained without difficulty. The Permanent Staff included an Adjutant, an R.S.M. and an R.Q.M.S., who were ex-Regulars. Headquarters, which, as before, were at Maidstone, were established in 1856 or 1857 in the Militia Barracks recently built in Union Street.

The West Kent Militia became a Light Infantry Regiment on February 7, 1853, with an establishment of 10 companies. Henceforth it was styled The West Kent Light Infantry Militia. Its facings remained Kentish grey in colour.

Except for the period of the Crimean War, when it was embodied and served in Ireland, the Regiment assembled only for annual training. During the remainder of the year the personnel lived at home, carried on with their civilian occupations and performed no drills. Training normally took place at Maidstone. The men were accommodated in the Militia Barracks or in billets in the town; the officers lived and messed in the Star Hotel. Many of the parades and inspections were held on the square of the Cavalry Barracks. Sham fights were carried out in Mote Park or on Penenden Heath. The recruits assembled some weeks before the trained men so that they could be put through their preliminary drills before the rest of the personnel arrived.

The Militia Barracks were used for the last time in 1875. After annual training that year the orderly-room, stores and property were transferred to 46th Brigade Depot, where the Headquarters of The West Kent Light Infantry Militia were then established. The Militia Barracks were subsequently converted into private houses.

In May 1876 The West Kent Light Infantry Militia expanded to two battalions of six companies each. The Commanding Officer of the 1st Battalion became Lieutenant-Colonel Commandant; the senior major was promoted to take command of the 2nd.

Both battalions assembled at Maidstone for training on October 15, 1877. The Officers' Mess was in a marquee pitched in a corner of 46th Brigade Depot square, an arrangement which proved rather chilly at that time of the year. On October 30, Colours were presented to the newly-formed 2nd Battalion on the Square by Lady Sydney, wife of the Lord Lieutenant of Kent. Afterwards the officers entertained their friends at luncheon in the mess marquee.

During the training periods of 1878, 1879 and 1880 the other ranks of both battalions were accommodated at 46th Brigade Depot, partly in the drill-shed and partly in tents on the barrack field. The Officers' Mess was in the Assembly Rooms, which stood opposite the entrance to the Depot.

The important changes in the title, uniform and training of The West Kent Light Infantry Militia, which occurred in 1881, are dealt with in the next chapter.

5. *The Rifle Volunteers*

Although Volunteer units existed during earlier periods of national peril, they were not recognised by Act of Parliament until 1794, when an invasion by France seemed to be imminent. Among the corps raised for that emergency were the Blackheath Cavalry, the Maidstone Volunteer Infantry Regiment, and a Volunteer contingent at Bromley. The last two were formed in 1798. The Loyal Greenwich Water Fencibles, which were trained to convey troops on the River Thames, were raised in 1803[1].

With the abdication of Napoleon in 1814 the period of danger came to an end. Parliament voted its thanks to the Volunteers for their services, and many of the units were disbanded. Some of them remained in existence as Rifle Clubs.

In 1859, after the Crimean War, an Act of Parliament authorised the formation of Rifle Volunteer Corps. These were numbered in each county according to the date of their formation. They chose their own uniform, provided their own arms and equipment, and defrayed all expenses except when called upon for active service. The members were not subject to military law. The officers received their commissions from the Lord Lieutenant of the County. In some towns the Corps were strong enough to constitute a battalion, but the usual arrangement was that a number of Corps were grouped by localities into Administrative Battalions, each Corps remaining independent except for the purposes of administration and drill.

The Rifle Volunteer Corps were usually the outcome of inaugural meetings, which took place in such halls as the Assembly Rooms of the Green Man Hotel at Blackheath. Typical of these meetings was that held at Maidstone on August 29, 1859. Many well-known personages were present. It was decided that enrolment should begin forthwith, and that drills should be carried out at the Grammar School or on the square of the Militia Barracks on two mornings and two evenings a week. Lord Romney offered a piece of ground in Mote Park for use as a rifle range.

In Kent the Rifle Volunteer Corps were grouped into five

---

[1] The Standard of the Blackheath Cavalry, and two drums used by the Greenwich Fencibles, are now in Holly Hedge House, Blackheath (See Chapter 4, Section 5). The drums are known as "The Nelson Drums" because they were piled about the coffin of Lord Nelson when he lay in state in 1805 in the Painted Hall of Greenwich Hospital (now the Royal Naval College).

THE ORIGINS OF THE REGIMENT

Administrative Battalions. The 1st had its Headquarters at Blackheath; the 2nd at Tonbridge; the 3rd at Maidstone; the 4th at Canterbury; and the 5th at Cranbrook. When the county was divided into two Infantry Sub-districts in April 1873, the 1st, 2nd and 3rd Administrative Battalions were included in No. 46, and the 4th and 5th in No. 45 Sub-district. The Corps in No. 46 (West Kent) Sub-district were:—

1st A.B.	2nd A.B.	3rd A.B.
3rd Lee	14th Tonbridge	1st Maidstone
4th Woolwich Town	17th Tunbridge Wells	12th Dartford
13th Greenwich	23rd Penshurst	15th Sutton Valence
18th Bromley	33rd Sevenoaks	19th Rochester
25th Blackheath	35th Westerham	31st Leeds Castle
27th Deptford		39th West Malling
28th Charlton		45th Rochester
32nd Eltham		
34th St. John's (Deptford New Town)		

All the Corps in the 1st Administrative Battalion and most of the Corps in the 3rd wore dark green uniform. In the 2nd the uniform varied at first, some Corps wearing green, some Kentish grey, and others a heather-coloured material; in about 1866 they were all ordered by their Commanding Officer, Colonel Viscount Hardinge, to adopt dark green.

The 3rd Administrative Battalion was dissolved in 1874. Of its seven Corps the 12th (Dartford) was transferred to the 1st A.B. The 15th (Sutton Valence) and the 19th (Rochester) were disbanded. The other four went to the 2nd A.B.

The 26th (Royal Arsenal, Woolwich) Corps, which constituted a battalion, was transferred from No. 49 (the Middlesex and Metropolitan) to the West Kent Sub-district in 1876.

There were several other changes between 1876 and 1879, and a final re-organisation of the Volunteers took place in the spring of 1880. By July 1881 the 2nd Administrative Battalion had been renamed the 1st Kent Volunteer Corps, with an establishment of eight companies; the 1st Administrative Battalion had become the 3rd (West Kent) Volunteer Corps (11 companies); and the Woolwich Arsenal and the Woolwich Town Corps had been combined to form the 4th Kent Volunteer Corps (10 companies).

CHAPTER 2

CONSTRUCTION
1881—1886

1. *The Formation of The Queen's Own (Royal West Kent Regiment)*

WITH effect from July 1, 1881, the Infantry of the Line and the Militia of Great Britain and Ireland were formed into Territorial (County) Regiments. These Regiments bore a territorial designation corresponding to the county or locality with which they were connected. In England most regiments consisted of four battalions, the 1st and 2nd being Line battalions and the remainder Militia.

By this re-organisation The 50th or The Queen's Own Regiment and The 97th or Earl of Ulster's Regiment became the 1st and 2nd Battalions, and the West Kent Light Infantry Militia the 3rd and 4th Battalions of the Royal West Kent Regiment (Queen's Own), as follows:—

1st Battalion (50th Foot)	Colchester
2nd Battalion (97th Foot)	Natal
3rd Battalion (West Kent Militia)	Maidstone
4th Battalion (West Kent Militia)	Maidstone
Depot	Maidstone

The day before this re-organisation was due to become effective, certain alterations in the titles of the new regiments were sanctioned. One of them was that " The Royal West Kent Regiment (Queen's Own) " was changed to " The Queen's Own (Royal West Kent Regiment)." Because of an error, probably in transcription, for some years the designation " The Queen's Own (Royal West Kent) Regiment " was used by the Line battalions. In official correspondence the title was " Royal West Kent Regiment.'

The General Order, which announced the formation of Territorial Regiments, laid down that all battalions of a regiment were to wear the same uniform, badges and facings. The only distinction was that the Militia would have an " M " on the shoulder-straps (subsequently altered, for other ranks, to " 3 " or " 4 " — the number of their battalion). The details of the badges and devices that were adopted by The Queen's Own can be found in Appendix A. Three cherished items were retained: the Royal Crest, the Lion and Crown (on the buttons of the officers and as collar badges), which had been worn by The 50th; the motto *Quo Fas et Gloria Ducunt,* which came with The 97th; and the cap and helmet badge, the White Horse of Kent with *Invicta,* which was brought by the Militia.

There was some concern about the facings. The General Order stated that Royal Regiments would wear blue facings, but made no mention of the velvet cloth, which was worn by the officers of The 50th. This caused Lieutenant-Colonel A. E. Fyler, the Commanding Officer, to write the following letter to the Adjutant-General: —

"Colchester Camp,
28th May, 1881.
Sir,
With reference to the alterations laid down in G.O. 41 of 1881, para. XI, I have the honour to request that H.R.H. the Field-Marshal Commanding-in-Chief may be pleased to consider the case of the Regiment under my command, and sanction the retention of the velvet facings now worn by the officers.

When for distinguished service in the field The 50th were in 1831 made a Royal Regiment, and granted the title of " The Queen's Own," the black facings were changed to Royal blue, and by special permission the velvet was retained.

The record of this permission having been lost, His Royal Highness was pleased to confirm the retention under authority dated 21st January, 1875 (copy of which is hereto attached).

The blue velvet facings have always been looked upon by The 50th as a special mark of distinction; and as by the latter part of para. XI above quoted, certain regiments are permitted to retain the black line through their lace, I hope His Royal Highness may be pleased to give this application his favourable consideration."

The reply was: —

"Horse Guards,
28th June, 1881.
Sir,
With reference to the letter from this Department of the 9th inst., as per copy, I have now the honour, by desire of the Field-Marshal Commanding-in-Chief, to acquaint you that His Royal Highness has approved of velvet facings being worn by the officers of the Royal West Kent (Queen's Own Regiment)."

On the formation of the Regiment, each Line and Militia battalion retained its Queen's and Regimental Colour. Those carried by the

1st had been presented to The 50th Foot on board the "Himalaya" in Melbourne Harbour on November 5, 1863. The pair borne by the 2nd had been received by The 97th Foot at Halifax, Nova Scotia, on November 15, 1880. The 3rd continued to carry the Colours which had been presented at Aldershot on November 21, 1855, to the West Kent Light Infantry Militia. The 4th bore the pair which had been received by the 2nd Battalion The West Kent Light Infantry Militia at Maidstone on October 30, 1877.

The 19 Battle Honours, which had been awarded to The 50th and The 97th Foot, were emblazoned on the Regimental Colour of the 1st and 2nd Battalions. They were:—

Honour	*Awarded to*	*War or Campaign*
THE SPHINX superscribed "EGYPT"	The 50th	Egypt, 1801
VIMIERA CORUNNA ALMARAZ VITTORIA PYRENEES NIVE ORTHES PENINSULA	The 50th	Peninsular, 1808-14
PUNNIAR	The 50th	Gwalior, 1843
MOODKEE FEROZESHAH ALIWAL SOBRAON	The 50th	Sutlej, 1845-46
ALMA INKERMAN	The 50th	Crimea, 1854
SEVASTOPOL	The 50th and The 97th	Crimea, 1854-55
LUCKNOW	The 97th	Indian Mutiny, 1858
NEW ZEALAND	The 50th	New Zealand, 1863-66

The choice of a Slow March for the Regiment presented no difficulty. All four battalions unanimously adopted "The Men of Kent," which had been played by The West Kent Militia for many years.[1] The selection of a Quick March was not so easy. The 97th had used "Paddy's Delight." Since 1869 the Quick March of The 50th had been "A Hundred Pipers." It so happened that this tune was also popular in The 97th. "A Hundred Pipers" was therefore chosen for the Line battalions; but the Militia preferred to keep their own Quick March, "The Low-backed Car." The 1st Battalion retained "Garry Owen," which had been the Quick March of The 50th prior to 1869, for playing the battalion on to parade.

The 50th and The 97th each had a Colonel of the Regiment. The

---

[1] The words of the ballad had been written in about 1760.

1st and 2nd Battalions also had their own Colonels until 1885. On July 17 of that year General The Honourable Sir Francis Colborne K.C.B., vacated the Colonelcy of the 1st Battalion; whereupon General J. M. Perceval, C.B., who had been appointed Colonel of The 97th on March 21, 1874, became the first Colonel of The Queen's Own (Royal West Kent Regiment). A Roll of Colonels from 1881 to 1914 is given in Appendix B.

A paper called "The Queen's Own Gazette" had been published by The 50th Foot since January 1, 1875, when Lieutenant-Colonel A. C. K. Lock was commanding. Its first Editor was Lieutenant Brock. It had been printed at the Headquarters of The 50th by Corporal Hunt until February 1877, when Sergeant Richardson had taken on the task of operating the press. Richardson had handed over this duty to Private Taylor in May 1878. When the 1st Battalion went overseas in August 1882, the printing press was sent to the barracks at Maidstone. The Adjutant of the Depot became the Editor, and "The Queen's Own Gazette" became the Regimental Journal for the whole Territorial Regiment. Taylor continued as printer until he was discharged in August 1884. The work was then carried out by "The Maidstone and Kent County Standard" as a temporary measure. By 1886 the paper was again being printed at the Depot.

There was some delay in the selection of colours for games. At a meeting of the officers of The 50th Foot at Colchester in March 1881, it was decided that the colours for cricket and tennis should be Royal blue and Kentish grey. When the Territorial Regiment was formed the 2nd Battalion seems to have agreed to this. But the 1st Battalion apparently suggested that any flannel that was made in future should be of Royal blue and sky blue (the colours of the facings of The 50th and The 97th). A factor may have been that the correct shade of grey cloth was difficult to obtain. Be this as it may, the Regimental colours had certainly become Royal blue and sky blue by 1886, when shirts of these colours were adopted, at its inception, by the football team of the 2nd Battalion. The grey of the West Kent Militia was retained in the Regimental tie, the colours of which were registered as Royal blue and Kentish grey stripes. (See footnote to Appendix A.)

2. *50th Regimental District and the Regimental Depot*

Another change that occurred on July 1, 1881, was that the term "Sub-district" was replaced by the words "Regimental District" with the former number of the senior Line battalion. Thus No. 46 Sub-district became known as 50th Regimental District.

The Headquarters of 50th Regimental District remained in the barracks at Maidstone. The staff included a brevet-colonel in command, an Adjutant, a Quartermaster, an R.S.M. and an R.Q.M.S. The first officer to command the District was Brevet-Colonel Hales

Wilkie, who had served in The 97th Foot from 1854 to 1859 and had been in command of No. 46 Sub-district since March 2, 1878. He was succeeded by Brevet-Colonel D. R. Barnes (late 14th Foot) on December 31, 1881. Barnes' tour of duty was cut short by ill-health; he was relieved after 14 months by Colonel W. J. Chads, C.B. (late Wiltshire Regiment). The latter did much to foster *esprit de corps* and make the new organisation a success. A roll of officers who commanded 50th Regimental District is in Appendix B.

The Depot of The Queen's Own (Royal West Kent Regiment), as 46th Brigade Depot was now called, also remained in the barracks at Maidstone. It was commanded by the Officer Commanding 50th Regimental District, and still consisted of two Depot Companies — I and K — from each of the Line battalions. The instructors in these four companies trained the Line recruits. The Militia recruits were drilled in separate squads by the Permanent Staff of the 3rd and 4th Battalions. Under a new regulation they were put through their preliminary drills and their first rifle course immediately on enlistment, instead of in a body some weeks before the annual training of the Militia battalions began. If there were a large number of them, some Militia officers were called in to supervise their training.

The two big ceremonial parades of the year at the Depot were the Annual Inspection, which was made by the Officer Commanding the South-eastern District, and the Queen's Birthday Parade. For the latter all the personnel in barracks turned out in review order and fired a *feu-de-joie*. Normal Church Parade services were held in Holy Trinity Church. For special services the troops marched to All Saints'

Annual courses, rifle meetings and shooting matches were fired on Boxley Warren Range until it was condemned in April 1886. A new range at Boarley Farm was then taken into use. A few months later a Miniature Range was constructed in barracks behind the gymnasium.

Much was done between 1881 and 1886 to alleviate the monotony of the winter evenings in barracks. A Minstrel Troupe was formed and, with the assistance of the Militia band, entertained the men twice a month in the gymnasium or the drill-shed. The sergeants frequently gave Quadrille Parties. In 1882 a shop was opened in the Reading Room for tea, coffee, cakes and groceries. This was a boon to the total abstainers and the recruits, many of whom disliked using the Canteen, where beer and tobacco were sold. Another factor which made life more amenable was that many of the men who were enlisting lived within easy reach of Maidstone, and were able to spend Christmas, Easter and other short holidays with their families. In December 1883 over 500 Kent men were serving in The Queen's Own.

Football matches against outside teams were first played in December 1883. The Depot side wore Royal blue guernseys. The Maidstone Church Institute and the boys of Maidstone Grammar School were the earliest opponents. Both games, which were drawn, were played on the barrack field. A stony path across the field limited the pitch to 100 yards in length and 50 yards in width.

From January 1, 1884, the internal organisation of the Depot was changed. The four companies were re-lettered, A, B, C and D, and officers, instructors and dutymen were, on joining, posted to them irrespective of the battalion from which they came. At the same time, all the N.C.O.s serving with the Home battalion and the Depot were placed on one combined promotion roll.

In the autumn of 1885 a report that the Depot was to become a School of Military Ballooning clouded the scene. The Royal Engineers inspected the site and even made the plans. But nothing came of the project. The shadow passed, and Maidstone remained the Home of the Regiment.

3. *The 1st Battalion*

When the Regiment was formed the 1st Battalion, under the command of Lieutenant-Colonel A. E. Fyler, was quartered in A and B Lines at Colchester. On November 22, 1881, it moved by rail to Aldershot, the Mecca of soldiering in England. The battalion's new home was in E, F, K and L Lines at North Camp, where it formed part of the 3rd Brigade.

That winter, route marching and garrison duties were the main occupations of the troops. On March 29, 1882, the Aldershot Division was inspected on the Queen's Parade by Field-Marshal H.R.H. The Duke of Cambridge, Commander-in-Chief of the Army. In April there was an impressive sham fight between the 2nd and 3rd Brigades in the vicinity of Cocked Hat Wood and Long Hill — an area not unknown to later generations of the Regiment. The great event of the early summer was the Royal Review, which was held on the Queen's Parade on May 16. Soon after 4 p.m. Her Majesty Queen Victoria arrived on the ground, and was received with a Royal Salute. The Queen then passed down the lines in a carriage drawn by four greys. The march past was led by the Cavalry. Then came the Royal Artillery, the Royal Engineers, the Infantry and the Commissariat and Transport Corps. The 3rd Brigade was led by Major-General H.R.H. The Duke of Connaught. The 1st Battalion went past Her Majesty in four double companies of 90 files to " A Hundred Pipers." The ceremony ended with an advance in review order.

In February Colonel Fyler had presented to the officers a cup made from the staves of the Colours borne by The 50th Foot from 1848 to 1863. This memento nearly met a tragic fate. At 11 p.m. on the night of June 27 the Officers' Mess Hut, in which it was kept, was seen to be on fire. The alarm was sounded, and the battalion turned out with commendable promptitude. By 1 a.m. the flames were out. All the property was saved except some linen and a few pieces of crockery.

On July 21 the battalion was ordered to mobilize for active service in Egypt. Approximately 350 of the personnel were found to be unfit or were too young to go. These were replaced, in part, by a draft of four officers — Captain Cautley and Lieutenants Alderson, Harrison and Maunsell — and 100 privates from the 2nd Battalion. Captain Grove was brought back from a course at the Staff College. Thirty-five Class I Reservists of the Regiment, who were called out, arrived from the Depot too late to be equipped. In the end the unit sailed about 80 short of establishment. Of those left behind, 317 were posted to the 2nd Battalion in Dublin; the remainder, including Bandmaster Gassner and the band boys, were sent to the Depot.

Mobilization was accomplished smoothly. The Regimental Colour was taken to the Depot.[1] The Officers' Mess silver was sent to Messrs. Cox and King, Agents. Thirty horses, five ponies and 16 mules were obtained for the transport section. By August 2 everything was ready for the final inspection by H.R.H. the Commander-in-Chief.

On the morning of August 3 the battalion marched to Farnborough Station and entrained for Portsmouth. There it embarked in the "Catalonia" at noon. The only other passengers were the Commander and Staff of the 2nd Division. Later in the day Colonel Fyler was informed that Her Majesty the Queen would personally inspect the troops before the ship sailed.

Shortly before 11 a.m. on August 4, the Royal yacht "Alberta" crossed from the Isle of Wight to Portsmouth. As Her Majesty came aboard the "Catalonia," the band played the National Anthem. The battalion was on parade between decks. Queen Victoria moved slowly down the ranks, and every man seemed to receive a kind glance or a nod. When she left the ship, a bugle sounded the "Advance." The troops hurried to the top deck; some even climbed into the rigging. As the "Alberta" cast loose, the battalion, led by the Commanding Officer, gave three cheers for Her Majesty. The Queen bowed in acknowledgement.

The "Catalonia" sailed at 11.40. The Royal yacht, instead of heading for Osborne, accompanied her out of the harbour. It was not until both ships had passed Spithead that the "Alberta" turned away. The last that the battalion saw of the Queen was the flutter of a white handkerchief.

4. The 2nd Battalion

In July 1881 the 2nd Battalion, under the command of Lieutenant-Colonel C. H. Browne, was in camp at Bennett's Drift, near Newcastle, Natal. Having been ordered Home, it began the march down-country on December 4. After a delay of nearly two months at Howick, the battalion embarked in the "Balmoral Castle" at Durban on February 13, 1882. When the ship arrived at Plymouth on March 16, the troops were transferred to H.M.S. "Assistance," which sailed later that day for Dublin.

---

[1] The Queen's Colour was apparently taken to Egypt.

CONSTRUCTION

The battalion disembarked at North Wall on March 18. At first, Headquarters and four companies were accommodated in Ship Street Barracks, with a detachment of 200 men in Royal Barracks. In November all eight companies moved to Beggars Bush. These quarters were the best in Dublin. The only disadvantage was that they were a long way from the Castle and other places for which guards had to be provided.

The two years in Dublin were marred by strikes and unrest. Extra guards had to be found to protect public property, and for many months an inlying picquet stood-by in barracks day and night. Because of these additional duties the men had little time for relaxation. Moreover, the disturbances prevented all ranks from enjoying the social life of the city. It was found possible however, to hold a Sports Meeting on the Landsdowne Running Track.

The battalion (less one company) moved to the Curragh on May 1, 1884. This was not looked upon as a change of station, as the camp was within the limits of Dublin District. The quarters were wooden huts in B Lines, which had not been occupied for some time. In October the battalion moved over to C Square, where the bungalows were of cement and the amenities were less primitive. The surrounding country was ideal for recreation of all kinds. Paper-chases were organised on most Saturday afternoons. Company football games were played nearly every day with balls provided from the Canteen fund. In the summer, cricket matches were arranged against other regiments in the station, and Sports Meetings were held in camp. The Tug-of-War team was able to get down to serious practice in front of the Lines; as a result it won first prize at the Royal Irish Military Tournament in Dublin on two occasions. Full advantage was taken of the Curragh Ranges, which were nearby. Two Rifle Meetings were fired on them, during which the Officers' and Eccles Challenge Cups were competed for. The latter had been presented by Lieutenant R. H. Eccles, late 97th Foot.

Colonel Browne, who had commanded for five years, was placed on half-pay on September 9, 1884.[1] He was succeeded by Lieutenant-Colonel D. J. D. Safford. A roll of Commanding Officers of all battalions of the Regiment is in Appendix B.

Lieutenant Alderson and 28 other ranks went to Aldershot on August 23, 1884, for a short course of training. They embarked at Portsmouth on the 28th for Egypt, where they joined the Mounted Infantry Camel Regiment which was being formed for the Nile Expedition. When the detachment returned on August 1, 1885, having lost two men in action and two from illness, the whole battalion turned out to welcome it. A few days later a very complimentary letter was received from the Officer Commanding the M.I. Camel Regiment. The outcome was that Lieutenant Alderson was detached to the Mounted Infantry for long periods during the next 17 years and gained accelerated promotion.

[1] Browne later commanded 23rd (The Royal Welch Fusiliers) Regimental District and was made a C.B.

The battalion left the Curragh in a special train on September 28, 1885, embarked at Kingstown in H.M.S. " Assistance," and disembarked at Chatham on October 2.

5. The 3rd and 4th Battalions

The Headquarters of the 3rd and 4th Battalions (Militia) were, as before, in the Depot Barracks. Each unit had its own Permanent Staff from the Line battalions, including a Quartermaster, an R.S.M., an R.Q.M.S., six colour-sergeants, eight sergeants and seven drummers. Neither had an Adjutant, but these duties were performed by the Adjutant of 50th Regimental District. Except for the band, most of which belonged to the Permanent Staff, the personnel still assembled only once a year for training.

The period of annual training had now been extended to four weeks. Both battalions assembled at the Depot on the same day to draw their equipment. They then went by train to Shorncliffe. During the first two weeks the range course was fired at Hythe. The other fortnight was occupied by field days and an inspection by the Officer Commanding 50th Regimental District. On the last day the personnel returned to Maidstone to hand in their kit before dispersing to their homes.

After annual training the band often fulfilled engagements for the summer season at such resorts as Margate or Broadstairs. In the winter it played at entertainments at the Depot and frequently marched the recruits to church.

The Honorary Colonel, George Byng, Viscount Torrington, died in the spring of 1884. He had held the appointment for 15 years. Major-General His Royal Highness Prince Arthur Duke of Connaught was gazetted in his stead on August 23, 1884.

6. The Volunteers

The 1st, the 3rd (West Kent) and the 4th Kent Volunteer Corps, the three Volunteer units in 50th Regimental District, were incorporated as Volunteer battalions in The Queen's Own (Royal West Kent Regiment) in April 1882. They were re-named the 1st, 2nd and 3rd Volunteer Battalions of the Regiment respectively on February 1, 1883. The details and lay-out of these battalions were: —

    1st Volunteer Battalion:
        Headquarters in the Corn Exchange, Tonbridge.
        Uniform: Green with green facings.
        Ranges: Hollingbourne and Tunbridge Wells.
        Companies: A and B at Maidstone; C at Tonbridge; D and E at Tunbridge Wells; F at Penshurst; G at Westerham; H at Leeds Castle.

The Headquarters of the Maidstone Companies were in the Bell Hotel, Week Street. The personnel fired on the range used by the Depot, and drilled in Vinter's Park or on the Depot Square.

2nd Volunteer Battalion:
Headquarters in a house in The Glebe, Blackheath.
Uniform: Green with black facings.
Ranges: Milton, near Gravesend, and a small butt at Eltham.
Companies: A and B at Lee; C and D at Dartford; E at Bromley; G and H at Blackheath; J at Deptford; K at Charlton; L at St. John's; M at Greenwich.

3rd Volunteer Battalion:
Headquarters at the Royal Arsenal, Woolwich.
Uniform: Green with scarlet facings.
Range: Plumstead.
Companies: All 10 at Woolwich. Most of the personnel were employed at the Royal Arsenal.

None of these battalions carried Colours.

Rochester and Chatham were not included in 50th Regimental District at this time.

The yearly compulsory training of the Volunteers consisted of only six company and three battalion drills, the firing of a short course, and attendance at the annual inspection. Although many men performed more drills and spent additional time on the range, such a low standard of compulsory attendance could not by itself be expected to produce an efficient unit. The important fact was that, by their system of evening and week-end drills and a continuous existence throughout the year, the Volunteer battalions maintained a corporate individuality far stronger than that of the Militia, which only "came out for training" for a few weeks annually.

Whenever practicable the Volunteers carried out seven days' training during the summer. The normal site for the camp of the 1st Volunteer Battalion was in Broadwater Forest, near Eridge. The 2nd went to Grove Park, Bromley. The 3rd seldom mustered for camp, probably because those men who were employed at the Royal Arsenal could not be spared in large numbers simultaneously. While the battalions were in camp they were inspected by the Officer Commanding 50th Regimental District.

On two occasions the 2nd Volunteer Battalion carried out special training at Easter. In 1884 it went by train to Faversham, marched from there to Dover and took part in a field day with other Volunteers. In 1885 it went to Maidstone, where the other ranks were accommodated in the drill-shed and gymnasium at the Depot, and the officers in the Assembly Rooms. There was a sham fight in Mote Park on the Saturday; a combined church parade with the Depot personnel and the Maidstone Volunteers in All Saints' on the Sunday; and a field day near Malling on the Monday.

7. Laying-up of Colours (50th and 97th Foot)

In 1882 there were two stands of Old Colours in the Officers' Mess at the Depot. These were the 1848-1863 (Crimean) Colours of The 50th Foot, and the 1857-1880 Colours of The 97th. The latter had been taken by The 97th to Gibraltar in 1880, and, when the Regiment was ordered to proceed on active service to Natal, had been deposited in Government House (the Convent) for safe-keeping; they had been brought home by a detachment which called at " The Rock " in March 1882. Some officers suggested that the Old Colours of The 50th should be placed over that Regiment's Crimea Memorial in Canterbury Cathedral. It was finally decided that both stands of Old Colours should be laid up in All Saints' Church, Maidstone.

The 1857-1880 Colours of The 97th Foot were laid up on All Saints' Day, November 1, 1883. The escort to the Colours was composed of the Depot staff and recruits. The Colour Party consisted of Lieutenants Maunsell and Baines and four colour-sergeants, all 97th men. The Maidstone Companies and the band of the 1st Volunteer Battalion attended the ceremony. Major Jameson handed the Colours at the chancel steps to the Chaplain, the Rev. T. Moore. The Vicar, the Rev. E. F. Dyke, addressed the congregation.

The 1848-1863 (Crimean) Colours of The 50th Foot were laid up on May 1, 1886. The 2nd Battalion, then quartered at Chatham, sent a large detachment, but of the 1st only six officers, who were on leave from Egypt, were able to be present. The Colours were carried by two 50th officers, Major Brock (Adjutant 2nd Volunteer Battalion) and Major Wynyard (Adjutant 50th Regimental District and 3rd and 4th Battalions). They were handed by Lieutenant-Colonel Bayly, of the 1st Battalion, to the Chaplain at the altar rails. An address was delivered by the Rev. Dyke. The Colours were then placed against a pillar on the north side of the aisle, and the troops filed past and saluted them for the last time.

8. The Battle Trophies of The 50th Foot

Three Sikh Standards had been captured by The 50th Foot in the Sutlej Campaign. Two of these had been taken by Corporal Edward Johnson, of the Grenadier Company, at the Battle of Ferozeshah. The third had been seized by Private Leonard Hale at Sobraon. After the campaign these trophies had been kept in the Mess Room of The 50th.

When the 1st Battalion was ordered to Egypt on active service in August 1882, the Standards were placed in the ante-room of the Officers' Mess at the Depot. As they were rapidly falling to pieces, the remnants were taken to the Army and Navy Stores to be set for protection in an air-tight case. The staves were used to form a beading round the interior and as an upright to support the cloth. Inside the case was fixed a small painting to show the Standards as they were when captured. The painting was a copy of a coloured photograph lent by Major-General J. Thompson, who, as a colour-sergeant, had been at the Battle of Sobraon. When the case was finished in April 1884, the memento was placed in the Depot Officers' Mess. It was moved from there to All Saints' Church on February 13, 1886.

CHAPTER 3

EGYPT AND THE SUDAN
August, 1882—June, 1886
1st Battalion and a Contingent from the 2nd Battalion

1.—*The Situation in Egypt*

EVER since the Sultan of Turkey had appointed Tewfick to be Khedive of Egypt in July 1879, there had been rivalry in the Egyptian Army between the Turkish and the Egyptian officers. Matters came to a head early in 1882, when Colonel Arabi, who was of Egyptian peasant stock, became War Minister. He gained control by stirring up hatred against all foreigners, especially the Turkish rulers. The situation became so tense that British and French naval squadrons steamed into Alexandria Harbour to safeguard the European residents. In spite of the presence of these ships, a riot broke out on Sunday, June 11. At least 150 Europeans were massacred. On the Monday many people sought refuge in the warships or in Consulates, and business was at a standstill. After the massacre, Arabi constructed batteries at Alexandria to threaten the squadrons in the harbour. The British admiral, Sir Beauchamp Seymour, requested him to demolish them. This amounted to an ultimatum. Arabi did not comply, and on July 11 the guns of the fleet opened fire. The Egyptian troops withdrew from the town.

A few days later British troops began to arrive at Alexandria from Malta and Cyprus. But by that time anarchy had spread throughout Egypt, and large numbers of armed men were flocking to join Arabi at Kafr Dowar, 15 miles east of Alexandria. Above all, it was known that Arabi was preparing to destroy the Suez Canal. This international water-way, which had been opened in November 1869, was largely controlled by British and French interests. Even so, the French National Assembly refused to grant money to ensure

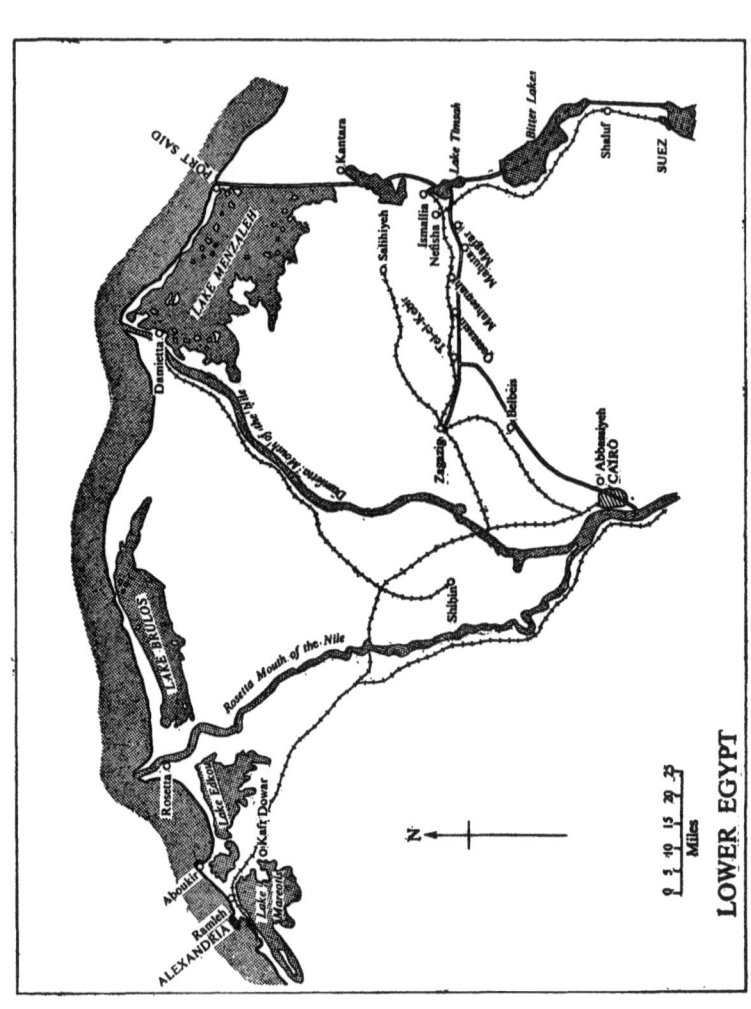

its safety. The British Government was forced to act alone. On July 20 the Cabinet decided to despatch an Army Corps to Egypt.

The Expeditionary Force, which was placed under the command of General Sir Garnet Wolseley, consisted of two divisions of infantry and a division of cavalry. The 1st Infantry Division was commanded by Lieutenant-General G. H. S. Willis. His 1st (Guards) Brigade was led by Major-General H.R.H. The Duke of Connaught, and his 2nd by Major-General G. Graham, V.C. The 1st Battalion was in the 2nd Brigade together with the 2nd Battalion The Royal Irish Regiment, the 2nd Battalion The York and Lancaster Regiment, and the 1st Battalion The Royal Irish Fusiliers.

The first ship of the Expedition departed from the Royal Albert Docks, Woolwich, on July 30. From then until August 11 the various vessels conveying the force sailed from the ports of the United Kingdom daily; the " Catalonia," with the 1st Battalion on board, left Portsmouth on August 4. The 1st (Guards) Brigade disembarked at Alexandria on the 13th, marched through the town and encamped near the sea at Ramleh. General Sir Garnet Wolseley landed on the 15th, on which day the " Catalonia " anchored in the harbour.

The key personnel in the 1st Battalion were: —
    Commanding Officer: Lieutenant-Colonel A. E. Fyler;
    Second-in-Command: Lieutenant-Colonel R. H. P. Doran;
    Adjutant: Captain M. Wynyard;
    Quartermaster: Hon. Lieutenant R. J. Roche;
    R.S.M.: Sergeant-Major W. Locks;
    R.Q.M.S.: Quartermaster-Sergeant W. Dawson.
A complete list of officers can be found in Appendix C.

2. *The Landing at Ismailia*

General Wolseley's orders were to suppress the military revolt in Egypt and re-establish the power of the Khedive. His intention was to capture and occupy Cairo, the capital. His plan was to seize the Suez Canal before it could be blocked, land at Ismailia and approach Cairo from the east. To do this, it would be necessary to give Arabi the impression that the attack was to be launched from another point. A second consideration was the importance of gaining control as soon as possible of the Sweet-water Canal, which ran from the Nile, near Cairo, to Ismailia and would be the main source of drinking water.

In order to draw Arabi's attention from the Suez Canal, Sir Garnet Wolseley ostentatiously issued orders for a landing at Aboukir. The Guards Brigade re-embarked on August 18, and on the morning of the 19th the warships and transports put to sea from Alexandria. They arrived in the afternoon in Aboukir Bay, where they anchored in regular lines, the warships being nearest to the shore. The " Catalonia " lay opposite a formidable-looking fort. From the decks the battalion could see that the beach was defended by numerous earthworks, and the troops expected strong opposition when they landed that night. But after dark the orders were cancelled. One by one the ships quietly slipped away eastwards to Port Said. At dawn the whole fleet had vanished. The ruse was completely successful.

While the Egyptians were preparing to resist a landing at Aboukir, the Royal Navy had seized strategic points on the Suez Canal, including Ismailia, and had cleared nearly all of the shipping from the water-way. Three steamers, moving northwards, prevented the Expedition from entering the canal at Port Said until the morning of the 20th.

The " Catalonia " cast anchor just outside Port Said Harbour at daylight on the 20th. It was a Sunday, and after an early breakfast the troops were about to fall in for Church Parade, when Colonel Fyler was ordered to take 300 men to Ismailia to reinforce the detachment of Royal Marines, which had landed there. Church Parade was cancelled. Without delay A, B, C and D Companies were transferred to the torpedo-boat " Beacon." Closely followed by the brigade commander and 300 men of The York and Lancaster Regiment in the " Falcon," the small warship steamed down the Suez Canal without a pilot. After passing Kantara the companies lined the rails with their Martini-Henry rifles ready loaded, and the sailors manned the Gatling gun in the bows. But no enemy appeared on the banks. As the " Beacon " approached Lake Timsah, General Graham signalled that he wished the " Falcon " to take the lead. Night had now fallen, and only the occasional flash of guns from the " Carysfort " and the " Orion " lit up the lake. These ships were firing on some Egyptians who were attempting .to destroy the gates of the lock in the Sweet-water Canal at Nefisha.

When the " Beacon " reached Ismailia at about 10.30 p.m. the four companies of the 1st Battalion disembarked rapidly onto lighters and went ashore at a small pier. Leaving their valises and reserve ammunition under a guard at the landing-place, they marched across a bridge over the Sweet-water Canal to the positions held by the Royal Marines in Arabs' Town, the western suburb of Ismailia. There they made preparations to repel a sudden attack and bivouacked for the night.

Early next morning, August 21, Sir Garnet Wolseley arrived at Ismailia. He ordered General Graham to advance immediately and secure the vital lock gates at Nefisha. The four companies of the 1st Battalion led the attack, with a naval Gatling gun on each flank. To the right rear were the detachment of The York and Lancaster Regiment and some Marines. A bugler sounded the "Advance," and The Queen's Own moved forward as for a field day. The sun was hot. Their red tunics, thick blue trousers and heavy helmets added greatly to the men's discomfort. On approaching Nefisha, it was seen that the place had been abandoned. That the retreat of the enemy had been hasty was apparent, for 30 trucks full of stores and ammunition were standing in the railway station. The lock gates were still intact.

Nefisha was occupied without incident. Trenches were dug, and the station was put in a state of defence. One Gatling gun was sited to fire west up the Ismailia — Zagazig Railway, the other along the line which ran to Suez. Later in the day a reconnaissance revealed the presence of the enemy some four miles to the west. That night the troops remained alert, but the Egyptians made no attempt to reoccupy the village. On the evening of August 22, the four companies of the 1st Battalion, having been relieved by a detachment of Royal Marines, marched back to Ismailia.

The arrival of the other four companies of the battalion had been delayed by a mishap to the " Catalonia." Soon after she left Port Said on the 20th, the ship ran aground on the west bank of the Suez Canal. All efforts to move her failed. At about 11 a.m. on the 21st, Brevet-Lieutenant-Colonel Leach and 134 men transferred to the gunboat " Decoy." Most of the remainder of the troops, under Lieutenant-Colonel Doran, were taken on by the " Cygnet." Both parties disembarked at Ismailia after dark and bivouacked in an open space near the Sweet-water Canal. The following evening they moved into the public gardens in the centre of the town, where A, B, C and D Companies joined them a few hours later. The animals and transport wagons were still in the " Catalonia."

3. *Qassassin*

A score of transports and several warships were now moored in Lake Timsah. As every man, horse, gun and article of equipment had to be landed in lighters at the one small pier at Ismailia, the disembarkation of the Expeditionary Force was a slow process. On August 23 the Royal Engineers laid a railway line from the landing-place to the station, and troops and stores were sent forward to Nefisha in readiness for a further advance.

The country between Ismailia and the Nile was a desert of sand. Across it ran side by side the Sweet-water Canal and the Railway to Zagazig. There was no road for wheeled transport. The sand was soft and loose near Nefisha, but it gradually became less deep till, at Tel-el-Kebir, it was fairly firm. During the day the sun blazed from a cloudless sky. At night the air became chilly. Shelter from the sun was necessary in the daytime; a blanket was required at night. The water from the Sweet-water Canal was potable when filtered.

An alarming drop in the level of the Sweet-water Canal caused General Wolseley to risk an early advance so as to gain possession of his vulnerable water supply. At dawn on the 24th the cavalry rode out from Nefisha, reached Magfar without difficulty, and found that the enemy were in a prepared position at Mahuta, where they had dammed the canal and blocked the railway. Sir Garnet halted to wait for reinforcements. The Guards Brigade was ordered to make a forced march to Mahuta, and the 1st Battalion to move forward and take over the defence of Nefisha.

Parties of the battalion were scattered on various fatigues in Ismailia, so that it was noon before it could start. There was no time for the men to eat their dinners, and they took part of the half-cooked meal with them. In the midday heat those troops who had been working all the morning soon felt the weight of their accoutrements and clothing. Some fell out as they plodded through the deep sand between Arabs' Town and Nefisha. Sergeant Howard was brought in unconscious; he died next morning.

The arrival of the Guards at Mahuta had the desired effect. When Wolseley resumed his advance on the 25th the Egyptians were seen to be retiring. The cavalry pressed forward as rapidly as possible, and Mahsemah, with a large camp still standing, was soon captured. On the 26th the canal lock at Qassassin was occupied by a patrol of The 4th Dragoons. Later in the day part of the 2nd Brigade marched into Qassassin; the cavalry returned to Mahsemah.

The 1st Battalion remained in Nefisha for four days. The men who were not required for protective duties were employed in unloading railway trucks, in digging out transport wagons that got stuck in the sand, and in erecting tents. The 28th brought another hurried move. The Egyptians launched an attack on the troops at Qassassin, and the battalion was ordered to move up by forced marches. The message was received in the evening, when the transport had just come in from fatigue duties. Captain Carr's Company was left in charge of the camp, and the first march, of 12 miles, began at 10.45 p.m. After a few hours' rest at Mahuta, the seven companies set off again at 8 a.m. on the 29th in attack formation. They had not gone far when General Willis, who was riding back from the front, met Colonel Fyler and told him that there was now no need to hurry as the enemy had been driven back by a cavalry charge the previous evening. The companies halted where they were, had dinners when the water-carts came up, and resumed the march to Mahsemah in the cool of the evening. The last five miles were covered early on the morning of the 30th. At Qassassin, the battalion rejoined the 2nd Brigade.

There was now a pause in the military operations while dams and other obstacles were removed from the Sweet-water Canal, and stores were accumulated at Qassassin. The latter was a lengthy undertaking, for as yet there were not enough pack mules or camels, the transport wagons were mainly too heavy for the loose sand, and the railway line had been blocked in several places. Although the Royal Navy organised a service of boats on the Sweet-water Canal, it was difficult to bring up even the full scale of rations. Tents did not arrive until September 3. Worse still, there was not enough drinking water, because the canal had been polluted by the Egyptians and it was impossible to filter sufficient quantities.

The troops at Qassassin were kept busy. Boats, wagons and, later, railway trucks had to be unloaded; defence works and emplacements for the guns had to be constructed. Occasionally a cavalry skirmish would cause a little excitement, while on September 6 most of the 2nd Brigade and some divisional troops marched past

General Willis. The toil in the heat of the sun and outpost duties in the chill of the night, all on a diet of tinned meat and bad water, undermined the health of the battalion. Many men fell sick with typhoid or enteric fever or dysentery. Several died.[1] The numbers were also diminished by operational commitments. For though Captain Carr's Company rejoined from Nefisha, Major Bayly's, Captain Armstrong's and Captain Jones' Companies returned to Mahuta, Mahsemah and Nefisha respectively to guard the line of communications. Lieutenant Alderson, Quartermaster-Sergeant Saddler and a dozen others were attached to a small contingent of Mounted Infantry, which had been formed.

* * *

Realising that the British preparations were nearly complete, Arabi determined to attack. On September 9, two Egyptian forces advanced on Qassassin simultaneously from Tel-el-Kebir in the west and from Salihiyeh in the north. The British were nearly taken by surprise. After the dawn stand-to a detachment of cavalry, riding out to post vedettes, saw the Egyptians approaching in strength. At 6.45 General Willis ordered the "Fall-in" to be sounded. By 7.10 the troops had occupied their prearranged positions. The 1st Battalion (less three companies), the 2nd Battalion The Duke of Cornwall's Light Infantry (divisional troops), some Royal Marine Artillery and two 25-pounder guns were south of the Sweet-water Canal. To the north of it were the 3rd Battalion The King's Royal Rifle Corps (divisional troops) with their left resting on the canal. On their right were the Royal Marines and the York and Lancasters. The Royal Irish Regiment was on the extreme right opposing the Salihiyeh force. Two field batteries (16-pounders) were in pits north of the camp.

Arabi had placed most of his guns on a low ridge north-west of Qassassin, whence they opened accurate fire. Shell after shell fell into the British lines, though many of them failed to burst in the soft sand. Under cover of this fire the Egyptian infantry advanced to within 1,200 yards. Some of them crossed to the south bank to carry out a turning movement; but the fire of the British infantry and the 25-pounders prevented them from completing the manoeuvre. When it became certain that the threat on the south of the canal could be held, The D.C.L.I. were moved across to support The Royal Irish on the right. On this flank however, the Egyptians made no attempt to press home the attack.

General Wolseley now assumed the offensive. He ordered the infantry and the 16-pounder batteries to advance about 1,000 yards. The 1st Battalion carried out this move in attack formation — two companies extended, two in support and one in reserve — with its right resting on the canal. The Egyptians retired slowly. At this stage the cavalry, which had come up from Mahsemah, rode forward so as to separate the Tel-el-Kebir force from the attackers who had

---

[1] See Roll of Honour. Those whose deaths were caused by disease contracted at Qassassin and on the line of communications were probably:— Sergeant Adams, Lance-Corporal Pearson and Privates Carpenter, Collins, Cotterell, Davis, Hayward, Morrison, Murray, Roe and Smith, G.

timidly approached from Salihiyeh. Seeing this, Sir Garnet ordered a further advance of the infantry. The Egyptians rose in alarm, and were closely followed by the cavalry and the Royal Horse Artillery until they were within three miles of Tel-el-Kebir. South of the canal the five companies of the 1st Battalion halted when they had advanced only a short distance through some cotton fields, so as to cover the south-western flank of the camp. Then, having been refreshed by biscuits and water from the carts, they returned to Qassassin for a late breakfast.

British casualties in this affair were three men killed, and two officers and 78 other ranks wounded. None of these was Queen's Own.

4. *The End of the Campaign*

The position selected by Arabi for his final stand was about a mile east of the village of Tel-el-Kebir. The defences consisted of a line of earthworks extending northwards from the Sweet-water Canal. They included a deep, wide ditch, a breast-work from four to six feet high, and a number of strong redoubts. In the rear were numerous shelter trenches. Work was still in progress on the northern part of the line.

By September 12, Wolseley's Corps had concentrated about Qassassin, with the exception of: — one company of the 1st Battalion with one troop of The 19th Hussars at each of the three most important villages on the line of communications (Mahsemah, Mahuta and Nefisha); the 1st Battalion The Manchester Regiment at Ismailia; and the 4th Brigade at Alexandria. Patrols had found that Egyptian picquets were not posted outside the earthworks of Tel-el-Kebir after dark. This discovery, and the fact that the ground between Qassassin and Arabi's position was open and practically flat, influenced Sir Garnet's planning. He decided on a night advance and a frontal attack at dawn. Strict secrecy was maintained so as to ensure complete surprise.

The two infantry divisions — the 2nd comprised the 3rd (Highland) Brigade and another brigade made up of divisional troops — were to advance with the mass of Field Artillery between them. They were to move up to the Egyptian fortifications without firing a shot. The Cavalry Division, Mounted Infantry and Royal Horse Artillery, on the extreme right, had orders to sweep round the enemy's rear as soon as he was engaged, and to be ready for an immediate pursuit. Each infantryman was to carry a hundred rounds of ammunition, the unexpired portion of the day's ration and the full ration for the morrow. The transport, except the water-carts, would follow at daybreak. Fifty men of the 1st Battalion were to be the escort to the Reserve Ammunition Column, which would move in rear of the 2nd Division on the left. The rest of the five companies of the battalion, which were at Qassassin, one troop of The 19th Hussars, and two companies of The Royal Engineers were to remain behind to guard the camp under Brigadier-General C. B. P. Nugent, the Chief Engineer. His orders were to cover the rear of the attacking force and to protect Qassassin, with all its stores, from a possible assault from Salihiyeh.

For several days there had been rumours that the five companies of the 1st Battalion would not take part in the attack, but it was only after Wolseley had issued his orders that they knew for sure that this was to be their lot. So as to soften the blow, the 50 other ranks who were to escort the Ammunition Column were selected so that all five companies would be represented at the battle. Lieutenant Maunsell was placed in command of this escort.

At 5 p.m. on September 12, the baggage and knapsacks of the attacking force were stacked alongside the railway. After dark all tents were struck. Camp fires were left burning by each unit as it moved off to the forming-up position. By 11 p.m. the troops were all in their correct places, where they lay down, waiting for the order to march. At 1.30 a.m. on the 13th the famous advance on Tel-el-Kebir began.

At Qassassin the night passed without incident. At dawn on the 13th the garrison stood-to as usual. Only distant artillery fire could be heard. Soon after the stand-down, the alarm was given by the outpost found by Captain Carr's Company. A bugler came running in with the message that a large force of Egyptian cavalry was drawn up in front. All available men were sent forward to the outpost, but before they could take up their positions the enemy turned and withdrew. The camp was not threatened again.

During the morning there was news of the fight at Tel-el-Kebir. The 1st and 2nd Divisions had nearly reached the earthworks before the Egyptian sentries saw them and fired a few shots. The whole mile of the enemy trenches had then blazed with the flashes of musketry. The signal for storming had sounded. The Highland Brigade on the left and the 1st Division on the right had rushed in to assault. The defenders had resisted stubbornly. As soon as it was light enough the mounted troops, increasing their pace, had swung round to the rear of the enemy. The Artillery had come into action. In 20 minutes the battle had been won and the Egyptians put to flight. Arabi, who had been in bed near the railway station when the attack began, had managed to escape. The losses of the enemy in killed alone had been not far short of 2,000. British casualties were 57 killed and nearly 400 wounded.

After its defeat Arabi's army scattered in groups throughout the country. Arabi himself, with a few senior officers, boarded a train at Belbeis. On reaching Cairo he prepared to set fire to the city. Sir Garnet Wolseley, anxious to save the capital from this fate, ordered the mounted troops to press on to Cairo with all speed. When they reached Abbassiyeh on the evening of September 14, the men and horses were exhausted, having ridden 65 miles over sand in two days. Nevertheless, the Egyptian garrison yielded unconditionally. Two squadrons of cavalry and a detachment of mounted infantry then rode into the capital to accept the surrender of the Citadel. Arabi gave up his sword that night. The Guards Brigade occupied Cairo next day.

It was not till September 23 that the five companies of the 1st Battalion entrained at Qassassin. They arrived in the capital that evening and bivouacked for the night at the railway station. Next morning they marched to the 2nd Brigade's camp on Ghezireh Island, where the other three companies joined them on the 25th. That afternoon the whole battalion lined a portion of the route when the Khedive re-entered Cairo from Ramleh, where he had been under British protection. On the 30th the Expeditionary Force (less detachments at Alexandria, Port Said and Ismailia) took part in a Victory March through Cairo. For this ceremony the battalion wore grey uniform, which had been issued three days before.

The Egyptian Medal, 1882, was awarded to all those who served with the Expeditionary Force between July 16 and September 14; and a clasp to those who attacked the enemy's trenches at Tel-el-Kebir. The officers and other ranks of The Queen's Own who received the clasp were: — Captain Grove, who held a Staff appointment; Lieutenant Johnson, who was attached to the Commissariat and Transport Staff; Lieutenant Alderson and the dozen other ranks, who were with the Mounted Infantry; and Lieutenant Maunsell and the 50 other ranks who escorted the Ammunition Column. In addition, the Khedive had a medal, called the Khedive's Bronze Star, struck and issued to the whole Force. A list of Honours and Awards can be found in Appendix D.

5. The Army of Occupation and Cyprus

Before the Expeditionary Force dispersed, the Khedive's Government requested that 12,000 of the men should stay in Egypt to maintain law and order. A, B, C and D Companies of the 1st Battalion remained with this Army of Occupation. Headquarters and the other four companies were ordered to Cyprus.

A, B, C and D Companies were quartered in the summer palace of the Khedive at Ras-el-Tin, Alexandria. The palace was on the north-eastern arm of the harbour, well away from the heat and noise of the town. The detachment was commanded by Lieutenant-Colonel Doran with Major Bayly as Second-in-command, Lieutenant Maunsell as Adjutant, and Lieutenant Harrison as Paymaster. The troops were mainly employed on guards and garrison duties. Their recreations were swimming, fishing, rifle shooting and amateur theatricals.

The detachment received its Egyptian Medals at a parade at Ras-el-Tin on March 28, 1883. Lieutenant-General Sir Archibald Alison, who was commanding the Army of Occupation, inspected the parade and addressed the troops; the medals were pinned on by

Colonel Doran. The Khedive's Bronze Stars were distributed at a combined parade in Alexandria on June 30. His Highness the Khedive attended the ceremony and personally presented their stars to all officers and to two N.C.O.s and two men of each corps.

A cholera epidemic broke out in the Nile Delta in June 1883. The disease mainly affected the native population, but, as a precaution, all troops were confined to barracks for six weeks. To entertain the detachment at Ras-el-Tin during this period, a Minstrel Troupe was formed. When the danger was over, the sergeants gave a mammoth party for the senior N.C.O.s of all the corps and departments stationed in Alexandria and Ramleh, including The 19th Hussars.

The Khedive arrived at Alexandria from Cairo on the morning of June 21, 1884, for a short stay at his summer palace. Having been met at the railway station by several celebrities, he drove to Ras-el-Tin. A, B, C and D Companies were drawn up at the gates of the palace to receive him. A Royal Salute was given, and the drums played the Khedivial Hymn. That evening the officers attended an informal reception held by His Highness.

Early in August 1884 the detachment was ordered to move to Cairo to prepare for active service in the Sudan. The journey was made by train on August 7. Quarters were taken up in the Citadel.

*   *   *

The 1st Battalion (less A, B, C and D Companies) entrained at Cairo on October 8, 1882, for the journey to Cyprus. It arrived very early next morning at Alexandria, embarked in the S.S. " Caspian," and went ashore at Limassol on the 12th. The troops marched to Polymedia Camp. Colonel and Mrs. Fyler took up residence in the Greek Consulate at Limassol.

The Port of Limassol is on the south coast of the island. Polymedia is some three miles north of it, on ground which slopes up gradually from the sea. The camp consisted of about 60 wooden barrack huts and some larger buildings for the Hospital, Canteen, Ablution-rooms and Officers' Mess. To the south of the men's lines were the transport stables and a tented camp for the officers. The rifle range was close to the west side of the camp, near the road to Mount Troodos. Field firing and minor tactical training could be carried out on an area adjoining the Salt Lake, five miles farther inland.

The Reservists, who had been called out for the Egyptian Campaign, left for England on October 23. They were replaced in January 1883 by a draft of men who returned from sick leave. The band boys, some married families, and Major Robinson with the Regimental Colour, had arrived earlier. Bandmaster Gassner brought out the Regimental property and heavy baggage .

The Egyptian Medals were presented at Polymedia by Major-General Sir Robert Biddulph, the High Commissioner for Cyprus, on March 20, 1883. Later in the day the Queen's Colour was trooped, and the gratuity money for the campaign, ranging from £34 for a lieutenant-colonel to £2 for a private, was distributed. There was brisk business in the Canteen that evening. The Khedive's Bronze Stars were received after the Queen's Birthday Parade on Limassol Racecourse on May 24.

With the exception of Limassol Race Week, there were few entertainments for the troops outside camp. In camp the main relaxations were cricket, theatricals and band concerts. A small open-air swimming bath was opened at Polymedia in March 1884.

In June each year there was a general exodus from Limassol for the summer months. Carts, mules and camels took the road inland for Mount Troodos. The troops marched up in several parties, the 36 miles being covered in three stages by night. The sick and the families travelled in ambulances and covered carts. At Troodos all ranks and the families lived in tents. Winter quarters at Polymedia were re-occupied in October.

Lieutenant-Colonel A. E. Fyler retired with the honorary rank of colonel on November 17, 1883. Lieutenant-Colonel Doran did not succeed him, as he was about to retire at his own request. Brevet-Lieutenant-Colonel E. Leach was promoted to command. He became a colonel in February 1884.

At Troodos on August 8, 1884, Colonel Leach received a telegram informing him that A, B, C and D Companies had moved from Alexandria to Cairo, that the remainder of the battalion was to return to Egypt forthwith, and that the whole unit was to join an Expedition which was being sent to the Sudan. The troops and families left Troodos on the evening of the 30th, reached Limassol on September 1, embarked in the troopship "Orontes" and landed at Alexandria on the 3rd. The two halves of the battalion were re-united in the Citadel at Cairo on the morning of the 4th. The families went on to England in the "Orontes."

6. The Nile Expedition

The trouble in the Sudan had been caused by a boat-builder named Mohammed Ahmed, who set himself up to be the Mahdi, the successor of the Prophet Mahomet. His mission was to march on Egypt and overthrow the Turkish rule. In order to suppress the revolt, the Egyptian Government had re-enlisted 10,000 of Arabi's former soldiers. A number of the more important posts in this Army of the Sudan were filled by British officers. In September 1883 a force led by one of them, Colonel W. Hicks, had been annihilated south of Khartoum by the Mahdi's men. This disaster had placed all southern Sudan at the mercy of the Dervishes. Khartoum itself was in peril. At this juncture the British Government recommended the abandonment of all territory south of Wadi Halfa. The Khedive's Ministers reluctantly adopted this course, and Major-General C. G. Gordon was sent to Khartoum to extricate the Egyptian garrisons from the Sudan. In

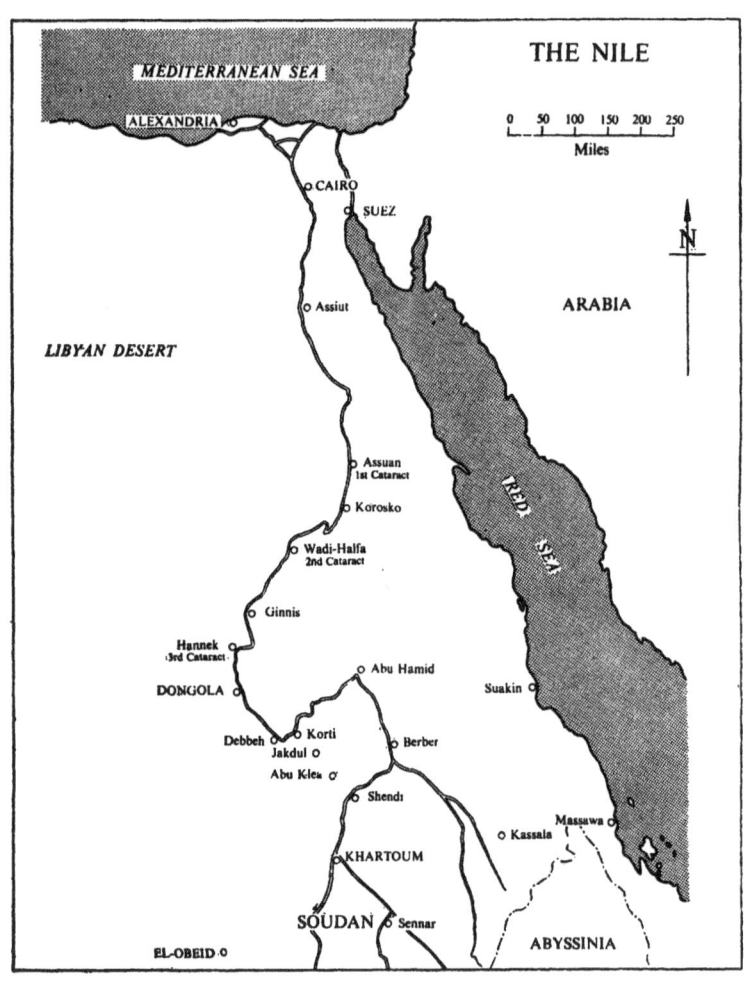

May 1884 the rebels captured Berber, thus cutting off Khartoum from Egypt. In August the British Government resolved that an Expedition should be sent to rescue Gordon.

The Nile Expedition, as it is generally called, consisted of: —
The 19th Hussars (less one squadron at Cairo).
A Mounted Infantry Camel Regiment, composed of 400 volunteers from the regiments in Egypt.
A Camel Corps, composed of 1,200 volunteers from the Cavalry, Foot Guards and Rifle Brigade, and divided into the Heavy, Light and Guards Camel Regiments.
1st Battalion The Royal Irish Regiment.
2nd Battalion The Duke of Cornwall's Light Infantry.
1st Battalion The Royal Sussex Regiment.
1st Battalion The South Staffordshire Regiment.
1st Battalion The Black Watch.
2nd Battalion The Essex Regiment.
1st Battalion The Queen's Own (Royal West Kent Regiment).
1st Battalion The Gordon Highlanders.
One Company Royal Engineers.
A Naval Contingent of sailors and marines.

The command of the Expedition was given to General Wolseley, who had now been created a peer. His orders were to reach Khartoum and bring away General Gordon. His plan was to proceed up the Nile and establish his force before the end of the year at Shendi, about a hundred miles down-river from Khartoum. The final effort to rescue Gordon would be made from there.

The first step was to concentrate the mounted troops and the infantry at Korti. Barges and steamers of Thomas Cook and Son, the tourist agents, were engaged to transport them from Assiut to the 2nd Cataract (Rapid) at Wadi Halfa. Thence the infantry would go in 800 small boats, similar to naval whalers. The mounted troops would make this stage of the journey by march route along the banks of the Nile.

As soon as the 1st Battalion was assembled in the Citadel at Cairo, preparations began to enable it to take the field. Grey uniform was issued to those who were not in possession of it. By September 9 the whole unit was ready for inspection by Lord Wolseley. Orders were then received that it was not to depart until the 1st Battalion The Royal Irish Regiment arrived from India.

In the middle of September Captain Morse, three sergeants and 42 rank and file left the battalion for Wadi Halfa. On the 27th, Lieutenant Alderson and 28 other ranks of the 2nd Battalion arrived there from Dublin. These two Queen's Own contingents were attached to B and D Companies of the Mounted Infantry Camel Regiment respectively and remained separate throughout the campaign. The personnel of this M.I. Regiment wore grey serge tunics, yellow ochre riding breeches, dark blue putties, coffee-coloured pith helmets and brown leather bandoliers — quite a colourful attire.

The advanced-party of the 1st Battalion left Cairo by train for

Assiut on November 9. The main body, 738 strong, marched out of the Citadel the following night and entrained at Boulac Dacrour Station.[1] All ranks wore red tunics, blue serge trousers and pith helmets; grey serge uniform was probably taken as a change of clothing. A rear-party of one officer and 108 other ranks, who were unfit for active service, remained in Cairo (Kasr-el-Nil Barracks).

The key personnel in the battalion were:—
Commanding Officer: Colonel E. Leach.
Second-in-Command: Lieutenant-Colonel J. L. Tweedie.
Adjutant: Lieutenant F. Wintour.
Quartermaster: Hon. Lieutenant R. J. Roche.
R.S.M.: Sergeant-Major W. Locks.
R.Q.M.S.: Quartermaster-Sergeant W. Dawson.

A complete list of officers can be found in Appendix C.

The battalion reached Assiut on the morning of November 11. The officers and the band boarded the S.S. " Masr," the largest of Cook and Son's flotilla of steamers. The remainder of the personnel embarked in four large barges. A further wait for the Royal Irish gave the troops an opportunity to visit the rock tombs above the town. The river journey began on the 13th. The " Masr," towing two barges, led the way, followed by a second steamer with the other two barges in tow. The stream was fast and the barges heavy, so that the average distance covered in a day was only about 30 miles. Each night was spent near a village, and the troops were allowed ashore until 7 p.m. to fish, wash clothing or listen to the band.

The convoy arrived at Assuan on the afternoon of November 24. Here was the first of the large cataracts, and the men and stores were disembarked. As soon as two trains were available, six companies were taken round the rapid. Headquarters, the band and the other two companies entrained next morning. The voyage was then resumed in a steamer, a barge and several small craft. Having passed Korosko on the 26th, the various vessels arrived at Wadi Halfa between November 28 and December 1. The battalion encamped on a sandy plain close to the river.

Wadi Halfa had become a temporary base for the Expedition as well as a permanent depot of commissariat and ordnance stores. It was something of a bottle-neck, because troops and provisions arrived from the north more quickly than they could be sent by train round the 2nd Cataract to Gemai. During the enforced delay E and H Companies were sent on to Sarras for fatigue duty. Major Robinson, Corporal Camber and two privates became ill with enteric fever. They died in hospital after the battalion had departed.

The battalion (less E and H Companies) moved from Wadi Halfa to Gemai by train in several parties between December 12 and 15. At Gemai each company in turn embarked in whalers — 12 men,

[1] Major Grove, who had recently returned from England, was Station Staff Officer at Boulac Dacrour. He remained on the Staff throughout the campaign.

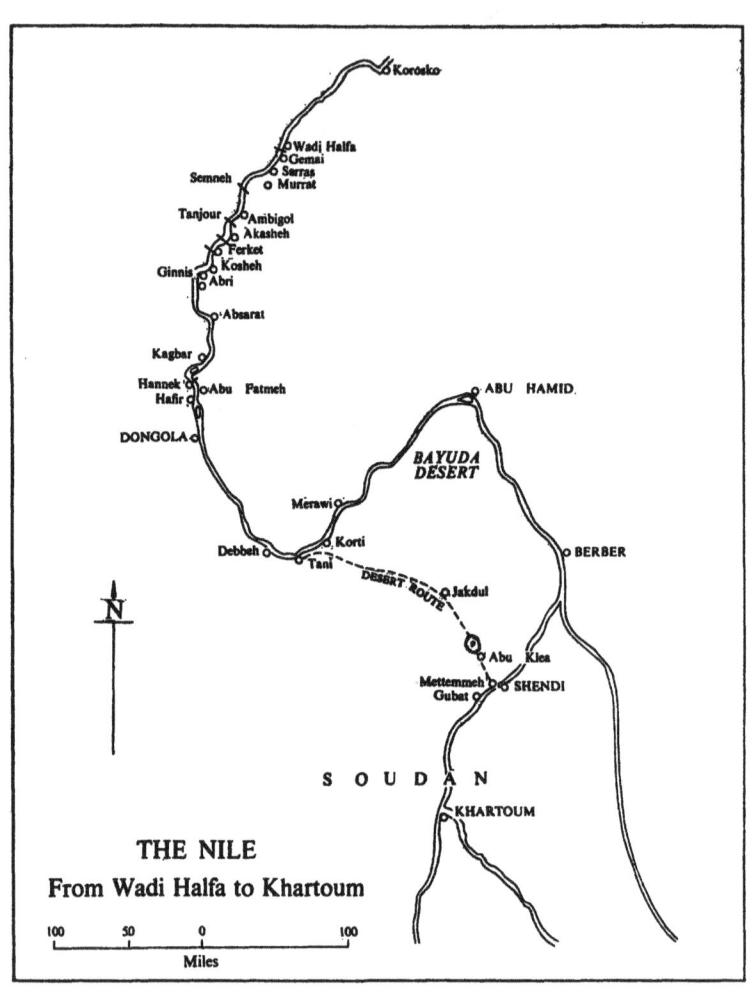

THE NILE
From Wadi Halfa to Khartoum

with their equipment and ammunition, to a boat. Rations for a hundred days were taken aboard at Sarras, where E and H embarked.

The stretch of the Nile from Gemai to Korti contained a series of dangerous rapids and difficult reaches, including the 3rd Cataract at Hannek. The whalers, which were suitable for rowing and sailing before the wind, had either to be carried round or hauled up them by ropes, called track-lines. Some Canadian boatmen, known as *voyageurs*, had been engaged to assist in the negotiation of the rapids; five or six were attached to each company of infantry. Egyptian labourers were stationed at the worst places to help with the portage. To provide for the needs of the personnel during the nightly halts, a series of posts had been established at intervals of about 30 miles. Cooking had to be done by the men at their bivouacs, fuel being bought from natives.

The first serious obstacle was the Lower Semneh Rapid, where, package by package, the cargo of each whaler had to be unloaded and carried round to smoother water. The track-lines were then passed over the rocks and, two or three crews manning one line, each boat was hauled up the cataract and run in to the bank opposite its cargo. This procedure was repeated at each rapid. Between the obstacles the whalers had to be rowed against a current as strong as the Thames in spate. Sometimes, when there was a fair breeze, a few hundred yards would be gained by making use of the sails. In this way the first 62 miles were covered in 18 days. For the next 100 miles the passage was smoother. At the 3rd Cataract a portage of more than three miles was necessary. After that came a long reach of clear water. The final stretch was a series of rapids as difficult as those south of Wadi Halfa. Eventually the companies reached Korti at various times between January 21 and 25, 1885. During the journey two men slipped as they were hauling their whalers over the rocks and were drowned.

A Special Order issued by Lord Wolseley recorded :—

" The following battalions in the order given have completed the journey in the quickest time:

1st Battalion The Royal Irish Regiment.

1st Battalion The Gordon Highlanders.

1st Battalion The Queen's Own (Royal West Kent Regiment).

. . . The Royal Irish and Royal West Kent Regiments have distinguished themselves by the care they have taken of their boats and of the boat supplies placed in their cargo . . . "

At Korti the battalion went to a Rest Camp, which was situated in a grove of trees near the left bank of the Nile. Many of the men were suffering from blistered hands. Some, including Major Bayly, whose hands had become raw, had been left temporarily in hospitals on the way. The clothing was in a deplorable condition, especially the trousers, which were worn through, and the boots, which had been torn by the jagged rocks.

7. The Desert Column

Because the infantry was behind schedule and Gordon was known to be short of supplies, Lord Wolseley had already sent forward his mounted troops and the 1st Battalion The Royal Sussex Regiment by a short cut across the Bayuda Desert to Mettemmeh, opposite Shendi. He now ordered the River Column to continue the journey in whalers. As a reward for their exertions on the way up the Nile, The Royal Irish and the 1st Battalion were detailed to wait at Korti as a reserve for the Desert Column. It is with that force therefore that we are hereafter concerned.

The main body of the Desert Column, including Morse's and Alderson's contingents of M.I., left Korti on January 8, 1885. It reached the wells at Jakdul on the morning of the 12th. Leaving the Light Camel Regiment and 150 men of The Royal Sussex to guard the wells, the column resumed its march. On the morning of the 16th, during the halt for breakfast, a message was received from The 19th Hussars, who were reconnoitring, that some Dervishes could be seen in the hills north-west of the oasis at Abu Klea. The Camel Corps and the M.I. Camel Regiment moved off on a broad front. When they approached the pass which led to the oasis, the forward troops dismounted and advanced on foot. The Dervishes retired to a prepared position. As it was too late to attack that day, Brigadier-General Sir Herbert Stewart, who was commanding, decided to bivouac for the night. He sent Morse's contingent of M.I. and a Gardner gun to take up an outpost position, and ordered the remainder of his force to construct a zeriba of brushwood and saddles.

During the dawn stand-to on January 17, Morse's party was called in. Whereupon the Dervishes re-appeared with drums beating and banners waving. After breakfast the zeriba was strengthened and a guard was detailed to remain in it with the camels and baggage. At nine o'clock the Column formed square with the M.I. Camel Regiment at the left front corner. As the square moved forward on foot the enemy opened fire on the front and both flanks.[1] The advance continued unchecked. When the square was opposite the left flank of their position and threatened to enfilade it, the Dervishes rose from the long grass. Armed with heavy swords and spears, they rushed towards the corner where the M.I. Camel Regiment was posted. The square halted. The troops fired volleys into the charging throng. The Dervishes swerved and penetrated the left rear corner. A hand-to-hand fight took place inside the square for 10 minutes. Then the enemy withdrew sullenly into the hills. Their losses had been very heavy, not less than 1,100 lying dead on the battlefield. The British casualties were 74 killed and 94 wounded. Of Alderson's contingent, Corporal Miles was killed by a spear; Private Neighbour was wounded in the leg.

[1] Some of the Dervishes were armed with Remington rifles captured from Colonel Hick's force.

When the dead had been buried the Column went on to Abu Klea, where it bivouacked in square at the oasis. That night a party went back to fetch the camels, the baggage and the occupants of the zeriba. On the morning of the 18th a small fort was built, and a company of The Royal Sussex was detailed to remain in it to protect the wounded. In the evening the main body started for Mettemmeh, a distance of 23 miles. On the 19th, when it was still four miles from its destination, an action similar to the fight at Abu Klea developed. The Dervishes were again repulsed, and the Column rode on to the Nile, where it took up a defensive position at Gubat. In this second action British losses were 23 killed and 98 wounded. Among the wounded was Private Swinbourne, of Alderson's contingent of M.I. He died on the 27th.

On January 21, four of Gordon's steamers arrived at Gubat from Khartoum. The commander of one of them brought news which made it imperative that Gordon should be brought away at once. There was some delay while wood was collected for the steamers to burn. On the 24th Colonel Sir Charles Wilson, with 20 Royal Sussex in scarlet tunics, set out for Khartoum in two of the vessels. When they came in sight of the town on the 28th, they saw that Government House and the buildings near it had been ransacked. No Egyptian flag was flying. Convinced that Khartoum had fallen, Wilson put about. On the way back he learned that Gordon had been killed on the 26th.

*   *   *

The Desert Column could not maintain its isolated position for long unless it was reinforced. Lord Wolseley decided to send forward his infantry reserve. He also ordered Major-General Sir Redvers Buller, V.C., to replace Stewart, who had been wounded on January 19.

The 1st Battalion The Royal Irish Regiment left Korti in several parties between January 28 and 31. They dropped two companies at Abu Klea and arrived at Gubat on February 11, having marched on foot the whole way.

As there was a scarcity of transport camels, further reinforcements could not leave Korti until February 10. On that day the Headquarters and A, E and G Companies of the 1st Battalion departed. Besides the C.O., the Adjutant and the Quartermaster, the officers who went were: Major Carr, Captains Jones and Evans, and Lieutenants Mann, Minchin, Sangster and Williams. Every man carried 70 rounds of ammunition, full water-bottle and rolled greatcoat. Extra water, reserve ammunition, rations for eight days, blankets and waterproof sheets were conveyed by 121 camels. Each night, on reaching the bivouac ground, square was formed and sentry-groups were posted. The men slept with their accoutrements on and rifles by their sides. Having marched 96 miles in six days, the small force arrived at the wells at Jakdul on the 16th.

By then, as the Mahdi's men were advancing on Gubat from Khartoum, Buller had withdrawn the Desert Column. When it reached

Abu Klea, he found that there were too few transport camels to evacuate the wounded, and he was compelled to wait at the oasis until more animals arrived from Jakdul.

So, at dawn on February 20, the Headquarters, A Company (Major Carr) and G Company (Captain Evans) of the 1st Battalion set off with a convoy for Abu Klea. All ranks were mounted on camels — not the most comfortable means of conveyance. The order of march was: one troop of The 19th Hussars; part of the Light Camel Regiment; the detachment of the 1st Battalion; a long string of camels carrying ammunition and water; a rear-party of the Light Camel Regiment. The first night was spent at Djebel El-Nus, 24 miles from Jakdul. Next day Lieutenant Williams and a score of A Company were left in charge of stores and water in a fort on the *djebel*, and the convoy rode a further 24 miles to the hills just short of Abu Klea. There the camels were handed over to the Desert Column. The infantry returned to Jakdul on foot in three marches. Williams' detachment remained at the water station at El-Nus to await the Desert Column.

Buller vacated Abu Klea after dark on February 23. At 6.40 the outposts were withdrawn. An hour later the Desert Column, probably including Morse's and Alderson's contingents of M.I., marched from the oasis. There were barely enough camels to carry the stores and the wounded, so that officers as well as other ranks were on foot. The camp fires were left burning, and the bugles sounded " The Last Post " as usual. The Dervishes did not interfere with the withdrawal.

When Buller arrived at Jakdul on the 26th, he received orders that the whole of the force in the desert was to return to Korti. Most of the troops began the journey back next day. The Headquarters and A, E and G Companies of the 1st Battalion marched out on the morning of the 28th for Megaga Wells, a distance of 27 miles. They remained there for nine days to guard the water while the garrison of Jakdul was passing through. They then destroyed the wells, and, in company with some of The Royal Irish, reached Korti on the morning of March 15, very ragged and rather drawn. Lord Wolseley met them a short distance from camp.

8. *The Return of the Expedition*

The River Column had also been ordered to withdraw. For it was now Wolseley's intention to distribute his troops along the Nile, from Merawi through Dongola to Hannek, until the beginning of the next cold season, when he would attempt the recapture of Berber. Meanwhile the erection of summer quarters was the chief consideration. Very soon the temperature would rise to well over 100 degrees, and tents would offer little protection against the strong, hot winds which would blow from the Bayuda Desert.

The place selected for the camp of the 1st Battalion was near the village of Tani, on the left bank of the Nile below Korti. The men set to work to build themselves cool, airy huts of mud-bricks or straw. Each hut accommodated 25 rank and file and had a verandah round it. Bedsteads, made from mimosa poles by the natives in the neighbouring villages, were issued. Two other infantry battalions, one troop of The 19th Hussars and part of the M.I. Camel Regiment were also accommodated in the camp. This force was organised into a mobile column, ready to go out at short notice if the enemy approached. Once the huts had been constructed there was little for the men to do, and boat races, concerts and a gymkhana were organised. On most evenings the band, whose instruments had arrived from Wadi Halfa, played in "Kentish Town." Before long the inactivity, the bad water and the heat affected the health of the personnel. Captain Birch, Lieutenants Williams and Anderson, and a dozen rank and file died of enteric fever or pneumonia.

In the spring the British Government abandoned its plan for further offensive action in the Sudan, and Lord Wolseley was ordered to withdraw his troops to Egypt. The evacuation was timed to begin on May 21, starting from the camp farthest up the Nile. The intention was kept secret as long as possible, since anarchy was certain to follow the withdrawal. On vacating the various stations, all stores likely to be of use were to be taken away. The remainder, such as bedsteads, were to be given to those natives who had been most friendly.

Tani was vacated on May 28. Some hours before the main body departed, the Mounted Infantry and the troop of The 19th Hussars rode down the left bank of the river as a flanking party. The three infantry battalions provided their own protection, while a steam pinnace followed behind the last whaler. The force bivouacked for the night at Debbeh. Subsequently, each unit moved independently. The 1st Battalion, under the Second-in-command, as Colonel Leach had been invalided to England, reached Dongola on June 1.

At Dongola the battalion, with one troop of The 19th Hussars and two guns, was detailed to be the absolute rearguard of the Expedition. Their orders were to wait until all camps farther south had been cleared, and until all stores and steamers had passed the 3rd Cataract at Hannek. This took about five weeks, during which the battalion lived in a dusty, insect-ridden camp. In the daytime it was so hot that all ranks remained in their straw huts, unless an escort was required to accompany a convoy to Abu Fatmeh. In the evenings they sometimes found enough energy to play a game of rounders or cricket. Every day refugees, fleeing before the threat of the Mahdi's approach, streamed through the town, carrying as many of their chattels as possible.

The rearguard left Dongola on July 5. That evening the battalion, in whalers, reached Hafir, where it occupied a camp in a large palm grove. Next day three companies moved on with the troop of The 19th Hussars to Abu Fatmeh. The rearguard remained in these stations for 10 days, while the steamers were passed down the Hannek

Cataract. When the retirement was resumed four companies, under Major Bayly, went down the cataract to Kagbar, and the remainder of the battalion moved to Abu Fatmeh. On the 17th Colonel Tweedie disconnected the telegraph at Abu Fatmeh and took his four companies to Kagbar. Bayly's detachment went on to Absarat. The troop of Hussars kept pace with these moves along the east bank of the river; the Gunners had already marched for Wadi Halfa. Below Absarat the whole battalion retired together. The rearguard arrived on the 21st at Abri, where its protective duties ended.

Having shot the rapids near Ferket, in which some of the Quartermaster's stores were lost, the battalion disembarked at Akasheh and handed in the whalers. The railway had by now been extended from Sarras to within a few miles of Akasheh. The troops marched to railhead, entrained there, and arrived at Wadi Halfa in two parties on July 24 and 25.

The Nile Expedition was at an end.

The Egyptian Medal with clasp " Nile, 1884-5,' was awarded to the officers and other ranks who took part in the Expedition.[1] An additional clasp, " Abu Klea," was received by the personnel of the Desert Column who were present at that battle.

9. *The Battle of Ginnis*

After the withdrawal of the Nile Expedition, one regiment of cavalry, one battery of artillery and four battalions of infantry were stationed at and south of Assuan. These British troops, together with some Egyptian units, formed the Sudan Frontier Force, which was commanded by Brigadier-General (local Major-General) F. W. Grenfell. Of this force the 1st Battalion, a battery of Egyptian artillery and part of the Egyptian Camel Corps composed the garrison of Wadi Halfa.

The village of Wadi Halfa contained little more than a sugar factory, a bazaar and a railway station. The battalion was accommodated in mud huts, which had neither doors nor windows. There were an Officers' Mess, a Canteen and a Hospital, all made of mud-bricks. The parade ground, of loose sand, was in the middle of the camp. Cooking was done in field kitchens, the rations consisting mainly of bully beef and preserved vegetables. For amusement the men had cricket, rounders, swimming and boating. The officers formed a yacht club, though most of the members had had a surfeit of sailing during the long trip to Korti and back.

Soon after their arrival at Wadi Halfa all ranks of the battalion were issued with khaki drill uniform.

[1] Many of the 1st Battalion were already in possession of the Egyptian Medal and so received the clasp only.

In August 1885 information came in to Wadi Halfa that the Mahdi's adherents, intent on the conquest of Egypt, had reached Dongola. Lieutenant Rowe was sent up the Nile in the steamer "Lotus" to locate them. He reported that the Dervishes were moving northwards in large numbers along the east bank. By October they were assembling near the village of Ginnis, only a short distance from Kosheh Fort, the most advanced British outpost.

In order to check this hostile advance the Sudan Frontier Force was ordered southwards. Most of the 1st Battalion, having left the heavy baggage and spare kit in the Nile Depot Store, moved by train to Akasheh on November 7. Lieutenant Annesley and 25 men were dropped at Ambigol Wells to augment the garrison of a small fort. One sergeant and 12 men were detached to man a blockhouse at Murrat Station. Captain Maunsell remained temporarily at Wadi Halfa, where he was in command of the newly-formed British Camel Corps.

On December 2, about 800 Dervishes made a daring raid on the railway at Ambigol Wells. They pulled down the field telegraph and besieged the fort, which Lieutenant Annesley's detachment and a handful of Royal Engineers were defending.[1] That night a party of the 1st Battalion The Royal Berkshire Regiment arrived by train from Wadi Halfa just before the raiders tore up the line. On December 3, Privates Harridine, Ralph and Simpkins, with some men of The Royal Berkshires, volunteered to make their way to the train and brought in some ammunition and medical stores. Next day Ambigol was visited by a mounted patrol, which managed to enter the fort under heavy fire. An officer and two men of this patrol rode out again to take news of the raid to Tanjour, the nearest British post. A relieving column left Akasheh that evening and reached Ambigol at daybreak on the 5th. The raiders dispersed.

The Dervishes then began to raid in the neighbourhood of Ferket. On December 12, Captain Evans' Company was sent southwards from Akasheh to reinforce the garrison. Early next morning the other companies and The Royal Berkshires followed by the desert route. There was no opposition, but the march, of 16 miles in great heat, was particularly arduous. At Ferket the Ambigol and Murrat detachments rejoined the battalion.

During the next few days several other units arrived at Ferket from the north. Lieutenant-General Sir Frederick Stephenson, who was commanding the British Army of Occupation, came from Cairo to take charge of the operations. He considered that the British troops should fight in " red." Consequently a party from each company of the battalion had to go back to Wadi Halfa to draw scarlet jackets and blue trousers from the Nile Depot Store.

By the 28th the whole Frontier Force, together with the 1st Battalion The Green Howards from Assiut, had concentrated in the area. The infantry were organised as two brigades. The 1st Brigade (Brigadier-General W. F. Butler) consisted of The Royal Berkshires, The Queen's

[1] The senior officer in the fort was Captain J. A. Ferrier, R.E.

Own and the 2nd Battalion The Durham Light Infantry; the 2nd Brigade of The Green Howards, The 1st Battalion The Cameron Highlanders and the 9th Egyptian Battalion. A battery of Egyptian Artillery was attached to the 1st Brigade, and a battery of screw guns to the 2nd. The mounted troops were The 20th Hussars and the British and Egyptian Camel Corps.

The Dervishes had assembled on the south bank of the Nile, which here ran from west to east. They were occupying a fortified village (Kosheh) about a mile west of Kosheh Fort. Their main camp was at Ginnis, some two miles farther west. Between the two villages were groups of mud houses surrounded by palm trees. Stephenson's plan of attack was for the 1st and part of the 2nd Brigade to make a detour and seize a rocky ridge which overlooked Kosheh and Ginnis from the south. The Cameron Highlanders would then sweep westwards from Kosheh Fort along the river bank, and, together with the rest of the 2nd Brigade, drive out the Dervishes at the point of the bayonet. The stern-wheeler " Lotus," manned by a detachment of the 1st Battalion under Lieutenant A. Wood Martyn, was to move up river slightly in advance of The Cameron Highlanders and engage the fortified houses at Kosheh. The mounted troops were to operate on the left flank.

On December 29, the Frontier Force advanced to a bivouac 700 yards north of Kosheh Fort. Opinions were divided as to whether the Dervishes would fight or not, but at nightfall several bullets fell amongst the outposts and all doubts were dispelled. Breakfasts were issued at 4 a.m. on the 30th. Blankets and greatcoats were stacked. Reserve ammunition, water and rations for one day were loaded on to camels. At five the 1st Brigade was on the march in a southerly direction. Just before daybreak it wheeled to its right. The going was bad — mainly rocky spurs and loose sand. As the leading companies of battalions approached the ridge from the south, they deployed into line. On reaching the top they took cover, while the supporting companies halted on the reverse slope. The 1st Battalion was on the right, The Royal Berkshires and the guns in the centre, The Durham Light Infantry on the left. Part of the 2nd Brigade with its screw guns was already in position to the right.

At 6.10 the screw guns opened fire. The Dervishes, taken by surprise, streamed out of their camp towards the ridge. The ground was undulating and afforded them excellent cover, from which their riflemen poured in a hot but ill-directed fire on to the 1st Brigade. Their spearmen attempted to charge the left of the line, but they were checked by some well-aimed shells from the Egyptian battery and steady volley firing by the infantry. The 1st Battalion was then ordered to prolong the line to the left. As the men moved off, fixing bayonets as they went, the British and Egyptian Camel Corps rode over the ridge. The Dervishes met them hand-to-hand and fought bravely until their right flank was turned by The 20th Hussars. They made good their retreat in the gullies.

By this time The Cameron Highlanders had captured Kosheh village, The Green Howards and the 9th Egyptian Battalion had joined them, and the whole of the 2nd Brigade, advancing west along the river bank, was in sight of the main camp. The 1st Brigade now moved down the slope to attack Ginnis. The enemy abandoned their camp without a fight and were pursued by the mounted troops in the direction of Abri. Two guns, a large amount of ammunition and a dozen banners were captured in Ginnis.

The enemy's losses were estimated at 600 killed. British casualties were eight killed and 33 wounded, none of them Queen's Own.

After the battle the Dervishes dispersed, and the units of the 1st Brigade were ordered to return to their previous stations. When the 1st Battalion arrived back at Wadi Halfa on January 9, 1886, it received the welcome news that it was to be relieved of its duties with the Sudan Frontier Force.

Since the battalion had left Cairo for the Nile Expedition in November 1884, five officers,[1] one colour-sergeant and 36 rank and file had died of disease or accident. Besides these, the Regiment had lost four rank and file of Alderson's contingent of M.I.— including one killed in action and one who had died of wounds.

Those who took part in the operations south of Wadi Halfa between November 30, 1885, and January 11, 1886, were awarded the Egyptian Medal and the Khedive's Bronze Star (if they had not previously received them).

Meanwhile, in England, a medical board had found Colonel Leach unfit to return to Egypt. Lieutenant-Colonel J. L. Tweedie was appointed to succeed him in command as from December 23, 1885.

The 1st Battalion left Wadi Halfa for Alexandria on January 13 in six barges towed in line ahead by one steamer. Four days later the flotilla reached Assuan, where the troops encamped for a week. The next stage, to Assiut, was carried out in two steamers, each towing barges. The remainder of the journey was by train. From Alexandria Station the battalion marched to a camp at Ramleh.

Two notable events occurred during the four months at Ramleh. On April 30 the sergeants entertained their friends at a Grand Ball in the Salle Storari, Alexandria, the hall being decorated with Sudanese trophies and banners captured at Ginnis. On May 27 the battalion trooped the Colour during the Queen's Birthday Parade in Alexandria.

On June 10, 1886, the battalion embarked in the S.S. " Poonah " for Gibraltar.

[1] This includes Major Carr, who died of dysentery at Wadi Halfa on January 19, 1886.

―――――― CHAPTER 4 ――――――

DEVELOPMENT
1886—1899

1. Regimental

THE Campaigns in Egypt and the Sudan brought two Battle Honours to the Regiment—"EGYPT, 1882," and "NILE, 1884-5." Queen Victoria approved of the 1st and 2nd Battalions being permitted to emblazon these two distinctions on their Regimental Colour.

The many cross-postings which had taken place between the Line battalions during the two campaigns, and the comradeship which had grown between the Regulars, Militia and Volunteers, blended the Territorial Regiment into a homogeneous organisation. The Regimental Spirit was evinced by two ventures. First, on July 16, 1886, a dinner for the past and present officers of the 1st and 2nd Battalions was held at the Hotel Metropole, London. Forty-one officers attended; Major-General E. D. Harvest, late 97th Foot, was in the chair. The occasion was such a success that the dinner became an annual event, usually at the Grand Hotel, Trafalgar Square. The second undertaking was the formation of a Regimental Cricket Team. Some matches had been played in 1884 and 1885 by sides made up of players from the Depot and the Militia and Volunteer battalions. In 1886, with the 2nd Battalion at Chatham, a more representative team was placed in the field, and games were played against seven clubs, including The Mote, Linton Park and The Buffs. In 1887 matches were arranged with The Mote and the School of Military Engineering, Chatham. Subsequently some games were played each summer. The first Regimental Cricket Week was arranged in 1891, the opponents being The Mote, Hayle Place and Linton Park.

A Memorial Window to the 75 members of the Regiment who lost their lives in Egypt and the Sudan was erected in All Saints' Church by their comrades in the 1st and 2nd Battalions. This window was unveiled on June 4, 1887, by Colonel E. Leach, C.B., who was at the time Assistant-Adjutant-General at Eastern Command. A Guard of Honour, consisting of men of the 2nd Battalion and dutymen from the Depot, lined the central aisle of the church. All the officers and other ranks who could get away from Chatham, the Depot Staff and recruits, the Militia band, and a strong detachment from the Maidstone Companies of the 1st Volunteer Battalion were present. The remainder of the church was filled by guests and the people of Maidstone.

The Colonel of the Regiment, General J. M. Perceval, C.B., was transferred to the Suffolk Regiment in February 1888. He was succeeded by General W. R. Preston. That officer's tenure was short; he went as Colonel to the Royal Munster Fusiliers in October 1890. The vacancy was filled by Lieutenant-General (Honorary General) Fowler Burton, C.B., who had been gazetted to The 97th Foot in August 1839 and had served with it throughout the Crimean War and the Indian Mutiny.

Colonel Safford, who had recently commanded the 2nd Battalion, succeeded Colonel R. A. Manners (late Royal Scots) in command of the Regimental District in July 1889. This was an important landmark, for thereafter the District was always commanded by an ex-Commanding Officer of one of the Line battalions.

The production of "The Queen's Own Gazette" continued in spite of several setbacks. In April 1887 the printer was posted from the Depot to the Home battalion, and the paper consisted of only a single sheet. From November 1887 to March 1888 it was not published at all, owing to lack of support. It re-appeared in its usual form in April 1888, when it was set up by Corporal Weeks at the Regimental Printing Press. The worst disaster occurred in February 1896, when Corporal Hibbert was the operator. For, early one morning the wooden building, in which the paper was printed, was gutted by fire.[1] Although much of the type was saved, it was impossible to carry on with the production in barracks, and a contract was made with Messrs. Dickinson of Maidstone. In 1897 the work was transferred to *The Kent Messenger,* who have produced the Q.O.C. ever since.

The Lee-Metford Magazine Rifle replaced the Martini-Henry in the Home battalion and at the Depot in 1890; in the 1st Battalion, then at Meerut, in February 1893; and in the Militia in 1894. There was no general change in dress during the period, but the 1st and 3rd Volunteer Battalions adopted scarlet uniform with blue facings in 1894 so as to come into line with the Regular and Militia elements. The 2nd Volunteer Battalion continued to wear green.

The new rifle could not be used with safety on the range at Boarley Farm, so the troops at the Depot had to go elsewhere to fire their annual courses. From 1891 to 1895 they went either to Dymchurch or Lydd, where two companies at a time were accommodated for 10 days. This was found to be unsatisfactory, and for the next four

[1] The fire occurred at 4 a.m. on February 21, 1896. The building was used also as the Quartermaster's Store and the Tailor's Shop. Some property of the 3rd Battalion and individual officers was destroyed; back numbers of the Q.O.G. were damaged.

years the courses were fired on the Milton Ranges at Gravesend. At the end of 1899 a new range at Boxley was taken into use. It had been constructed near the old one at Boarley Farm, but at an angle so as to give a greater safety zone behind the butts.

A Corporals' Room was opened at the Depot in January 1891, so that the junior N.C.O.s no longer shared the Canteen and Restaurant with the dutymen and recruits.

An attempt was made in 1891 to bring Rochester and Chatham into the Regimental Recruiting Area. The application was refused on the grounds that the locality was included in the 3rd (The Buffs') Regimental District, although it was 15 miles from the boundary. This anomaly was not removed until 1900.

A Memorial Screen to those of the 1st Battalion, who were killed or died of disease in the Punjab Frontier Campaign,[1] was unveiled in All Saints' Church on December 10th, 1898, by Major-General E. Leach, C.B., then G.O.C. Barbados. Every battalion of the Regiment, except the 1st, sent a contingent. The Guard of Honour was provided by the 2nd Battalion, and the Mayor and Corporation of Maidstone attended in state.

By 1891 cycling had become popular in the Home battalion and at the Depot. Few, if any, of the troops had civilian clothes, so they were permitted to wear a modified uniform when riding bicycles off duty. Another sport which was introduced into the Regiment was boxing, Recruits' Contests being held at the Depot as early as 1894. The first Regimental success at boxing on record is the victory of Corporal Pond in the Middle-Weights at the Thames District Competition in March 1897. Association football was the most popular game, and the Depot team won the Maidstone Football League in the seasons 1894-95 and 1896-97. The outstanding achievement was the winning of the Army Football Cup by the 2nd Battalion in March 1893. The following members of that battalion played football for Kent:—

1887. Lieutenant Pedley, Lieutenant Burbury and Corporal McGregor.

1893. Sergeant McGregor, Sergeant Sharp, Sergeant W. E. Bass, Corporal Spooner and Private McGregor.

2. *The 1st Battalion in Gibraltar, Malta and India*

The 1st Battalion arrived in Gibraltar on June 15, 1886, for a tour of three years. For most of this time it was accommodated in Casemates Barracks, but for the last 11 months it occupied South Barracks. The garrison, which consisted of four battalions of infantry besides ancillary services, was commanded by Major-General M. Walker, V.C., who carried out the annual inspections.

The only training that was possible on " The Rock " was shooting on the ranges at North Front and route marching. Garrison and Battalion

---

[1] See next Chapter.

Rifle Meetings were held each year. Ceremonial parades, including the Queen's Birthday Parade, took place either at North Front or on the Alameda.

With so many troops in the station, garrison duties were not heavy, and the troops had ample time for recreation. Cricket matches, gymkhanas, athletics meetings, bathing, fishing, and trips to places of interest in Spain occupied the summers. The monotony of the winter months was relieved by assaults-at-arms, weekly concerts in the Garrison Recreation Room, and visits to the Theatre Royal to see performances put on by the Amateur Dramatic Club. In the autumn of 1888 a Queen's Own Minstrel Troupe was formed.

On September 20, 1886, General The Honourable Sir Arthur Hardinge,[1] the Governor and Commander-in-Chief, presented Egyptian Medals to those officers and other ranks who were at the Battle of Ginnis and had not already received the medal. The presentation took place on the Alameda Parade Ground.

The outstanding social event was the Ball given by the officers in the Assembly Rooms on April 25, 1887. The staircase was draped with flags, including Dervish banners captured at Ginnis. At the top of the stairs were the battalion's Colours, with the drums piled beneath them. Bunting, half of Royal blue and half of sky blue (the regimental colours), was hanging round the gallery. H.R.H. Prince Albert of Wales, who was in Gibraltar at the time, and H.E. the Governor were among the 300 guests.

The battalion moved to Malta in the "Himalaya." Disembarkation took place on August 19, 1889, when six companies marched to their quarters on the east of the Grand Harbour as follows: — Headquarters and one company in Fort Ricasoli, one in Fort Salvatore, one in Vittoriosa Barracks, and three at the Zabbar Gate and Couvre Porte. The other two companies went to a camp at Pembroke. In the absence of Major-General Hales Wilkie, who was on leave, the Commanding Officer assumed temporary command of the infantry brigade. This consisted of six Regular battalions and the Royal Malta Regiment of Militia.

Except for range courses, which were fired at Pembroke, there was little training during the first summer, and the troops spent much time in bathing and boating. A few games of cricket were played at Fort Ricasoli and the Zabbar Gate. An Aquatics Meeting was held in September at Rinella Bay, inside the Grand Harbour. In the autumn, football became the main sport. Some of the men attended the Race-meetings on the Marsa Racecourse.

Lieutenant-Colonel W. H. Bayly took over command from Lieutenant-Colonel J. L. Tweedie, D.S.O., in December 1889.

The battalion moved over to Manoel Island, in Marsamuscetto Harbour, in March 1890. Headquarters, the Officers' Mess and the parade ground were inside Fort Manoel. Most of the other ranks were accommodated in huts, which had recently been erected on the

[1] Brother of Viscount Hardinge, who was commanding the 1st Volunteer Battalion.

grassy slopes outside the fort. Two companies were still detached at Pembroke.

Two peaceful years were spent on Manoel Island. Each spring the Malta Rifle Meeting took place at Pembroke, when the battalion acquitted itself well; indeed, it carried off the Challenge Cup in 1891. From April till June companies went in turn to Pembroke Camp for three weeks to fire the range courses. The summers were devoted mainly to regattas and swimming in Marsamuscetto Harbour, and to gymkhanas and cricket matches at the United Services Sports Club at Marsa. After the weather broke in September, route marching and tactical training began, the latter being carried out from tented camps in the north of the island. Altogether it was an uneventful but not unpleasant life.

Fort Manoel and the huts were meticulously inspected by H.R.H. The Duke of Cambridge, Commander-in-Chief of the Army, on February 8, 1891. He was accompanied by His Excellency the Governor, Lieutenant-General Sir Henry Smyth. They were received by a Guard of Honour and lunched in the Officers' Mess. In a speech after lunch the Duke said that he was very satisfied with the condition of the fort, the huts and the institutes.

Major-General Hales Wilkie died of heat apoplexy on December 24, 1891. As he had served in The 97th and had commanded 50th Regimental District, arrangements were made for the battalion to march in the funeral procession.

On the morning of January 2, 1892, two tugs took the battalion round to the Grand Harbour, where it embarked in the "Serapis." Already on board was a large draft from the 2nd Battalion. During the afternoon several friends came to say good-bye; and as the "Serapis" sailed slowly out that evening the band of each fort and ship played "A Hundred Pipers" as she passed. Extracts from a farewell article in *The Malta Chronicle* will show that The Queen's Own had made a good impression:—

". . . During the two years that this crack regiment has been in the garrison they have ever taken the foremost place, alike on the parade ground, on the Marsa, and in the boudoir . . . Not vainly did they hold the reputation of being the best dressed regiment in the garrison, a reputation trivial in itself, perhaps, but in their case significant, as emphasizing their general reputation for smartness and efficiency. Officers and men alike, the Royal West Kent will long be remembered in this garrison as one of the best regiments that has ever served in Malta . . . "

The "Serapis" arrived on January 19 at Karachi, whence the battalion went by rail to Meerut. On arrival, Colonel Bayly was informed that the whole battalion was to set out for the hill station at Chakrata on March 1.

The march up to the hills took 20 days. Each morning camp was struck before dawn, and the next bivouac area was reached in time for breakfast. Mild forms of exercise or shoots occupied the remainder of the daylight hours. At Chakrata, cricket, football and gymkhanas kept the troops fit for the first two months. Several field days took place in June. The monsoon put an end to most outdoor activities during July and August. With the appearance of snow on the summit of the neighbouring mountains in October, it was time to return to the plains. During the march back, which began on November 7, an exercise in siege warfare was carried out at Pur in co-operation with artillery and cavalry.

After the exercise Colonel Bayly said farewell to the battalion[1]. Major T. H. Brock succeeded to the command on December 23, 1892.

The battalion arrived back at Meerut on December 30. Headquarters and six companies were accommodated in the British Infantry Lines. The other two companies were on detachment at Delhi, where they lived in the fort. This was a particularly unhealthy spot, as the smell and dampness from the River Jumna caused fever and ague, and the companies were changed over frequently.

At Meerut the hot weather usually began in May, when all officers and other ranks who could be spared went on leave, and the convalescent personnel were sent up to the hills to recuperate. Those that remained at Headquarters carried out the routine duties in a temperature of over 100 degrees. By November, when the hot weather normally ended, the whole battalion had re-assembled at Meerut. Training began in December with field days on neighbouring areas, and culminated in the Meerut District Manoeuvres in February or March. The courses and rifle meetings were fired on a range close to barracks. The Meerut Assault-at-Arms, in which the battalion won the tug-of-war competition on two occasions, was held in January or February.

In the spring of 1895, 10 members of the battalion left Meerut for service with the Chitral Relief Force. Of these Lieutenants Marshall and Smith acted as Transport Officers in the Commissariat Department; Sergeant Haysmore and four privates did duty with Nos. 5 and 6 British Field Hospitals; Corporal Ailwood joined No. 3 Section of the Chitral Road Commandant's Office; and two privates served with other regiments. They all rejoined in October, when the force was dispersed. They were awarded the India Medal with clasp " Relief of Chitral, 1895."

The battalion left Meerut by train on February 24, 1897. After an uncomfortable journey of four days it arrived at Peshawar and marched to the British Infantry Lines, which it shared with the 1st Battalion The Buffs. The remainder of the garrison consisted of two Indian battalions, one Indian cavalry regiment and two batteries of artillery.

Peshawar is on the North-West Frontier of India, some 50 miles from the Malakand Pass. Two years back the local tribesmen, thinking that the Chitral Expedition was an invasion of their territory, had fiercely though unsuccessfully opposed its advance at the Malakand. Since then there had been no hostile acts. As conditions on the Frontier appeared to have returned to normal, the usual hot weather routine was put into operation. Two companies of the battalion went

---

[1] Colonel Bayly later commanded 50th Regimental District.

up to the hill station at Cherat in April, and 10 officers, including Colonel Brock and the Quartermaster, Captain Mansfield, left India on long leave. Other officers departed on short leave or courses. The first sign of trouble occurred on June 21, when Mr. Ross, a prominent business man, was murdered by a *ghazi* (religious fanatic). June 22 was the day of Queen Victoria's Diamond Jubilee. To begin the celebrations in Peshawar, an elaborate breakfast had been arranged by the Mohammedan community. But because of the crime many people were unwilling to enter the city, and the breakfast did not take place. In the evening however, an open-air concert organised by the battalion was attended by Major-General E. R. Elles, the District Commander, and a number of ladies who had not gone up to the hills.

A month later the hill tribes rose in revolt. On July 31 the battalion left Peshawar for active service on the North-West Frontier.

3. *The 2nd Battalion at Chatham, Portland, Shorncliffe, Enniskillen and Dublin*

The 2nd Battalion settled down quickly at Chatham. This was the first time that a Queen's Own Line battalion had been stationed in Kent since the formation of the Territorial Regiment, and all ranks were keen to create a close association with the county, the Militia and the Volunteers. Cricket matches were arranged against the Militia and several Kentish clubs, such as Rochester, Sittingbourne and Faversham. Shooting competitions took place with the Volunteer battalions. Many guests from the county were invited to the Athletics Meetings which were held on the Great Lines. But socially the most important event was the Ball given in the Officers' Mess on June 3, 1887. For this occasion a large marquee and a neighbouring house were linked by covered ways to the Mess, so that the 300 guests could dance in comfort.

Training consisted mainly of route marching, minor tactical schemes on local areas, and field firing exercises and range courses, which were fired at Gravesend by two companies at a time.

A battalion football team was started by Lieutenant Alderson in 1886. Wearing shirts of dark blue and light blue halves, it played against other battalions in Kent and the Depot. It was not a good team at first, but within a few years it became famous in the Southern Counties and in the Army.

Colonel Safford was placed on half-pay in June 1887. He handed over command to Lieutenant-Colonel J. A. Murray.

When the battalion left Chatham Major-General J. H. Dunne, who commanded Chatham District, had these words about the move published in District Orders:—

" . . . For 700, mostly young, soldiers to leave a station in their own county, where they have been quartered for two and a half years and have made many friends, without a single man drunk or absent, is a triumph over temptation which the Regiment may almost be as proud of as any of the 20 victories enrolled upon their Colours."

This statement opens a revealing window on military life in the 1880s.

A special train took the battalion to Portland on February 7, 1888. Verne Citadel Barracks, in which it was accommodated, were quite comfortable in spite of their grim name. They contained a good drill square and tennis and racquets courts, and there was a large field for games. The great disadvantage was that they were on the top of a steep and wind-swept hill. A small detachment of one officer and some 40 other ranks was maintained at Weymouth, which was four miles away. The nearest Army rifle range was at Chesil Beach, but the Naval Range at Portland was normally used. The annual inspections were made by the Officer Commanding Southern Command, General The Honourable Sir Leicester Smyth.

In November 1888 and again in January 1890 a detachment of one officer and some 35 other ranks went to Aldershot to attend a course organised by the 1st Mounted Infantry Regiment, of which Captain Alderson was Adjutant. During June 1890 a gun crew, under 2nd Lieutenant A. Martyn, took a three-barrelled Nordenfeldt to Portsmouth for a Southern Command training exercise. This is the first recorded occasion on which any battalion of the Regiment was armed with a machine gun.

Lieutenant-Colonel C. E. Partridge assumed command in March 1890.

Officers and men joined enthusiastically in the sporting life of Dorsetshire. Cricket and football matches were played against most of the clubs in the county, including Dorchester, Poole, Blandford, Weymouth College and Sherborne School. The Tug-of-War and Bayonet Exercise teams gained renown at local Assaults-at-Arms. The football team won the Dorset County Football Cup once, and the County Six-a-Side Tournament four times; eight of the team played football for Dorsetshire on various occasions.

The battalion marched out of Verne Citadel on February 10, 1891, and embarked in the " Assistance " at Portland. It disembarked at Dover next day and entrained for Shorncliffe, where it was accommodated in A Lines. The change was very welcome, for there were plenty of amusements in Shorncliffe Camp itself, and the entertainments of Folkestone and the social amenities of Kent were within easy reach. There was a fine field for games and athletics. Adequate training areas were close at hand. Excellent rifle ranges were available at Hythe.

New Colours were presented on the Brigade Drill Field by H.R.H. The Duke of Cambridge on June 23, 1891. In the absence of the Archbishop of Canterbury through indisposition, the Colours were consecrated by the Rev. E. F. Dyke, Vicar of All Saints', Maidstone. Lieutenant Doyle received the Queen's Colour, and Lieutenant Moody the Regimental. The R.S.M. was Sergeant-Major Beale. In the final march past the battalion was followed by other troops of the garrison, and by the 3rd and 4th Battalions of the Regiment, which were in D

Lines at the time for their annual training. Amongst former officers of The Queens' Own present on the ground were Major-General Hales Wilkie and Colonels Leach and Tweedie. Afterwards, the officers entertained over 100 guests to lunch in their Mess. That evening the sergeants gave a Ball in the Garrison Gymnasium, which was attended by representatives from every corps in the garrison, and from every battalion of the Regiment. These New Colours replaced the pair which had been presented to The 97th Foot in 1880. The Old Colours were not laid up until November 1909 (See Chapter 9, Section 1).

A firm friendship was formed with the Militia battalions while they were at Shorncliffe for their annual camps, and also with the 1st and 2nd Volunteer Battalions, which were there for training in 1892 and 1891 respectively. Shooting and cricket matches were arranged with them; training exercises were carried out together.

Civilians as well as the troops supported the battalion football team, which played games not only against most of the military sides in the neighbourhood but also against many of the prominent clubs in Kent — such as Maidstone, Ashford, Folkestone and the Royal Arsenal, Woolwich. In 1892 the team entered for the Football Association Cup, beating Chatham in the 1st Round and losing 0-2 to Millwall Athletic in the 2nd. The matches against talented civilian players moulded the side into a skilful combination. Yet the only notable sporting successes were at Tug-of-War. Twice, in 1891 and 1892, the battalion team won this competition at the Army Athletics Meeting at Aldershot, and in 1892 it was victorious at the Royal Military Tournament at the Agricultural Hall, London.

The move to Northern Ireland began on January 30, 1893, when the battalion went by rail to Dover and embarked again in the "Assistance." The ship arrived at Moville in Lough Foyle late on February 2. That evening three companies were taken in steam tugs to Londonderry. Next day the remainder of the battalion disembarked on to lighters and entrained for Enniskillen, whence one company went on to Belturbet.

Londonderry is 50 miles north, and Belturbet 30 miles south of Enniskillen. Of the three, Enniskillen was the worst station. There were no adequate training areas or ranges, and the four companies, which were accommodated in the Fort, fired the annual courses at Eglinton, near Londonderry. Ceremonial parades had to be carried out on the Fermanagh County Cricket Ground. A deep ditch ran through the middle of the football pitch, and the troops' cricket field was usually waterlogged. Consequently the main recreations were boating and fishing in Lough Erne. Belturbet was a little better. The town itself was quiet and offered no amusements, but a ground was placed at the disposal of the detachment for football practice, and the surrounding country was suitable for paper chases. The Londonderry detachment had the best of it. The three companies lived in comfortable barracks, which were pleasantly situated on a ridge overlooking the River Sillies. The town was large, with a theatre and other amenities. Furthermore, it was a garrison town, and good football and cricket pitches were available on the Military Recreation Ground.

With such long distances between detachments, it was difficult to nourish *esprit de corps*. In the circumstances it was fortunate that the football team was able to boost morale by winning the Army Cup. The team had entered for this competition when it was started in 1888-89, and in the last year at Portland had reached the 4th Round. During the first full season at Shorncliffe the issue had been quickly settled by a defeat in the 2nd Round. The 1892-93 contest had begun more hopefully with three well-deserved victories. The interruption in practice caused by the move to Ireland, and the lack of a suitable ground at Enniskillen then made further success doubtful. But before going to Belfast for the 4th Round the players put in some hard training. They managed to win. The semi-final was at Crewe against the 2nd Battalion The Scots Guards, who had won the Cup in the two previous seasons. The result was a win in extra time. The final was played on the Army Athletics Ground at Aldershot on March 29, 1893, against the 1st Battalion The Sherwood Foresters. After extra time the score was 1-1. When the teams met again next day, The Queen's Own scored the only goal of the match. The Cup was received by Lieutenant Burbury, the captain. The players were:—

Goalkeeper	Lance-Sergeant W. Pepper
Backs	Corporal W. Jones Musician J. Ball
Half-backs	Sergeant W. E. Bass Lieutenant F. W. Burbury Sergeant G. Taylor
Forwards	Private W. McGregor Sergeant J. McGregor Sergeant J. Sharp Lance-Corporal W. Richardson Corporal J. Spooner

The team was trained by Armourer-Sergeant J. Hadgkiss.

So as to give the side the practice that was necessary if it was to repeat its victory in the Army Cup, tours were arranged in England in December 1893 and December 1894, while the players were on leave. In spite of this preparation, the team went no farther than the 4th Round. A change of station seemed to be the only hope of further success.

Lieutenant-Colonel J. C. Cautley assumed command in March 1894.

The battalion moved to Dublin by train on November 4, 1895. It was accommodated in Royal Barracks. The first reaction of all ranks was that it was good to be stationed in a city where there was an abundance of entertainment. But they quickly realised that life had its sterner aspect, with route marches three times a week, lectures and war games at the Royal Institute, and numerous guards and other garrison duties to be done. Only two weeks after its arrival the battalion was put through a searching inspection by Field-Marshal Lord Roberts, who was commanding the Forces in Ireland. Nor was the first annual inspection, made by Major-General Viscount Frankfort de Montmorency, G.O.C. Dublin District, less exacting. It was carried out in marching order in barracks and in drill order on the Fifteen Acres in Phoenix Park. In addition, rehearsals soon began for Guards of Honour, which had to be found for Garden Parties at the Vice-regal Lodge, for Drawing Rooms at the Castle, and for the Dublin Horse Show.

Range courses and field firing were carried out from Kilbride Camp, whither half the battalion at a time went for two or three weeks. This camp was a 17-miles' march, mainly uphill, from Royal Barracks; the only link with Dublin was a steam tram. Field training began in March with company tactical schemes on local areas. Battalion training followed. Each August the 9th Dublin Brigade, to which the battalion belonged, went to the Curragh. From there it marched farther afield for inter-brigade and inter-divisional exercises. The practice, begun at Portland, of sending detachments to Aldershot for courses in Mounted Infantry duties was resumed. In April 1897 the battalion went through a test mobilization.

Colonel Cautley retired on account of ill-health in August 1896. Lieutenant-Colonel E. A. W. S. Grove rejoined from half-pay to take over.

A Garrison Torchlight Tattoo was held in Phoenix Park in March 1897 to commemorate the sixtieth year of Queen Victoria's reign. The actual Diamond Jubilee celebrations, on June 22, were marred by disturbances in the city; the parade in Phoenix Park was limited to a *feu-de-joie* and a march past in column. Another special occasion was the visit of the Duke and Duchess of York in August 1897. The battalion furnished the Guard of Honour which received them at Kingstown, lined a portion of the route as they drove through Dublin, and found another Guard of Honour at a Garden Party which they attended at the Vice-regal Lodge.

With opponents like the Bohemians, the Hibernians and Shelbourne to practice against, the football team quickly returned to its old form. In 1895-96 it had three early victories in the Army Cup, and went on to beat the 2nd Battalion The Black Watch in the semi-final on Preston North End's ground. The final was played at Aldershot on Easter Monday, April 6, 1896. The 1st Battalion The Royal Scots won 3-1. After this the team fell away, though it managed to reach the semi-final in 1897-98.

On June 30, 1898, after two and a half strenuous years in Dublin, the battalion went via Holyhead to Aldershot, where it occupied a camp on Rushmoor Hill. It took part in the Queen's Review on Laffan's Plain on July 7, and lined a portion of the route to Farnborough Station on Her Majesty's departure. For the next nine weeks it carried out brigade and divisional exercises from camp. At the end of August it went by rail to Homington, near Salisbury, for Army Manoeuvres[1]. These ended near Weyhill, where the troops entrained for Chatham.

---

[1] These were the famous Grand Manoeuvres of 1898. Manoeuvres on such a large scale had not been held for many years.

DEVELOPMENT 53

An advanced-party had gone on ahead to take over the barracks, so that everything was ready when the battalion marched in late on September 9. Only 10 years had passed since the last tour at Chatham, and some of the older hands were familiar with the routine of garrison duties, route marches and shooting on Milton Ranges. All ranks looked forward to a long stay in their home county. Fate intervened.

In June 1899 the battalion set out on a recruiting march through West Kent. The route was from Chatham to Maidstone — Hadlow — Tunbridge Wells — Tonbridge — Sevenoaks — Westerham — Green Street Green — Bromley — St. Mary's Cray — Dartford — Farningham — Malling — Chatham. The march took 16 days. The nights were spent in tents pitched in parks or other suitable places. At each camp a Torchlight Tattoo, organised by Bandmaster Ingham and Sergeant-Drummer Inglis, was performed. The people gave the troops an enthusiastic reception at every town and village; the gentry bestowed hospitality on them. Eleven recruits were attested during the march, while a hundred other youths handed in their names. This number was disappointingly small, but the secondary object of the march — to promote a closer union between the Regiment and the County — was undoubtedly achieved.

A few weeks after it arrived back in barracks, the battalion was placed under orders to proceed overseas.

4. *The Militia Battalions*

Except for the years 1893, 1895 and 1897 the annual training of the Militia battalions took place as usual at Shorncliffe. While they were there in May, 1886, The Duke of Connaught, as Honorary Colonel, paid his first visit to them. In 1887 they paraded with the troops of the garrison on June 21 to celebrate Queen Victoria's Golden Jubilee; on the 24th the officers gave a Jubilee Ball in the gymnasium. In 1891 and 1892 they trained with the 2nd Battalion, which was at Shorncliffe at the time. In 1899 the Militia again took part in field days with Regular troops, some of the exercises being watched by H.R.H. The Duke of Cambridge, and Major-General Sir Leslie Rundle, who was commanding the South-Eastern District.

The first two weeks of the annual training in 1893 and 1895 were spent in camp at Lydd, where the range course was fired. During the other fortnight manoeuvres were carried out with the 18th Militia Brigade and other formations of the South-Eastern District. The annual training of 1897 requires a more detailed description. The first two weeks were spent in camp at Lodge Hill, Chattenden (near Chatham), during which the range courses were fired at Gravesend. The troops then set out on a march through West Kent. The route was Meopham — Seal — Wrotham Heath — Maidstone. Training exercises were carried out on the way, and camp was pitched each night. Queen Victoria's Diamond Jubilee was celebrated at Seal on June 22, when a *feu-de-joie* was fired and a Torchlight Tattoo was given at night. A detachment of some 220 all ranks, with the Colours and the band, went to London for the day and lined part of the processional route on the north side of The Mall, near Marlborough Gate.

In 1894, after the Lee-Metford Magazine Rifles had been issued, the Militia recruits ceased to fire their range course while they were at the Depot. Instead, they went to camp for an extra 14 days and completed their recruits' course before the trained men arrived.

From April 1, 1894, the 3rd and 4th Battalions were amalgamated into one unit. The 12 companies remained in being, so that the reduction in establishment was limited to one battalion headquarters. The title became The 3rd Battalion The Queen's Own (Royal West Kent Regiment).

5. *The Volunteer Battalions*

By 1886 the Volunteer battalions had become an important part of the Regiment. They obtained their permanent staffs, which included an Adjutant, an R.S.M. and a number of instructors[1], from the Line battalions. They sent representative detachments to the principal Regimental ceremonies. They supplied players to assist the Regimental cricket side. In every possible way they maintained a close association with the Regulars and the Militia.

The main event in the Volunteers' year was the eight days' annual training. For a number of years the camps were held in the battalion areas, the 1st choosing sites at Brasted, Penshurst or Somerhill Park near Tonbridge; the 2nd at Grove Park or Plaistow Lodge near Bromley; and the 3rd at Erith or St. Paul's Cray. In the early 1890s the battalions began to go farther afield — to such places as Minster, Shorncliffe, Bisley and even Gosport. From 1894 onwards the Volunteers trained by brigades or larger formations. These combined camps were held at Aldershot, Shorncliffe or near Ashford.

Attendance at annual camp was not obligatory. Further voluntary training was sometimes carried out during the Easter and Whitsun week-ends, usually at the Depot. At Easter 1891 the 2nd Volunteer Battalion took part in an exercise near Brighton, and in 1896 it joined 5,000 other Volunteers in a field day near Winchester. The most important Easter was that of 1890, when both the 1st and 2nd spent the holiday at Maidstone. The other ranks were accommodated in the drill-shed, the gymnasium and vacant barrack rooms at the Depot, while the officers slept at the Bell Hotel and the New Inn. A concert was arranged in the Corn Exchange on the Saturday night;

[1] The number of instructors depended on the lay-out of the battalion. For example the 3rd, with only one drill station, had fewer than the 1st and 2nd.

all ranks marched to All Saints' Church for a service on the Sunday; the two battalions joined in a training exercise at Blue Bell Hill on the Monday. At Whitsun 1899 the 3rd marched through part of West Kent, the route being Woolwich — Dartford — Gravesend — Maidstone.

Annual inspections were made by the Officer Commanding 50th Regimental District. These normally took place while the battalions were in camp. But after 1890 the 2nd and 3rd were sometimes inspected on the Polo Ground of Charlton Court, the seat of Sir Spencer Maryon Wilson (see page two). In 1899 the inspection of the 1st was carried out at the Depot, that of the 2nd in a field near Shooters' Hill, and that of the 3rd on Woolwich Common.

A spacious drill hall for the 3rd Volunteer Battalion was opened by Earl Stanhope, Lord Lieutenant of Kent, in Beresford Street, Woolwich, on June 14, 1890. As it contained a Canteen for the rank and file, and Messes for the officers and sergeants, it was very suitable for social functions, such as Prizegivings and Concerts.

There was a change in the lay-out of the 1st Volunteer Battalion in 1893. The Penshurst Company was disbanded, and a third company (F) was formed at Maidstone to replace it.

The 2nd Volunteer Battalion was gradually re-organised. In June 1888 Holly Hedge House, which stood on Blackheath, was acquired as Battalion Headquarters[1]. A drill hall was built in the grounds. It was centrally placed for Deptford, Greenwich, Charlton and Lee. By 1890 the various small drill stations in the area had been closed, and the eight companies affected were drilling at Holly Hedge House. There was a further change in 1892, when a company was raised from the students of the Goldsmiths' Technical and Recreation Institute at New Cross. At the same time the detachment at Dartford was reduced to one company instead of two. Thereafter, the only outlying companies were C at Dartford, D at New Cross and E at Bromley.

The 1st Volunteer Battalion had a reputation for skill at arms. It was the best Volunteer unit at shooting in Thames District in 1893, 1894 and 1898. The Bayonet Exercise Team of the Maidstone Companies won the 1st prize for Volunteer Corps at the Royal Military Tournament in 1892.

The 3rd Volunteer Battalion carried out the tests of a cycle mounting for Maxim machine guns in November 1891. The gun and carriage, mounted on cycle wheels, were drawn by two Humber cycles[2]. The ammunition was carried in the bandoliers of the crew as well as in the carriage. The weapon was fired from the mounting at the proof butts of the Maxim Gun Company at Erith. This appears to have been the first occasion on which a Maxim was fired by personnel of the Regiment.

[1] Holly Hedge House, with three acres of land, was leased for 30 years by the Right Hon. William Walter, 5th Earl of Dartmouth, on June 24, 1888. The freehold was conveyed to the 2nd V.B. for £2,600 on November 28, 1906.

[2] Cyclist Sections were formed in Volunteer Battalions in 1888 cr 1889.

CHAPTER 5

THE FIRST BATTALION IN THE PUNJAB FRONTIER CAMPAIGN AND THE ADEN EXPEDITION

July, 1897—November, 1902

1. The Rising of the Hill Tribes

IN July 1897 there arrived in the Malakand district of the North-West Frontier of India a *mullah* (priest) who professed that he could work miracles. The Mad Mullah, as he came to be called, preached a Holy War, declaring that he would expel the British within eight days. With astonishing speed he gained an incredible hold over the tribesmen. On the 26th, followed by a fanatical mob, he moved towards the British fort and camp at the Malakand Pass.

The "Alarm" was sounded at the Malakand at 10 p.m. It was only just in time. A few minutes later the tribesmen rushed wildly at the fort from several directions. They were beaten off, but returned again and again until 4.30 a.m., when they withdrew into the surrounding hills. During the following day large parties of hostile natives could be seen closing in on the Malakand from all points of the compass. This information was telegraphed to Nowshera. That night, and again on the night of the 28th, the assaults on the Malakand were fiercely resumed. They were repulsed with difficulty.

The 29th was *Jumarat,* a day on which the prophet watches over those who die in battle for the faith. As expected, the attacks were flung in after dark with greater ferocity. At 2 a.m. one group of tribesmen reached the defences and began to pull down some of the sangars. In this charge, it is said, the Mad Mullah was wounded. Be this as it may, the assaults suddenly ceased. Although they tried again on the 30th, the attackers seemed to have lost much of their zeal. Next morning two Indian battalions arrived from Nowshera, and the tribesmen gradually dispersed to their villages.

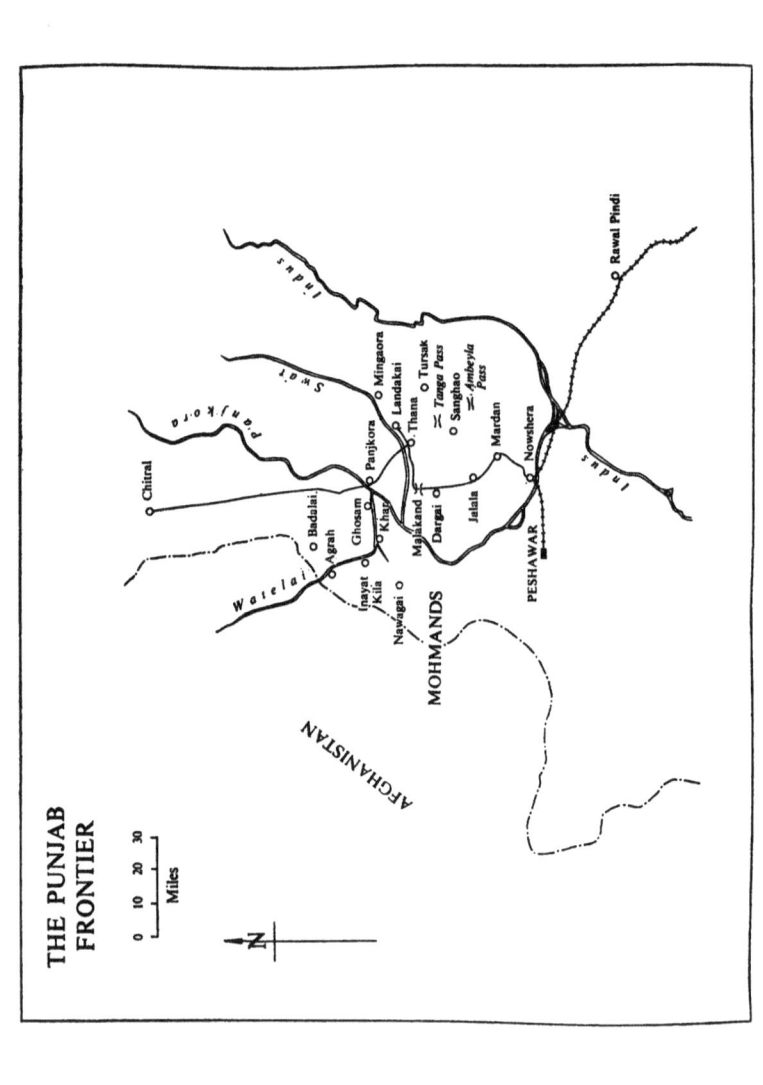

As soon as it became clear that the rising was a concerted attempt by all the neighbouring tribes to drive the British from the area, the Government of India began to assemble a force strong enough to suppress it. The force consisted of Divisional Troops and three Infantry Brigades. It was placed under the command of Major-General Sir Bindon Blood. Of the Peshawar garrison, the 1st Battalion was in the 1st Brigade; the 1st Battalion The Buffs and The 35th Sikhs were in the 2nd. The other units in the 1st Brigade, which was commanded by Brigadier-General W. H. Meiklejohn, were The 24th Punjab Infantry, The 31st Punjab Infantry and The 45th Sikhs.

The 1st Battalion entrained at Peshawar for Nowshera on July 31. Many of the officers were on leave or courses, and only Major Evans, two captains and seven subalterns were present. The dress was khaki drill tunics and trousers; putties; white pith helmets in khaki covers, with sun curtains at the back of the helmets; leather belts and pouches; and valises. The other ranks were armed with Lee-Metford magazine rifles.

At Nowshera the night was spent in loading tents, stores, kits and blankets on to the 105 pack-mules and 143 camels, which comprised the unit transport. The men had no sleep. After a hasty breakfast, the march of 16 miles along the dusty road to Mardan began. Towards midday the heat became oppressive, and some of the troops were very distressed when they reached camp. The next march, of 12 miles to Jalala, was made in the cool hours of the morning. Tents were erected at the side of the road, and the battalion had a long rest. Then on again through the sweltering plain to Dargai, a fort at the foot of the Malakand Pass. On leaving Dargai the road wound up-hill through the pass and turned eastwards into the valley of the River Swat. At Amandarra, five miles west of Thana, the battalion joined the 1st Brigade in the concentration area. During the march of 54 miles from Nowshera, Sergeant Tollman and two privates died of heat apoplexy.

While the battalion was at Amandarra seven officers arrived. Captain Hewett became Brigade Signal Officer. As Colonel Brock had not yet returned from leave the key personnel were:—
  Commanding: Major C. W. H. Evans.
  Adjutant: Lieutenant C. G. Pack-Beresford.
  Quartermaster: Hon. Captain A. E. Mansfield.
  R.S.M.: Sergeant-Major S. J. Barton.
  R.Q.M.S.: Quartermaster-Sergeant W. H. Noller.
A list of the officers is in Appendix C.

2. *The Malakand Field Force*

The rapid concentration of the Malakand Field Force, as Blood's Division was named, had caused the troops severe hardship. There was now a pause of 10 days, during which the commissariat arrangements were organised and the 1st Brigade was made ready for operations. Information was received that tribesmen were moving from the south into the Swat Valley, where the Mad Mullah was still preaching a Holy War. General Blood ordered Meiklejohn to advance into the valley and strike a swift blow.

The 1st Brigade, with The Guides Cavalry, The 11th Bengal Lancers, The 10th Field Battery (12-pdr. guns), Nos. 7 and 8 Mountain Batteries and a company of Sappers and Miners, moved forward to Thana on the afternoon of August 16. Camp was pitched in fields well away from the hills. That evening cavalry patrols located groups of tribesmen near Landakai, about three miles ahead.

The position held by the enemy was on a range of hills which overlooked the track from Thana. It was nearly two miles in length. The right rested on a steep, rocky spur overhanging the River Swat. Between this spur and the river was a narrow causeway, which was the only route into the Swat Valley. Barring the approach to the causeway was a low ridge. Beyond the range of hills was an open plain of swamps and rice fields.

At 6.30 a.m. on August 17 The Guides Cavalry and two companies of the 1st Battalion moved out from camp as an advanced-guard. The cavalry found hostile outposts in a group of ruined buildings on the low ridge. The two companies engaged these outposts, while the remainder of the battalion deployed and drove them back to their main position. It could then be seen that the tribesmen were occupying sangars and an old Buddhist fort on the range of hills. They were dressed in dark blue and white clothing. Many of them were defiantly waving gaily-coloured banners. Their bagpipes were playing inspiring tunes.

The 10th Field Battery and No. 7 (British) Mountain Battery now came into action on the low ridge, whence they opened fire at 1,600 yards, first on the Buddhist fort, and then along the whole length of the position. Covered by this shelling the two battalions of Punjabis, with No. 8 (Bengal) Mountain Battery and The 45th Sikhs in support, advanced towards the enemy's left flank. Realising that their line of retreat into the plain was threatened, the tribesmen attempted to reinforce this flank from their reserve near the causeway. This move was prevented by the volleys of the 1st Battalion. As the Punjabis approached the summit of the range, one desperate charge was made by a handful of *ghazis*. But the majority of the enemy lost heart. Many of them made good their escape into the plain before the Punjabis swung left and began to clear the position.

At 11 o'clock the 1st Battalion advanced, firing controlled volleys as they went. When they reached the top of the spur near the causeway, the remaining tribesmen vacated their sangars and the Buddhist fort, rushed down the hillside and fled across the rice fields. Some were shot as they tried to carry away their dead. The Guides Cavalry rode up to the causeway, filed along the narrow passage, each man leading his horse, and emerged at the other end. Seeing the enemy escaping across the plain, they galloped over the swampy ground in pursuit. No. 8 Mountain Battery completed the rout.

In this action the casualties in Meiklejohn's force were two officers killed, and two officers and seven other ranks wounded. None of them was Queen's Own.

After a quiet night at Landakai, the force marched into the Swat Valley. The road was rough and narrow, and only 10 miles were covered on the 18th. Next day, after another march of 10 miles, the troops reached Mingaora.

This part of the valley was covered with fine crops and large villages. Many of the inhabitants had remained in their houses and willingly provided grain, chickens and pigeons to supplement the rations. During the next four days all the villages in the vicinity accepted the terms of submission, namely, to hand over any arms or government property in their possession, to demolish their fortified towers, and to supply what fodder and wood the force required during its stay. Among the weapons handed over were nine rifles lost in the defence of the Malakand.

The column began the march back on August 24. It reached Thana on the 26th, and on the 27th went on to the Malakand Pass. Here the 1st Battalion occupied Crater Camp; eight more officers rejoined, having returned post-haste from leave in England. One of them was Major Western, who assumed the duties of Second-in-command. Colonel Brock reached Bombay, but was unable to travel further owing to illness, so Major Evans continued in command. Captain Mansfield fell sick, and Lieutenant Isacke became Quartermaster.

*   *   *

Early in September Sir Bindon Blood was ordered to punish the Mohmands. His plan was that his 2nd and 3rd Brigades, with cavalry and artillery, would move to Nawagai and enter the Mohmand country from the north-east. At the same time the Mohmand Field Force would leave the Peshawar area and march north. Having effected a junction, the combined columns would inflict such punishment on the tribe as might be necessary.

Leaving his 1st Brigade to hold the Malakand Pass and posts on the line of communications to Panjkora, Blood set out for Nawagai on September 4. By the 10th, Force Headquarters and the 2nd and 3rd Brigades had all crossed the narrow suspension bridge over the Panjkora River and had concentrated at Ghosam. From there the 3rd Brigade went on to Nawagai, linked up with the Mohmand Field Force and operated with it as intended. The plan for the 2nd Brigade was changed. On the night of the 14th its camp near Khar was strongly attacked, and Sir Bindon ordered Brigadier-General P. D. Jeffreys, who was commanding the brigade, to enter the Watelai Valley and punish the tribesmen.

Jeffreys marched north and encamped at Inayat Kila, whence the 2nd Brigade went out daily to destroy all villages within reach. This treatment seemed to break the spirit of the tribesmen in the Watelai Valley. They asked for peace, and were given up to the 29th to hand back some rifles which they had captured. During the lull the 1st Battalion was ordered up from the Malakand to relieve The Buffs, who were suffering a good deal from fever.

The 1st Battalion marched out from Crater Camp on September 21. On the first day difficulty was experienced in getting the camels across the Swat River. Several of them broke away from their strings, and some 50 kits fell into the water. These were recovered some distance down stream. Two more marches took the battalion to the base camp in the Panjkora bridgehead. The next stretch, to Khar, was of 16 miles over a road little better than a goat track. As they were leaving Khar, The Buffs came in. "What's it like up there?" asked one of The Queen's Own. "You'll be all right," replied a Buff, "so long as you don't go near no officers nor no white stones." He meant that the officers, being dressed differently from the men, were conspicuous targets. During the last nine miles to Inayat Kila heavy rain drenched the troops, but the hot sun in the afternoon and a tot of rum soon put matters right.

The camp at Inayat Kila was situated as far as possible from *nullahs* and rocky knolls, which might give cover to snipers. It was arranged in the form of a square, with the infantry and guns on the perimeter, and the cavalry and transport animals in the centre. Round the perimeter were a parapet with traverses and a trench. The parapet had been strengthened by large boulders, and sharp stakes had been driven into it to check rushes by an attacker. At night sentries were posted at intervals of 20 yards. Half of the men in each infantry company slept in the trench, with equipment on and arms through their rifle slings. The remainder of the infantry lay, dressed and accoutred, in bivouacs made from waterproof sheets and sticks. Magazines of rifles were charged and bayonets fixed from dusk till dawn.

For the first few days at Inayat Kila the battalion was occupied in escorting convoys of mules to villages, which had been destroyed, in order to bring back grain and fodder. As a rule the commodities were buried in vaults in the fields, and it required a practised eye to locate them. During these foraging expeditions the troops met with no opposition, but the tribesmen could be seen watching from the neighbouring hills. At night snipers sometimes fired into the camp. On one occasion Major Evans had a narrow escape when a bullet passed through the side of his bivouac.

As the rifles were not forthcoming, Brigadier-General Jeffreys resumed operations. At 5.30 a.m. on September 30, his force moved out to destroy the fortified villages of Agrah and Ghat. These villages consisted of stone houses with towers, in which the families lived with their armed retainers. They were perched on the lower slope of a steep and rugged hill. On the slope great rocks were interspersed with narrow terraces, which rose 10 to 12 feet one above the other. On either side of the villages were rocky spurs, strewn with boulders and loose stones.

The valley up which the troops moved was very rough and broken. Nothing was seen of the enemy for the first seven miles. Then The

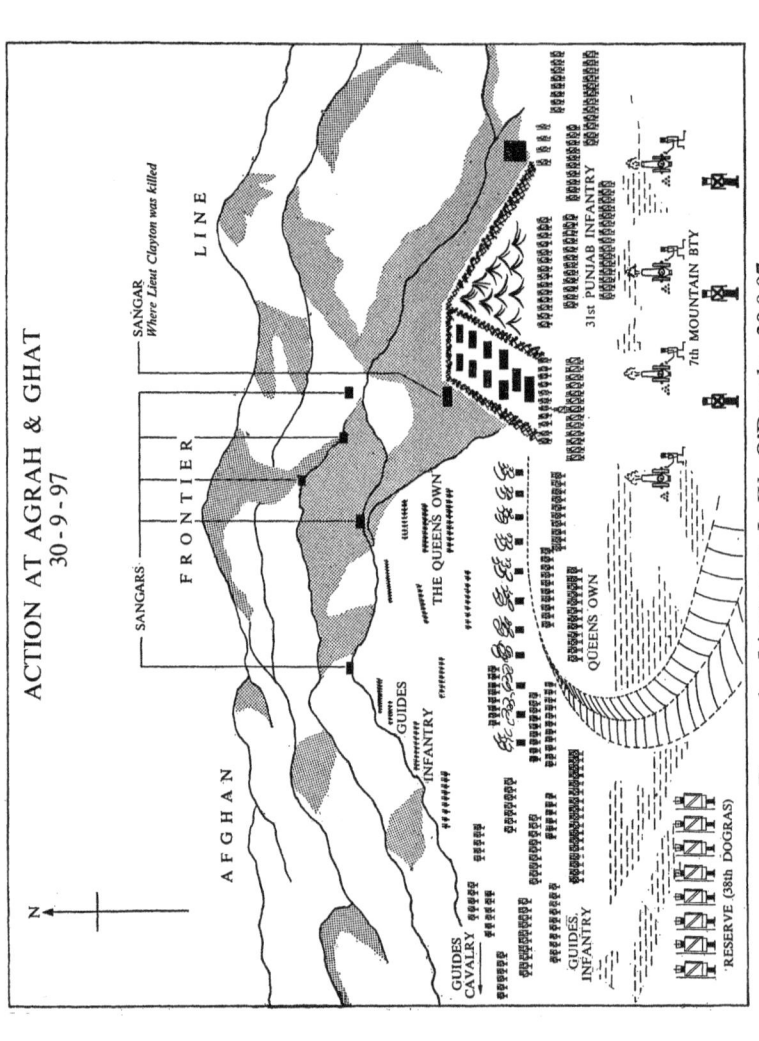

Guides Cavalry sent back word that several red standards were visible on some sangars near Agrah. The tom-toms of the villagers could be heard summoning their comrades from all parts of the valley. Large numbers of tribesmen came hurrying down a re-entrant on the left. They were checked by the arrival of the cavalry.

It was now clear that the enemy were in strength on the spurs on either side of Agrah and Ghat, and that these must be captured before the villages could be destroyed. While the cavalry continued to block the re-entrant, the brigade advanced into action. The Guides Infantry and the 1st Battalion attacked the spur on the left of Agrah. The 31st Punjabis (from the 1st Brigade) made for the spur on the right of Ghat. The 38th Dogras were in reserve.

The 1st Battalion advanced at a quick pace with The Guides Infantry prolonging the line to the left. The tribesmen opened fire from stone sangars, on which banners were fluttering in the wind. But when the troops got within a hundred yards of them and fixed bayonets, only a dozen *ghazis* stood to resist the assault. The rest retired up the rocky slope, and the position was taken without a single casualty. On the right, the Punjabis captured their spur after a sharp fight. The 38th Dogras remained in rear to protect No. 7 Mountain Battery, which, firing over the heads of the troops, shelled some sangars on the higher slopes.

The brigade stayed in these positions for about an hour, during which the Sappers and Miners destroyed the two villages. When the time came to withdraw, the Punjabis could not disengage without support. To assist their retirement, the 1st Battalion was ordered to move down the slope on its right and up to the spur above the village of Ghat.

As each company arrived on the spur it came under the fire of the tribesmen, who had moved down the hill to harass the withdrawal. The troops were hampered by the terraces, and the sub-units became separated. Part of C Company, led by Lieutenant Browne-Clayton, stormed a sangar, driving the occupants up the slope. About 15 men entered the post. But after four or five of them had been hit by bullets fired from higher ground, they were ordered to withdraw. At that moment Browne-Clayton was shot dead. Before his body could be passed over the rock wall, the tribesmen suddenly charged. Major Western, who was nearby, told A Company to advance, re-take the sangar and recover the body. Captain Style was the first to reach the post; he was closely followed by 2nd-Lieutenant Jackson and Lance-Corporal McGee. Colour-Sergeant Willis supervised the evacuation of the dead and wounded down the slope.

The 1st Battalion and the Punjabis then retired by alternate companies to the plain below, a steady fire being maintained as they fell back. Several times the tribesmen rushed to within 20 yards of the rear company, but they invariably withdrew again on being charged with the bayonet. The cavalry prevented them from following beyond the broken ground at the foot of the hill. The march back to camp was unmolested.

The total casualties in the brigade were two officers and 10 other ranks killed; six officers and 42 other ranks wounded. Of the 1st Battalion, Lieutenant Browne-Clayton, Drummer Berry, and Privates Hutson and Jones were killed; Sergeant Warner was mortally wounded; five officers and 19 privates were hit.[1] The other ranks, who had been killed, were buried at Inayat Kila. The bodies of the officers were taken to the Malakand for burial.

On October 3 the brigade went out to destroy the village of Badalai. The tribesmen offered no opposition. But on the way back they appeared in large numbers and closed in on the troops in a great crescent. The battalion, acting as right flank-guard, made good shooting at 500 yards with their magazine rifles. The cavalry prevented the enemy from following along the level ground. In this skirmish the casualties were two killed and 14 wounded. Amongst the latter were three other ranks of The Queen's Own[2].

Reinforcements, including the 2nd Battalion The Highland Light Infantry and four guns of the 10th Field Battery, reached Inayat Kila on October 4. The appearance of the 12-pounders was too much for the tribesmen. They again sued for peace. This time their sincerity was beyond suspicion. The captured rifles were surrendered, and all the neighbouring khans offered their submission at a full *durbar*.

While the peace was being negotiated, the men who were too ill to walk were sent to the Malakand. The convoy of about 60 wounded and the same number of sick left Inayat Kila on October 9, some being carried in cradles by camels and others in litters by natives. As the danger of attack on the long, straggling column was great, it was escorted as far as Panjkora by the 1st Battalion.

The battalion remained at Panjkora until October 24. During that time the remainder of the troops arrived from Inayat Kila. The whole force then marched back across the Swat River.

In his despatch Sir Bindon Blood wrote:— " The conduct and discipline of the troops in the Watelai Valley was in the highest degree satisfactory. The operations were carried out without tents and on a very low scale of baggage, while the rations, though abundant and excellent in all respects, were necessarily open to the objection of sameness. Notwithstanding these inconveniences, the troops remained uniformly cheerful, especially when active hostilities were going on..."

3. *The Buner Field Force*

When the 1st Battalion arrived back at the Malakand Pass it rejoined the 1st Brigade. Brigadier-General Meiklejohn was still in command, but the other battalions were now The 16th Bengal Infantry and The 20th Punjabis. At the end of October, the 1st

---

[1] Of those hit, sixteen were only slightly injured. The others were Captain Style, Lieutenant Isacke and Privates Bright, Buckland, Edwards, Jipps, Meagher and Sullivan.

[2] Sergeants Ashby and Regan, and Private Clipsham.

Brigade moved to Kunda Camp, near Mardan, where it spent two restful months under canvas.

On New Year's Day 1898 Sir Bindon Blood received orders to move against the Buner tribe, which had not yet acceded to the terms imposed on it for its complicity in the Malakand rising. For this operation Blood formed the Buner Field Force, consisting of Divisional Troops and the 1st and 2nd Brigades. Captain Hewett was Signal Officer at Force Headquarters; Lieutenant O'Dowda replaced him as Signal Officer of the 1st Brigade.

The Buner Field Force concentrated at Sanghao on January 6. Reconnaissances found that all the passes leading into Buner were held by the Bunerwals. Sir Bindon decided to send a mobile column to threaten three of the defiles, and to launch his main attack against the Tanga Pass. This was visible from Sanghao. The Bunerwals seemed to be expecting an assault that day; during the night their snipers fired into the camp without causing any casualties.

At 8 a.m. on the 7th The 20th Punjabis set out from Sanghao to scale a high peak to the north of the Tanga Pass, whence they could command the right flank of the position held by the Bunerwals. Half an hour later The Buffs moved forward with the artillery. At nine the 10th Field Battery began to bombard the main ridge. Under cover of the 12-pounders The Buffs extended, climbed an intermediate spur and opened volley fire at 1,400 yards. They were followed by No. 7 and No. 8 Mountain Batteries, which sent a hail of shrapnel all along the ridge and prevented the tribesmen from firing over the top of their sangars.

When this combined artillery and infantry fire had made its power felt, The Highland Light Infantry, The 21st Punjabis and the 1st Battalion advanced through a narrow ravine into a small basin. The 16th Bengal Infantry was in support. From the basin The H.L.I. and The 21st Punjabis clambered up the hillside on the left so as to link up with The 20th Punjabis. The 1st Battalion, led by A Company, scrambled in single file up a goat track, which led straight to the pass. For an hour the ascent went on. The Bunerwals, exposed to the fire of the artillery, offered little resistance until A Company was 600 yards below them. They then fired a few shots from their sangars and rolled rocks and boulders down on to the troops. There was no cover. But the adoption of fire and movement tactics enabled the climb to be resumed. A few minutes later the arrival of The 20th Punjabis on the peak to the north caused the defence to collapse abruptly. A Company pressed on, impeded only by obstacles which had been placed on the track, and reached the summit with a cheer. At 2 p.m. Lieutenant O'Dowda signalled to Force Headquarters that the Tanga Pass had been taken with the loss of but one casualty — a private of The Highland Light Infantry.

Sir Bindon Blood attributed this easy success to the endurance of the infantry; the careful and judicious leading by the officers; and the signalling arrangements made by Captain Hewett, which enabled him " to time the various movements with an accuracy which would not have been otherwise possible."

As soon as the battalion had re-formed, Major Evans led it down into the valley on the east of the Tanga Pass, where The Highland Light Infantry and The 20th Punjabis joined it. These three battalions bivouacked near a village for the night. As the transport animals could not get over the pass, the blankets and greatcoats were brought forward by coolies.

The morning of January 8 was spent by the troops in collecting grain, which was found in large quantities in every house in the village. That evening some mules, having managed to cross the pass, arrived with supplies. Although the Sappers improved the track, the transportation of the stores and baggage took three days. During that time one company of the 1st Battalion was posted in the pass to keep it open, and heliographic communication was maintained with Force Headquarters by a party of signallers.

Meanwhile the mobile column had captured a pass five miles south of Tanga and had also entered the Buner country. The 2nd Brigade now marched south to storm the Ambeyla Pass.

On January 10, leaving the 1st Battalion to guard the Tanga Pass, Meiklejohn moved unopposed to Tursak, the capital of Buner. The inhabitants were submissive. On the 12th, Headquarters, A, C, D and F Companies of the battalion escorted a convoy to Tursak; the other four companies joined them there on the 15th. The units at Tursak were then divided into two columns, which marched by separate routes through Buner. The tribesmen accepted the terms imposed on them, and promptly paid their fines and provided what grain was required. On January 18, all the villages having been visited, both the 1st and 2nd Brigades left the Buner country by the Ambeyla Pass. A long and dusty march brought the Force to Mardan, where it broke up.

All those who took part either in the Malakand or the Buner operations were granted the India Medal (1895) with clasp " Punjab Frontier, 1897-98." They also received a gratuity according to rank. A list of Honours and Awards can be found in Appendix D.

4. *Interludes in Bengal and Burma*

The departure of the 1st Battalion from the Punjab Frontier was unexpectedly sudden. It did not even return to its barracks at Peshawar. Having rested at Mardan for one day only, the troops marched to Nowshera, where they entrained for Dum Dum on January 25, 1898. The journey took seven days.

The barracks at Dum Dum consisted of five large two-storey buildings, and a fine bungalow in which were the Sergeants' Mess and the Regimental Institutes. The Officers' Mess was in Dum Dum House, where Lord Clive had once lived. There was a football pitch on the barrack square, and a cricket ground nearby. Calcutta was but seven miles away. One company was on detachment at Barrackpore.

On February 28, the battalion marched to Calcutta for the unveiling of a statue of Field-Marshal Lord Roberts. All ranks were accommodated in tents on the *maidan* near Fort William. The ceremony was performed by the Earl of Elgin, the Viceroy of India, the following afternoon. As the statue was unveiled, 4,000 troops presented arms and a salute was fired by the guns of the fort. The battalion marched back to Dum Dum early on March 2.

Punkahs were started in barracks on March 15, when also white uniform was taken into use for walking out. A number of officers and other ranks departed on leave, and 70 convalescent men went up to the hill station at Darjeeling. The remainder of the personnel were occupied during the hot weather in firing the annual rifle course on a range near Dum Dum. After the monsoon, football, hockey and, a new game, bicycle-polo, were played with a good deal of enthusiasm. The battalion Rugby team — the first to be turned out — entered for the Calcutta Cup Competition, but was beaten in the first round. Cricket was started when the cold weather returned in October.

The Punjab Frontier Medals were presented on the barrack square by Brigadier-General J. H. Wodehouse, commanding the Presidency District, on December 4. He personally pinned on the medals of the officers and sergeants; those of the rank and file were pinned on by the company commanders. After the parade, which ended with a march past in column and quarter column, the officers entertained their guests to lunch.

Lieutenant-Colonel (Brevet-Colonel) T. H. Brock, who had rejoined from sick leave in August, was placed on half-pay on December 23. Major C. W. H. Evans, D.S.O., succeeded to the command.

The battalion again marched into Calcutta to a camp on the *maidan* on December 28. This time it was for the Annual Proclamation Parade. Several rehearsals were carried out, and the actual parade took place on January 2 (the 1st, the usual day, was a Sunday). The troops were drawn up in line almost a mile in length, with the spectators forming a ring of four miles in circumference. At 8 a.m., on the arrival of the Viceroy, the Royal Salute was given. This was followed by a *feu-de-joie* and three cheers for the Queen-Empress. The Earl of Elgin then drove down the line, and the parade ended with a march past. The battalion returned to Dum Dum on the 8th, having undergone various inspections during the intervening period.

*   *   *

The move to Burma began on January 11, 1899, when four companies marched to Calcutta. They embarked in the Royal Indian Marine Steamship "Dalhousie" on the 13th and arrived at Rangoon four days later. The remainder of the battalion left Dum Dum on February 2, sailed from Calcutta in the R.I.M.S. "Canning" on the 4th, and disembarked at Rangoon on the 8th. After four days on shore D and E Companies, under Major Rowe, went on in the "Canning" to Port Blair, in the Andaman Islands.

At Rangoon the battalion (less two companies) was accommodated in wooden bungalows built on piles. The cantonment lay to the north of the town, which was out of bounds because of a small-pox epidemic. Facilities for games were practically non-existent; boating on a neighbouring lake was almost the sole recreation. Furthermore, the only form of training that could be carried out was the annual rifle course. This was fired on a range six miles from the cantonment, each company in turn camping in a grove of trees for the duration of the course. The troops found the tents considerably cooler than the bungalows. All things considered the situation was somewhat depressing.

For the hot weather a detachment of one officer and 70 other ranks went to the hill station at Wellington, near Ootacamund in India. Several officers, including Colonel Evans, departed for long leave in England. It was during that monotonous, oppressive summer that, after less than seven months in Burma, the battalion was suddenly ordered to Aden.

The move to Aden was a considerable nautical operation. On September 18, D and E Companies left Port Blair in the R.I.M.S. " Clive " for Rangoon, where the other six companies embarked. The " Clive " then took the whole battalion to Bombay. There the personnel and baggage were transferred to the troopship " Dunera," which sailed for Aden on October 5.

5. Aden

When the " Dunera " entered the harbour at Aden on October 15, 1899, orders were received for some 250 men to stay on board and proceed to Alexandria to join the 2nd Battalion, which had arrived in Egypt a month before and was well below strength. The remainder of the personnel, about 500 in all, went ashore in two parties. Three companies disembarked at Steamer Point, where they were accommodated in barracks just above the landing-place. Headquarters and the other five companies transferred to lighters, landed at the main quay and marched to Crater Camp.

Crater Camp, which was five miles by road from the town of Aden, was reached either through a narrow gorge or through a long tunnel. Triangular in shape, the barracks consisted of double-storey stone buildings, with the other ranks' accommodation on one side, the married quarters on another, and the various offices, messes and institutes on the third. The chief disadvantage, both at the Crater and at Steamer Point, was the shortage of water. Rain seldom falls in Aden, but when it does come it is collected in a series of storage reservoirs, called " tanks," made partly by excavation and partly by damming a deep *nullah*. These tanks were often empty, and most of the water for drinking had to be distilled.

Besides the battalion, the garrison of Aden comprised The 5th Bombay Light Infantry, which occupied barracks near the Crater, and some detachments of Garrison Artillery, which manned the forts at the harbour entrance.

Football, hockey and cricket grounds, of a sort, were available at the Crater. There was a good theatre at Steamer Point, in which boxing contests, concerts and assaults at-arms were held. Gymkhanas took place on the racecourse. In the town were an Officers' Club, in which the battalion band played frequently, and a club for the European other ranks. Sea-bathing was a popular pastime, though it was inadvisable in the deep water near Steamer Point owing to the presence of sharks. Some of the men became interested in sea-fishing. Others found cliff-climbing an outlet for their energy. A few ardent cyclists were able to obtain bicycles. At the Crater the Army Temperance Association, the Good Templars and the Rechabites each had a tent, and between them many enjoyable social evenings were organised. In the cooler weather the band gave a series of concerts on the *maidan*, near the town, for the entertainment of civilians as well as the troops.

Lieutenant-Colonel C. W. H. Evans, D.S.O., was placed on half-pay on March 21, 1900. Major C. E. C. B. Harrison, who was appointed to succeed him, was on active service with the 2nd Battalion in South Africa and was unable to get to Aden until September. Major Western was in command until July, when he himself sailed for South Africa and Major Rowe took over.

The progress of the war in South Africa was followed with great interest. So much so that on June 6 a holiday was granted to celebrate the capture of Pretoria. At reveillé the troops at the Crater were awakened by the band playing " God Save The Queen," and they spent the morning in decorating the barrack rooms with flags. In the evening the band played on the *maidan* to an enthusiastic audience. The native shops all round were illuminated by innumerable tiny oil lamps, which made a romantic scene as darkness fell.

During the hot weather of 1900 the battalion suffered considerably from fever, and the hospitals at Crater Camp and at Steamer Point became overcrowded. The women and children were also affected; several whole families fell sick. To make matters worse, plague broke out in the town, quite half of the population left the area, and there were no servants to pull the *punkahs*. The situation improved only when the cooler weather arrived.

In January 1901 an attempt was made to carry out field training in conjunction with The 5th Bombay Light Infantry. A Battalion Rifle Meeting, which continued for five days, also took place. This was held on the range near Steamer Point, where the annual courses were fired.

Their Royal Highnesses the Duke and Duchess of Cornwall and York,[1] who were on a tour of the Empire, arrived in the harbour in the Royal Yacht " Ophir " on the morning of Good Friday, April 5. In the evening a launch brought their Royal Highnesses to the Prince of Wales' Pier, where a Guard of Honour furnished by the

[1] On the accession of Edward VII the Duke of York became also the Duke of Cornwall.

battalion received them. After the Duke had inspected the guard, the Royal procession drove to the Crater. The route was lined by troops, one man to every 25 yards, the Europeans wearing white uniform and the Indians khaki drill. At the Crater the Duke laid the foundation stone of a new hospital. The Royal party then visited the famous tanks, and arrived back at the pier at about 6.30, when the Guard of Honour again presented arms. The "Ophir" departed at midnight.

When the hot weather closed in again in May, the usual exodus began of those whose turn it was for leave. Fifty sick men were invalided to England. The remainder of the battalion resigned themselves to a tedious six months. Suddenly the prospect was brightened by the chance of a spell of active service.

6. *The Aden Expedition of 1901*

The port of Aden had been taken over by the British in 1839. It had rapidly grown in importance as a trading post of the East India Company, and tribes in the hinterland had begun to send caravans of merchandise to the port for shipment. This led to a request by a number of the tribes to be placed under British protection. In 1891 the Aden Protectorate had been surveyed and mapped. Within its boundaries dwelt nine tribes. One of these was the Haushabi tribe, whose territory adjoined the Arabian frontier. Arabia was under Turkish rule.

Early in 1900 the Sultan of the Haushabi tribe reported to the Resident of Aden that Mohammed Bin Nasir Mukbil, who collected taxes for the Turks, had built a stone tower within the limits of the Haushabi territory. Correspondence took place between the British Foreign Office and the Porte at Constantinople, with the result that Mukbil was told to vacate the tower. But Mukbil did not do this. Eventually the Resident of Aden received orders from the Foreign Office that the tower was to be destroyed.

The outcome of all this was that on July 12, 1901, Colonel Harrison was instructed to prepare an expedition for active service in the Aden Protectorate. His orders were to proceed to the Haushabi territory and demolish Mukbil's tower. This stood near the village of Ad Daraijah, about 60 miles north-west of Aden and only a few hundred yards from the Arabian frontier. On no account were any of his troops to cross the border into Arabia. The composition of his force was to be: —

    219 all ranks of the 1st Battalion.
    216 all ranks of The 5th Bombay Light Infantry.
    Six mountain guns (7-pounders) carried on camels.
    A company of Bombay Sappers and Miners.
    A section of a Field Hospital.
    The Aden Troop of native levies, about 100 strong.

The detachment of the 1st Battalion was placed under the command of Major Rowe. It was organised as three companies. No. 1, under

ACTION AT AD DARAIJAH

Lieutenant Hastings, consisted of men from B, E and H Companies. No. 2 was composed of men from D Company and was commanded by Lieutenant Snow. The personnel of No. 3 were drawn from the other four companies, with 2nd-Lieutenant Keenlyside in command. The Transport Officer was 2nd-Lieutenant Hudson. The detachment wore khaki drill uniform and topees; every man was issued with a pair of goggles and a spine pad.

The Expedition, officially named the Ad Daraijah Field Force, assembled at Sheikh Othman, nine miles north-west of Aden, on July 15. Here Colonel Harrison, who had been unwell for some time, was prostrated by the heat and was sent back to Aden by the Medical Officer. The command of the force devolved on Major Rowe.

For the first 30 miles, to Musemir, the route was little more than a bridle path across the desert, and the baggage, rations and forage were carried by a string of over 400 transport camels. Owing to the heat and the deep sand, only short marches were made each morning. Camp was then pitched, and the troops spent the remainder of each 24 hours in tents. Water was brought up each day by another string of camels, which was controlled by Sergeant Kill. As the distance from Aden increased so the daily journeys to and fro of this water-convoy lengthened. In spite of all precautions, two rank and file of the battalion and one gunner died of heat apoplexy during the early days of the march; 2nd-Lieutenant Keenlyside and 20 men, stricken by the sun, were compelled to return to Aden. On the 23rd the force reached Musemir, where a halt was made for a day and a base camp was formed. The desert had now been left behind, and the expedition was about to enter the hilly country of the Haushabis. The village of Ad Daraijah was 16 miles ahead.

The Force moved on in light order on the 25th to Mileh, a village seven miles south of Ad Daraijah. All reports received up till then agreed that Mukbil had some 2,000 Arabs with him, of whom 400 were occupying Ad Daraijah and the rest were guarding the tower. In the afternoon Major Rowe and the company commanders went forward with a small escort of the mounted levies to reconnoitre the position. He found that Ad Daraijah was situated on a low ridge, the approach to which was concealed by a belt of trees. From the village the ground sloped up in a north-easterly direction to a hill, on which was a small fort. On higher ground to the north of the village were two large sangars. Mukbil's tower was beyond the sangars. The first task was to capture the village and the small fort. Major Rowe's plan was that the detachment of Bombay Light Infantry should attack frontally so as to hold the enemy's attention, while Nos. 1 and 2 Companies of the 1st Battalion moved round to the right under cover of the trees and took the position in flank. The guns, escorted by No. 3 Company, would support the attack. The Aden troop would protect the left flank.

At 5.30 a.m. on July 26 the whole force moved off northwards from Mileh. When it had marched five miles, it reached some water pools in the bed of a *nullah*, where breakfast was cooked and issued. The infantry then advanced to the southern edge of the trees, with Nos.

1 and 2 Companies on the right and The Bombay Light Infantry on the left. The guns came into position on a knoll south of the trees. So far Mukbil's Arabs had shown no sign that they were aware of the impending attack.

The engagement opened with the guns firing at the fort. Immediately a number of Arabs made off up the hillside. Supported by accurate shelling the infantry attack went well. Despite considerable opposition Nos. 1 and 2 Companies, skilfully led by Lieutenant Hastings, seized the fort and cleared the ridge on which it stood at the point of the bayonet. Some of the enemy made a determined stand, but by 2 p.m. the Ad Daraijah position had been captured with the loss of five casualties. Two of the wounded were Queen's Own.

The Arabs had retired up the slope to their sangars, from which they maintained a hot fire. The guns were now brought forward to a position north of the village and began to shell the sangars. Nos. 1 and 2 Companies moved farther up the slope so that they could shoot more accurately. This fire fight went on until five o'clock, when a heavy thunderstorm came on and continued for an hour. The rain was so heavy that the opposing forces were hidden from each other. During the storm many of Mukbil's men seem to have quitted the arena, for when the guns resumed the shelling there was but a feeble reply. By dusk all firing had ceased.

Mukbil's casualties were estimated at 40. The Field Force lost a total of nine. Of these the 1st Battalion had Private Hoy killed and 2nd-Lieutenant Hudson, Sergeant Ailwood, Corporal Ward and Private Clarke wounded.

After this engagement the Field Force bivouacked in the village of Ad Daraijah, with sentry groups posted on high ground. During the night not a shot was fired, but further fighting was expected on the morrow. Several prisoners were brought in. They were all Turks, and from them it was learned that Mukbil had persuaded the garrison commander at Tayiz to send him reinforcements, alleging that the British were about to attack him in Turkish territory. This explained why the opposition had been so heavy.

At dawn on the 27th an ultimatum was sent to Mukbil demanding the surrender of the tower. The messenger returned with the information that neither Mukbil nor his men were anywhere in the vicinity. The Force therefore marched to the tower, the Sappers and Miners prepared their demolition charges, and soon nothing was left of it but a heap of stones and smouldering rafters. Later in the day some Arab traders rode in to Ad Daraijah. They reported that the Turkish commander was so incensed at having been misled that he had ordered Mukbil to be brought to him under arrest. As an act of courtesy the Turkish prisoners were taken to the frontier and released.

The Ad Daraijah Field Force began the journey back on August 3. The marches were carried out either in the cool hours of the morning or in the evening, and the 60 miles were covered in eight days with little discomfort. At Sheikh Othman Brigadier-General P. J. Maitland, the officer commanding at Aden, who had ridden out

to welcome the expedition, addressed a few words to each unit. To the detachment of the 1st Battalion he said:—
"When you left Aden, the first three or four marches were very trying . . . but you stuck to it pluckily, and your difficulties lessened as the distance from Aden increased . . . With regard to the very successful action at Ad Daraijah, I was extremely glad to hear such good accounts of your behaviour . . . I shall have much pleasure in so reporting to the Commander-in-Chief."

There is a tablet in All Saints' Church, Maidstone, to the memory of the three other ranks who lost their lives during the expedition.

*   *   *

One other notable event occurred before the battalion departed from Aden. This was the replacement of the Lee-Metford by the Long Lee-Enfield Rifle in November 1901. The main difference between the two weapons was that the rifling turned in the opposite direction.

After many farewell functions the battalion sailed for Malta in the troopship "Sicilia" on February 13, 1902. The relieving unit was the 2nd Battalion The Royal Dublin Fusiliers, who came from South Africa.

7. *Nine Months in Malta*

The "Sicilia" made a slow passage though the Suez Canal and did not anchor in the Grand Harbour, Malta, until February 24. Having disembarked in lighters, the battalion marched to Manoel Island, where it was accommodated in Fort Manoel and the huts which it had occupied from 1890 to 1892. Within a few weeks two large drafts, over 300 in all, arrived from England to complete the establishment.

Garrison life in Malta had changed little since 1892. The Command Rifle Meeting was still held on the ranges at Pembroke in May; football and cricket matches were still played on the grounds of the Marsa Sports Club; and bathing was still the chief pastime during the summer. There were two new sporting events, both held at the Marsa. The first was the Malta Horse Show, which took place in April. The second was the Garrison Athletics Meeting, which was held in May. In the latter the Battalion Tug-of-War Team won the Infantry Catch-Weight Competition.

In May, leaving some 50 men at Fort Manoel to perform the necessary duties, the battalion marched to a camp at Ghain Tuffieha for manoeuvres in the north of the island. The exercises lasted for five days and culminated in a scheme in which five Regular battalions, two battalions of the Royal Garrison Regiment[1] and The Royal Malta Regiment of Militia took part.

[1] The Royal Garrison Regiment consisted of retired officers and men who had re-entered the Regular Army for garrison duty.

Elaborate preparations were made on the island for the celebration of the Coronation of King Edward VII in June. Owing to the sudden illness of His Majesty, however, the *festa* had to be postponed until July 2, when the King was known to be out of danger.[1] A torchlight tattoo, in which 150 of the battalion took part, was the main military contribution.

His Excellency the Governor, Lieutenant-General Sir Francis Grenfell, paid a farewell visit to the battalion at Fort Manoel on November 21. The companies were formed up on the square in front of the Officers' Mess. In the absence of Colonel Harrison, who was in Cottonera Hospital, Major Rowe was in command of the parade. After passing down the ranks His Excellency addressed the troops. In his speech he expressed regret at the departure of so smart and so well-drilled a unit, and said that he was glad to see an improvement in the health of the men, which had been impaired by an unusually extended stay at Aden. In conclusion he trusted that after its long tour of 20 years' foreign service the battalion would enjoy, and benefit by, a spell at Home. Sir Francis then bade "Goodbye" to the officers individually, and the parade was dismissed.

On November 26 a draft of 250 other ranks for the 2nd Battalion, now in Ceylon, went aboard the troopship "Dunera." The remainder of the battalion embarked in the "Dominion," which was bound for Egypt with drafts for regiments which were stationed there. Both ships sailed at daylight on the 27th. They remained in sight of each other for two days and were moored close together at Alexandria for a few hours on the 30th. The "Dominion" then turned westwards for England, while the "Dunera" steamed on to Port Said and Colombo.

[1] The Coronation eventually took place on August 9.

CHAPTER 6

THE WAR IN SOUTH AFRICA

September, 1889—November, 1902

2nd Battalion and the 1st, 2nd and 3rd Volunteer Active Service Companies

1. *The Mobilization of the 2nd Battalion*

WHEN the trooping programme was issued in the summer of 1899, the 2nd Battalion was down to move from Chatham to Malta. The date was given as October 6, and the bulk of the men were sent on embarkation leave in the middle of August. The imminence of war in South Africa then caused drastic alterations in the programme. On September 8 a telegram arrived from the War Office: "Hold 2nd Battalion Royal West Kent Regiment in immediate readiness to embark for Egypt instead of Malta with families as soon as arrangements can be made." This was followed next day by orders to sail for Alexandria on the 13th to relieve the 1st Battalion The Royal Irish Fusiliers, which was being sent to Natal.

Those on leave were immediately recalled. Some 170 N.C.O.s and men, who were ineligible for service overseas, were detailed as a rear-party. The families — with the exception of 10, which remained at Chatham — and the heavy baggage were sent off on the 12th. On the morning of the 13th the battalion went by train to the Royal Albert Docks, Woolwich, and embarked on time in the "Avoca." The rear-party marched to the Depot for attachment 10 days later.

The "Avoca" arrived at Alexandria on the evening of September 23. The troops disembarked next day and marched to Mustapha Barracks, Ramleh, where the officers and other ranks occupied newly-built bungalows. The families, the messes and the canteen were accommodated in the older part of the cantonment. Within a few days some 50 N.C.O.s and men, under Lieutenant Bonham-Carter, were sent to Cairo for training in Mounted Infantry duties. On

October 23 a draft of nearly 250 men joined from the 1st Battalion in Aden to bring the strength up to 850.

When the battalion arrived the days were oppressively hot, and khaki drill uniform was quickly issued. Garrison duties were heavy, leaving the men little time for recreation. Perhaps this was as well, for the only amusements for them at Ramleh were sea-bathing and scratch games of cricket or football on the parade ground. For the officers there was a Sports Club nearby. Alexandria, with its garish entertainments, was four miles away.

As the months went by the prospect of active service in South Africa receded. Then, on January 13, 1900, the battalion was placed under orders to return Home for mobilization. Five more weeks passed. Eventually, on February 19, the troops and the families went aboard the "Dunera" in Alexandria Harbour. Even then, because of a gale, the ship did not sail until the 21st. Twelve days later, having disembarked at Southampton, the battalion was in Ramillies Barracks, North Camp, Aldershot.

Mobilization was completed in less than two weeks. The Reservists were received and allotted to companies; a Mounted Infantry Company was formed with personnel who had knowledge of horses; some 300 men, who were medically unfit or otherwise unable to go, were detailed as a rear-party; and khaki serge uniform was issued and fitted. "Comforts" for the troops (woollen garments, tobacco, papers), received from friends of the Regiment, were distributed. On March 16 the re-organised battalion went by train from Farnborough Station to Southampton, where it embarked in the "Bavarian," bound for South Africa.

Most of the rear-party — now known as The Details — moved to Shorncliffe when their duties at Aldershot had been completed. The others went to the Depot.

2. The Situation in South Africa

The cause of the dispute in South Africa was that the burghers of the Transvaal and the Orange River Colony — or Boers as they were usually called — had refused to grant political rights to the many people who had flocked into the country to dig for gold. On October 9, 1899, the Colonial Office in London had received an ultimatum from the Boer Government, and a reply had been despatched that the conditions demanded were "such as Her Majesty's Government deem it impossible to discuss." Hostilities had begun on October 11.

With well-planned strokes the Boers had invaded Natal and had forced the small British Army to retire into Ladysmith. They had also besieged Kimberley. Moreover, they had defeated at Colenso and Magersfontein two British forces which had been sent to relieve the beleaguered towns.

These reverses had caused the British Government to call upon the country to make a great military effort. Almost all the Regular

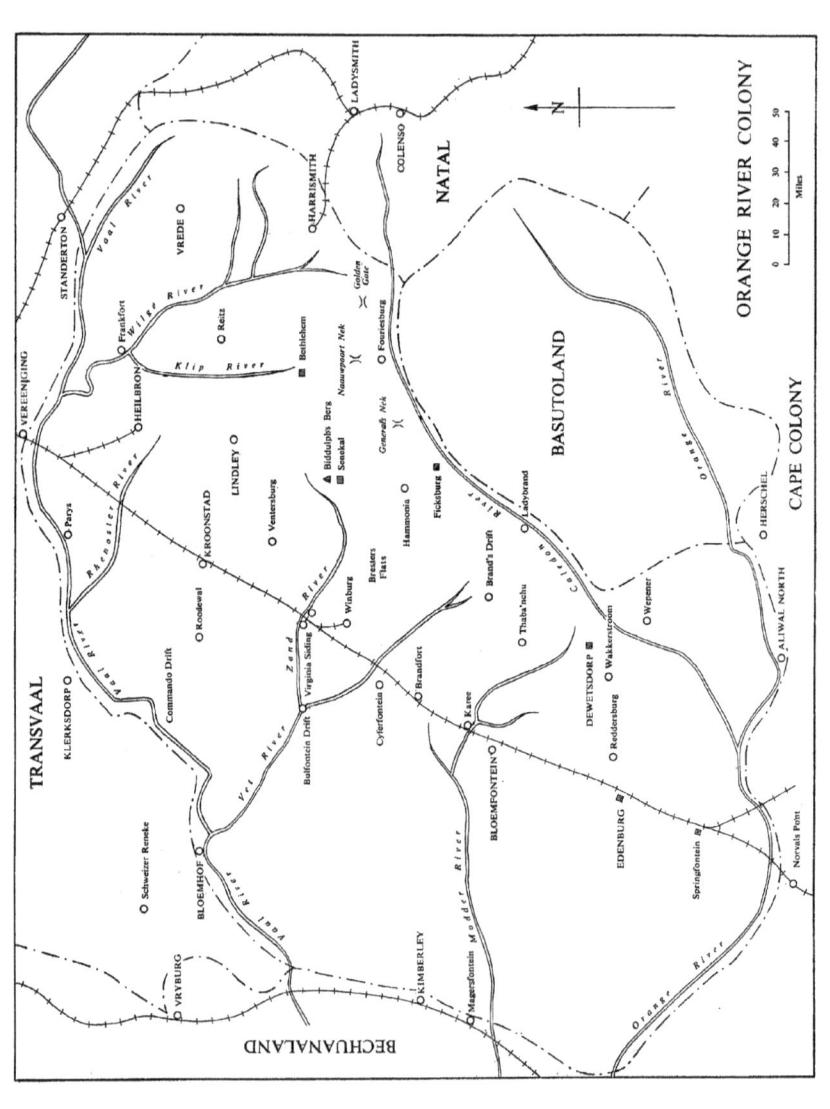

Army had been ordered to South Africa; some Militia battalions had been sent to replace the garrisons in the Mediterranean; the Army Reserve had been called out; another division (the 8th) had been hastily mobilized; and contingents of Volunteers had been assembled for service at the front. Above all, the direction of the campaign had been placed in the hands of Field-Marshal Lord Roberts, in whom the Army had implicit confidence.

Lord Roberts had decided to strike direct for Bloemfontein, the capital of the Orange River Colony, so as to relieve the pressure on the besieged towns. This move had brought an immediate change in the aspect of the war. Kimberley had been relieved on February 15. Eleven days later the bulk of the Boer Army in the Colony had been captured. Buller had joined hands with the Ladysmith garrison on February 28. On March 13 Bloemfontein had been occupied. Several detachments had then been sent out to the east of the Norvals Pont — Kroonstad Railway, and a post had been established at Karee, which commanded the crossings over the Modder River.

A Boer Council of War, attended by President Kruger of the Transvaal and President Steyn of the Orange River Colony, had been held at Kroonstad on March 17. The Council had agreed that their forces should be divided into several flying columns, one of which would ride on Bloemfontein to entice Lord Roberts out of it, while others would attempt to cut the railway from Bloemfontein to the south, which was the British line of communications. These columns would be mounted, without wagons, and were to act aggressively.

The first of these flying columns, or commandos, had encountered the strong outpost at Karee and had withdrawn. The others had been more successful. By April 8 only one of the British detachments east of the railway, that at Wepener, had remained intact. Against it Christian De Wet, postponing his intention to harry the line of communications, had concentrated his forces. By so doing he had permitted a stream of trains from Cape Colony to enter Bloemfontein with reinforcements, food and ammunition. Consequently, by the middle of April Lord Roberts was ready to begin his advance against the Transvaal. But before this could start, Wepener must be relieved and the Orange River Colony cleared of the commandos which threatened the railway.

Lord Roberts' plan was to send part of the Colonial Division to relieve Wepener, while 8th Division, which included the 2nd Battalion, concentrated near Edenburg as fast as its units landed from England and marched to Dewetsdorp to cut off De Wet.

3. *The Arrival of the 2nd Battalion*

The 2nd Battalion had a comfortable voyage in the "Bavarian." Some of the time was spent in shooting at barrels towed astern for rifle and revolver practice. Several men fell sick and three privates died. Orders had been received for disembarkation at East London, but on the way there from Cape Town a gun-boat came alongside with fresh instructions. The battalion ultimately went ashore in barges at Port Elizabeth on April 9. It met with enthusiastic applause as it marched to a camp two miles north of the town.

That night the troops slept in the open because there were no poles for the tents. This was their first experience of the bad staff work which was to cause them much discomfort and many unnecessary miles of marching during the campaign.

The key personnel in the battalion were:—
    Commanding Officer: Lieutenant-Colonel E. A. W. S. Grove.
    Second-in-Command: Major C. E. C. B. Harrison.
    Adjutant: Captain M. P. Buckle.
    Quartermaster: Hon. Lieutenant J. Couch.
    R.S.M.: Sergeant-Major W. E. Turner.
    R.Q.M.S.: Quartermaster-Sergeant G. Barnes.
    O.C. A Company: Captain A. Montgomery-Campbell.
    O.C. M.I. Company: Captain R. J. Woulfe-Flanagan.
    O.C. C Company: Captain H. L. C. Moody.
    O.C. D Company: Captain J. P. Dalison.
    O.C. E Company: Major L. Brock-Hollinshead.
    O.C. F Company: Captain A. Martyn.
    O.C. G Company: Major G. W. Maunsell.
    O.C. H Company: Captain N. H. S. Lowe.

A complete list of the officers, warrant officers and staff sergeants who disembarked, and of the officers who joined later, can be found in Appendix C.

Eight officers of the Regiment were already in South Africa with other corps or on the Staff. The first to arrive had been Brevet-Lieutenant-Colonel Alderson, who had gone out as Commander of a Mounted Infantry battalion with the 1st Cavalry Division. Lieutenants Hildyard and Long had followed, to be Quartermasters of Colonel Alderson's and Colonel Tudway's Battalions of M.I. respectively. Lieutenant Marsh, who had been seconded for service in West Africa since November 1897, was besieged in Mafeking. Major Wintour was Assistant Provost Marshal, 7th Division. Lieutenant James was in Cape Colony on special service. Lieutenant Hickson was attached to the 2nd Battalion The Buffs. 2nd-Lieutenant Hudson (1st Volunteer Battalion) had enlisted as a private in The Middlesex Regiment and was serving with the Mounted Infantry.[1]

The destination of the two trains, in which the 2nd Battalion left Port Elizabeth on April 12, was Edenburg. The march from there to the concentration area began three days later, in company with several other units of 8th Division. The men wore khaki serge uniform, putties, and pith helmets in khaki covers, which had red cloth tabs on the left side showing the name of the Regiment. Their equipment was of leather with water-bottle, mess-tin, haversack and ammunition pouches (the Mounted Infantry Company wore bandoliers). In addition to his Lee-Metford Rifle and 150 rounds, each man carried a blanket

---

[1] Hudson was later commissioned into the Line and served with the 1st Battalion in Aden.

rolled in a waterproof khaki-coloured bag provided regimentally; a sweater or second flannel shirt; and one pair of socks. In his haversack were a woollen cap, small kit and rations. His greatcoat, waterproof sheet and second blanket were carried in the transport wagons. The officers wore breeches instead of trousers, and carried field glasses, compasses and revolvers; otherwise they were dressed and equipped in the same manner as the other ranks. To begin with they carried rifles. Transport was a difficulty, for there were not enough animals for all of the water-carts and ammunition-vehicles. There were no horses at all for the M.I. Company, which had to march. The transport wagons were pulled by teams of 12 or 16 oxen, which were urged forward by natives with very long whips. The battalion's Maxim gun was mounted on a heavy, conspicuous carriage and was drawn by a mule or " intelligent N.C.O.," as the instructional handbook put it.

17th Brigade, to which the battalion belonged, concentrated at Reddersburg on April 17 and joined up with the remainder of 8th Division next day. It was commanded by Major-General J. E. Boyes. The other units in it were the 2nd Battalion The Worcestershire Regiment, the 1st Battalion The South Staffordshire Regiment and the 2nd Battalion The Manchester Regiment.

4. Wakkerstroom and Thaba'nchu

8th Division, commanded by Lieutenant-General Sir Leslie Rundle, and composed of the 16th and 17th Brigades, three batteries of Field Artillery and two battalions of Imperial Yeomanry, began its march to Dewetsdorp on April 19. Next day the advanced-guard, which was under the command of Colonel Grove, encountered enemy outposts near Wakkerstroom. These were driven back to their main position by the Worcestershires, who had one man killed and five wounded. The 2nd Battalion, which was brought up in support, came under shell fire but sustained no casualties. The Boers made considerable use of the " pom-pom," which threw its one-pound shells with great rapidity. Our artillery replied, but, as the shooting was at long range, little damage was done.

During the 21st, Rundle made an unsuccessful attempt to turn the flanks of a long ridge held by the Boers. Artillery fire was kept up by both sides. The enemy chiefly shelled the Supply Column, of which two natives were killed and several wagons were damaged. While this was going on, the battalion lay in a gully in reserve.

There was now a pause while Rundle awaited the arrival of Lieutenant-General J. D. P. French's Cavalry and Major-General R. Pole-Carew's Division from Bloemfontein. The intention was to surround the Boers at Wakkerstroom and cut their line of retreat towards Thaba'nchu. 8th Division's role was to bar the enemy's escape to the west and south, and, in the event of their withdrawing, to close in at once and pursue.

For the best part of two days the battalion occupied a hill south-east of Wakkerstroom. It was then moved back to a position near the Headquarters of 8th Division at Constantia Farm. All day on April 24 it lay on the *veldt* expecting a battle. Most of the men slept, but all were ready to put on their equipment at a moment's notice. No orders came. Pole-Carew failed to gain a passage over the Modder River before nightfall, and the operation was postponed until the morrow.

Before dawn on the 25th, Boyes' Brigade marched north-west for Roodepoort Hill, which it was to hold and thereby prevent the escape of the burghers to the west. But on approaching the hill, information was received from General Rundle that the Boers had slipped away from their main position during the night. All hope of encircling them had gone. After a rest and a bathe at a dam, which was greatly enjoyed, the brigade set out for Dewetsdorp. The sun was hot and drinking water was short, so that the troops were very tired when, at 10 p.m., they passed through the town to their bivouac. The battalion had marched 25 miles that day.

It was not only from Wakkerstroom that the Boers had retired. They had seen that the net was closing in, and had made a general retreat northwards. When Lord Roberts learned that the siege of Wepener had been raised, he directed 8th Division on Thaba'nchu.

17th Brigade bivouacked at the Modder River on the evening of April 26. Near the camp some cattle, which had been rounded up during the march, were being shot for food. One of the bullets, after hitting a bullock, was deflected into the chest of Private G. Kew. He died almost immediately and was buried that night. He had two brothers in the battalion. As the troops march out next morning, it was noticed that stones had been placed on his grave to preserve it.

When Boyes' Brigade reached Thaba'nchu, mounted troops had already found some Boers in the hills east of the town. On the afternoon of the 28th, The South Staffordshires and The Manchesters were sent to clear the high ground north of the Ladybrand road; The Queen's Own moved out to occupy a mountain south of it. Three companies of the battalion were already detached on outpost duty, and one was acting as escort to the Divisional Commander. The others ascended the hill in two parties, C and the M.I. Companies under Colonel Grove going by one route, and D and E under Major Harrison by another.

D and E Companies reached the top of the mountain before nightfall and gained touch with a detachment of the 2nd Battalion The East Yorkshire Regiment. Colonel Grove's party, which had a more difficult climb, was forced to bivouac for the night on a plateau about half-way up. It moved on again at daybreak. When it was about 500 yards from the summit, the left flank came under severe rifle fire. Two sections of the M.I. Company, under Lieutenant Bonham-Carter, were sent out to cover the advance, while the remainder clambered to the crest and began to return the fire. Three men were wounded during the ascent.[1] Captain Buckle, who had volunteered to find

---

[1] Those wounded were Privates Brooks, Johnson and White.

The East Yorkshires, was missing. After a time D Company moved round from the other side of the hill, thus making the position secure. In the afternoon the 2nd Battalion The Grenadier Guards arrived to relieve the four companies. The two sections of the M.I. Company, who had taken cover in a water-course, were unable to move. The rest made the descent with difficulty.

It was only a short respite. Before midnight the Brigade Major roused Colonel Grove to tell him that the battalion must march at once to cover the entry of a convoy, which had been attacked on its way from Dewetsdorp. So it was that the troops spent several uncomfortable hours, without greatcoats or blankets, at a *nek* (pass) five miles from Thaba'nchu. On the return to camp it was found that Lieutenant Bonham-Carter had been able to withdraw his sections after darkness fell. They had been delayed because one man, whose shin had been shattered by a bullet, had to be carried. There was also news of Captain Buckle. He was in the Field Hospital with wounds in the left wrist and thigh. His experience had been very trying. Soon after daybreak he had come under close fire from the Boers. Before he could find cover, he had been hit by a Mauser bullet. He had crawled behind a big stone, but each time he had attempted to move he had been fired at immediately. When night came, he had found the strength to slide and roll down the side of the hill and reach the British lines.

5 *Biddulphs Berg*

By the beginning of May Boer raids into the Orange River Colony had been brought to an end, and Lord Roberts was able to begin his march on Pretoria, the capital of the Transvaal. His axis of advance was the railway from Bloemfontein to Vereeniging. Sir Ian Hamilton's Mounted Infantry and Smith-Dorrien's Brigade acted as right flank-guard. 8th Division was ordered to remain in rear to prevent any large bodies of the enemy from returning towards the Wepener-Dewetsdorp gap, and then to follow the Boers if they withdrew northwards.

As the enemy made no attempt to attack his outposts, Sir Leslie Rundle decided to advance eastwards and northwards. By May 14, Boyes' Brigade was three miles north of Brand's Drift; 16th Brigade was north of Ladybrand. Three more marches brought 17th Brigade to Bresters Flats, where it remained for six days. Information had come in that Roberts had entered Kroonstad on the 12th. Small parties of Boers, who had willingly surrendered, confirmed reports that their commandos were falling back on Senekal.

Since it had left Thaba'nchu on May 7, the battalion had been living for the most part on the country. But the sheep and cattle were thin, and fuel — usually ox-dung — was very scarce. More often than not, dinner consisted of some dry flour tipped into the men's helmets. The best they could do was to mix it with a little water to make dough, which they fried in oil on their small fires. The heat and the lack of fresh vegetables produced an intense thirst, and in their need for water some of the troops filled their bottles from polluted water-courses, thus bringing on bouts of diarrhoea or dysentery.

Rundle's next move was to Senekal, the distance, some 45 miles, being covered in two days. Here Colonel Grove was taken ill and was sent to hospital at Bloemfontein. Command of the battalion devolved temporarily on Major Harrison.

At about noon on the 28th, Rundle received information that a detachment of the Imperial Yeomanry was surrounded in Lindley. He considered that the best way to draw off the Boers was to demonstrate towards Bethlehem. Leaving most of 17th Brigade in Senekal, he took that road at 2 p.m. with some Yeomanry, two field batteries, 16th Brigade (Major-General B. B. D. Campbell) and The Queen's Own. The Yeomanry reconnoitred to the north and came under fire from Biddulphs Berg, a group of *kopjes* (rocky hills) five miles from Senekal. The troops bivouacked for the night near a stream.

The Boers on the Biddulphs Berg *kopjes* were 1,500 strong with three guns and a pom-pom. Rundle's plan was to send the Yeomanry straight at the position, while two guns and a detachment of East Yorkshires moved to a hill to the south-west. The rest of the force, less a guard over the baggage, would make a flanking movement to the west and close in on the *kopjes* from the north.

The battalion was ready to move before dawn. But it was not till 8 o'clock that it left the bivouac with orders to follow the 2nd Scots Guards and the 2nd Grenadiers. The turning movement drew fire from two Boer guns, one of which was near a farm on the north-west of Biddulphs Berg. At 10.30 General Campbell ordered Lieutenant-Colonel Harrison[1] to detach one company (C) as escort to the field batteries, which opened fire on the farm and northern face of the *kopjes*. Covered by this fire the infantry deployed for attack. The Grenadier Guards advanced well extended; the Scots Guards moved to the right. The battalion took up a position in support, with D, E and F Companies under Colonel Harrison on the right of the guns, and G, H and M.I. under Major Maunsell on the left.

When the Grenadiers were about 1,200 yards from the farm, they were checked by shells from the Boer guns and by heavy rifle fire. The pom-pom joined in. The advance came to a halt, with the guardsmen lying on the open *veldt*. Then the enemy guns lifted and began to throw shell after shell on the position occupied by the battalion and the field batteries. At this stage a grass-fire flared up behind the Grenadiers. Some of their wounded, who lay helpless on the ground, were burned. The Queen's Own were more fortunate, for the flames passed diagonally in front of them. Many believed that the fire had been started by the Boers, but this they afterwards denied.

After the action had begun orders arrived from Lord Roberts to the effect that, as other troops were on their way to Senekal, 8th

---

[1] News had been received on May 28 that Major Harrison had been promoted to command the 1st Battalion.

Division was to march south on Ficksburg. This brought an end to Rundle's plan of threatening Bethlehem. The object of the operation had practically been attained however, for groups of Boers had already been seen coming from the direction of Lindley. At 3.30 p.m. Sir Leslie issued instructions for his troops to break off the engagement.

As the Guards rose from the ground the enemy redoubled their fire. Even so, the withdrawal was carried out admirably, the Grenadiers passing through the position held by the battalion. It was then seen that several of the wounded had been left on the scorched *veldt*, and an officer and a score of guardsmen returned to rescue them. Some of the Queen's Own assisted in this work, Colour-Sergeant Bullock, Corporal Dorrell, Lance-Corporal Humphreys and Privates Bishop, Bond, Crisp and Styles being particularly conspicuous.[1] After the troops had returned to camp, Civil-Surgeon Turner and Corporal Dorrell remained on the field all night attending to those who could not be brought in. The Boers sent some armed men to protect them, and took out brandy, coffee and soup for the wounded.

The Grenadiers lost 139 killed and wounded in this action, and the Scots Guards 24. Although the battalion had been under shell fire for a considerable time, casualties were only eight wounded.[2] The losses of the Boers were slight, though they had one important casualty — Commandant A. J. de Villiers, who was mortally wounded.

In a letter to General Boyes, Major-General Campbell wrote: —

"I have today testified in my report to the Lieutenant-General to the conduct of the 2nd West Kent Regiment, to their steadiness and discipline during the action, which was beyond praise.

The 2nd Grenadiers and Scots Guards will never forget the day when they stood together with the Royal West Kent and will always be grateful to that Regiment for the material aid rendered to them on that occasion."

After Senekal had been handed over to 12th Brigade, 8th Division moved south to join hands with General E. Y. Brabant's Colonial Division. The battalion marched into Hammonia on June 6. Everybody was in good spirits because news had been received that Lord Roberts had entered Pretoria. A double tot of rum was issued that evening.

6. *Prinsloo's Surrender*

For the next 10 days 8th Division, the Colonial Division and 12th Brigade were extended in defence of the line Ficksburg-Senekal. The main reason for holding this line was to prevent the enemy from moving west against the Bloemfontein — Kroonstad Railway. Hammonia was garrisoned by two companies of Imperial Yeomanry, The Queenstown Volunteers, four guns, The South Staffordshires and The Queen's Own, all under the command of Major-General Boyes. The Boers were in considerable strength in the vicinity, and Boyes maintained active patrolling by day and strong outposts by night.

---

[1] The list of Honours and Awards is in Appendix D.

[2] Privates Andrews, Ardrey, Cairns, Hoye, Latter, Ott, Smith, J. and Valder.

The bivouac occupied by the battalion was on a rough piece of ground at the foot of a hill which became known as "Boyes' Berg." Here it was that the 1st Active Service Company from the Volunteer battalions of the Regiment arrived just after dark on June 9.[1] It had come by rail from Edenburg to Winburg and thence by march route. Captain Buckle, whose wounds had healed very quickly, came with it.

On the night of June 10 the battalion was suddenly ordered to stand-to as the Boers were expected to attack. All animals were moved to cover, and the companies were placed in positions suitable for defence. The night passed quietly, but the incident caused General Boyes to revise his plans.

Major Maunsell was sent with four companies to occupy "Leinster Hill," about two miles to the north-west, while the other four were ordered to put "Boyes' Berg" in a state of defence. A field gun was to be placed on the summit of the latter. This was no mean task as it had to be taken off its carriage, tied to a tree which had been felled, and borne up a steep, rocky track. Ammunition and provisions for 10 days were also carried up. Sergeant-Instructor-of-Musketry Mitchell earned praise for the way in which his team man-handled the Maxim gun to its position. General Boyes heliographed his appreciation of these exertions.

During the three days that the battalion remained on "Boyes' Berg" and "Leinster Hill," Colonel Grove returned from hospital, thereby making it possible for Colonel Harrison to depart for England and thence to take command of the 1st Battalion in Aden.

*   *   *

Lord Roberts now issued orders for the hemming-in of all enemy forces in the north-east of the Orange River Colony. The principal towns were to be adequately garrisoned, and four flying columns were to be constantly on the move throughout the area.

This re-organisation caused half the battalion, under Colonel Grove, to be moved to Ficksburg. Two companies were on the summit of a *kopje* called Imperani Mountain; Headquarters and the other two, with one gun and some Imperial Yeomanry, were on a lower spur. The remainder of the garrison held Ficksburg Hill. The Boers had a gun on Zoutkop, three miles north of the town. This shelled the troops on the spur of Imperani Mountain for the first few days. Otherwise the only hostile act was a raid which occurred at 1.30 a.m. on July 4. The raiders infiltrated into a ditch in front of Ficksburg Hill and opened up a heavy rifle fire for half an hour. At the same time some shells were fired from Zoutkop. There were no British casualties.

Meanwhile the flying columns had been moving on Bethlehem and Reitz from the north. Knowing that they were not strong enough to resist, the Boer commandos had been falling back on the mountain stronghold near Fouriesburg and the Basutoland border. The tract

---

[1] See Chapter 7, Section 4, for information about the Volunteer Active Service Companies.

in which they sought refuge was bounded on the south by the Caledon River. The other three sides were walled by an almost continuous chain of hills, which was pierced only at five passes suitable for wagons. The chief of these were General's Nek, Naauwpoort Nek and the Golden Gate.

Lieutenant-General Sir Archibald Hunter, who had assumed command of the British forces in the area, proposed to close in on the Boers from the west and north simultaneously. After clearing the passes, the target was to be Fouriesburg, which had been proclaimed the new capital of the Orange River Colony. But, while Hunter was waiting for supplies, Christian De Wet slipped through with 2,600 men and made for the north. With him went President Steyn and the Government. To pursue them was not the main issue, however. There were still some 5,500 of the enemy inside the mountain stronghold. Hunter issued orders for a combined forward movement to begin on July 23.

Sir Leslie Rundle arrived at Hammonia on the 22nd with The Scots Guards and the 1st Battalion The Leinster Regiment. Next day he began to clear the hills to the north-east and east. D and H Companies from Ficksburg assisted in this operation by forming part of a force which drove the Boers from Zoutkop. Rundle then went on and occupied General's Nek. Naauwpoort Nek and two other passes were already blocked from the outside. This left open only the Golden Gate. Towards it two mobile columns were advancing with all speed.

General Rundle now ordered part of the garrisons of Ficksburg and Hammonia to follow him to Fouriesburg. On the morning of the 26th, F, G, the M.I. and Volunteer Companies, having left Hammonia at 10.30 p.m. the previous night and having marched 17 miles, arrived at Zoutkop. Together with five companies of The South Staffordshires, two guns and some Mounted Infantry, all under Colonel Grove, they marched again at 2 p.m. and halted for the night at General's Nek. There the other four companies, which had left Ficksburg at 4 p.m., joined them soon after midnight. The transport wagons came in later. Grove's force pressed on and linked up with 8th Division Headquarters.

The Boers were falling back on Slaap Kranz ridge, whither Hunter's flying columns were rapidly closing in. Rundle's infantry went into the attack, supported by the fire of six guns. The Scots Guards gained possession of a *kopje* which outflanked the enemy position, and E, G, H and the Volunteer Companies went forward to take part in a renewed assault. The Boars vacated the ridge under cover of darkness. This action was called " Wittebergen," the name of the nearest section of the chain of hills.

On the morning of the 29th General Hunter received a request from Commandant Prinsloo, the Boer leader, for a four days' armistice. This he refused. At 4.30 p.m. he received a second message, in which Prinsloo agreed to surrender unconditionally next day. Hunter accepted and ordered his force to suspend hostilities unless it was attacked. The news was received with great enthusiasm by the troops.

In the bivouac that night the battalion assembled and sang "God Save The Queen" and other patriotic songs. The celebration was mellowed by a double tot of rum.

A ceremony was arranged for the reception of the Boer prisoners-of-war on July 30. It took place on Nok Hill, where Prinsloo had made his last stand. A flagstaff was erected, with a Union Jack flying. Near it stood General Hunter and, later, Sir Leslie Rundle. One battalion was drawn up in a line facing the Generals, with cavalry on one flank and a battery on the other. This guard was relieved every two hours, The Queen's Own taking their turn at 12.30 p.m. The first prisoners to pass through were Prinsloo and Crowther, both fine-looking men. Then followed the commandos, which slowly filed down a steep mountain path and piled their arms and ammunition before reaching the guard. They were a motley throng. Some were mere boys, others white-haired, bearded men. All had two horses, many had three; the spare animals carried baggage, blankets and pots and pans. Having laid down their arms the prisoners were collected in one place, where a cordon with fixed bayonets was placed round them. Their horses were closely inspected, and the best were appropriated as remounts.

While the battalion was acting as the guard Sir Leslie Rundle told Colonel Grove that he greatly appreciated its services and conduct. He said that he had specially ordered it forward owing to his high opinion of it, and expressed the wish that his remarks should be communicated to the men.

*   *   *

After Prinsloo's surrender Rundle established his headquarters at Harrismith. The town was the terminus of the Natal Railway, and 8th Division became based on Durban. This brought the prospect of better conditions for the troops, whose clothing and boots had for some time been in a deplorable state. A large number of them were without trousers and were reduced to wearing sacks as kilts; boots were so badly worn that many had been marching with putties wound round their feet. Indeed, with their bushy beards — there was no way of shaving — some of the men would not have been recognisable as soldiers at all had they not worn helmets and equipment. Ragged they were, yet continual marching had made them so fit that they had become known as " Rundle's Greyhounds."

The battalion did not accompany Rundle to Harrismith. It was sent with 17th Brigade to search the Reitz — Vrede area for those commandos which had been outside the Fouriesburg stronghold. In this task the M.I. Company, now mounted on horses which had been taken at Nok Hill, was of great value. At Vrede Major Western and Captain Pack-Beresford joined from the 1st Battalion. Western became Second-in-command. Beresford took over H Company from Captain Lowe, who was acting as Brigade Intelligent Officer.

By September 4 the search had been completed, and most of 17th Brigade left Vrede for Bethlehem. The battalion marched to Harrismith. There new clothing and boots were issued, and the troops received

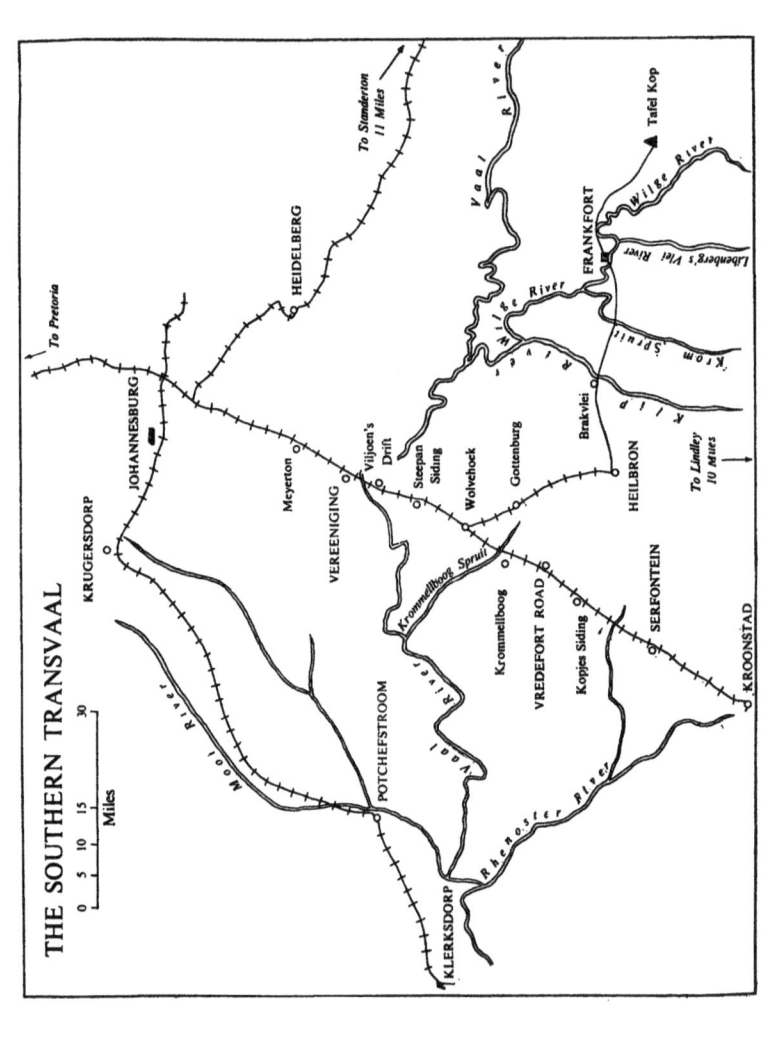

their full ration of food and tobacco. Amenities of all sorts could be bought from shops in the town. A newspaper arrived every morning. Above all, three weeks' mail was distributed. Thirty men went to join Colonel Alderson's Mounted Infantry in the Transvaal.

After nearly three weeks' rest, the battalion left Harrismith to take part with 17th Brigade in a combined sweep in the Frankfort — Heilbron area. At a bivouac some miles north of Bethlehem a draft of two officers and 140 other ranks joined from The Details at Shorncliffe. The sweep began on September 26. Touch was gained with several groups of Boers, who fell back under artillery and rifle fire. Next day the battalion formed part of the advanced-guard. On several occasions the enemy showed themselves and opened fire at long range. Twice the troops deployed for attack, but each time the Boers retired without making a stand. The M.I. Company, which operated on the flanks, had Private Barnes shot through the shoulder. The operation ended on the 28th.

7. The 2nd Battalion in Frankfort

It now seemed as though the whole enemy force still under arms in the Orange River Colony was in the quadrilateral Reitz — Frankfort — Heilbron — Lindley. In order to round it up, garrisons were placed in these four towns and in Vrede, Harrismith and Bethlehem, and on them were based mobile columns, which moved about in search of the Boers and destroyed all supplies that might sustain them. The garrison of Frankfort consisted of the 2nd Battalion, two field guns and the 33rd Company Imperial Yeomanry (East Kent).

A few days after the occupation of Frankfort, orders were received for the return to England of the 1st Volunteer Active Service Company. It left with an empty convoy on October 8. When it reached Norvals Pont on the 17th it was ordered to remain and guard the railway bridge. While it was there five of the men died of enteric fever. The company eventually embarked for home on April 9, 1901.

Frankfort stands on the north bank of the River Wilge. From the river the ground rises steeply to grassy, undulating country. The town, in which the main buildings were the church, the courthouse and the store, was held by G Company. The remainder of the unmounted men were in tents on the higher ground, with Headquarters, C and F Companies and the two guns on " Kent Hill," E on " Cemetery Spur," and D and H on " Beresford Kop." Round the camp was dug an entrenched perimeter about 500 yards in diameter. The mounted men — the M.I. Company and the East Kent Yeomanry — were in a valley between " Kent Hill " and " Beresford Kop." Colonel Grove was in command of the whole garrison. Supplies for one month had been brought into the town.

The area was so well scoured by the mobile columns that most of the Boers soon departed for less dangerous districts. But a few small groups remained in the neighbourhood of Frankfort, ready to pounce on any suitable target. In consequence the garrison had always to be on the alert, and numerous outposts had to be mounted at night. The town was in fact entirely cut off from outside communication until November 2. A native runner, who was chased by two Boers for the last six miles, then brought in about 20 letters. Thereafter, runners went to and from Heilbron weekly. They received £2 a trip. None of them was killed, though three had their ponies shot under them.

The main duty of the garrison was to prevent the Boers from entering Frankfort and obtaining supplies. Before long, however, provisions of all sorts became very scarce. Articles such as candles, matches and soap were practically unobtainable. Tea, sugar and porridge were strictly rationed. When flour was available, bread was baked in the town; at other times biscuits were issued. The meat ration — at one pound a day — was always maintained. Tobacco ran out on November 6, after which the troops smoked dried grass, tea leaves or compressed vegetables. In his distress at the absence of My Lady Nicotine, some wag in the battalion produced the following lament:—

"When cigarettes are ended, and tobacco is no more,
And the ration plug is finished at the Quartermaster's Store,
We do not sigh or grumble, we utter ne'er a sound,
But we makes our own tobacco from the weeds that grow around.
There's Frankfort mixture, Kent Hill twist, and Kopje Myrtle Grove.
They're smokes that ought to suit the taste of every sort of cove.
For when of genuine baccy we've finished every type,
Why everything's tobacco to the soldier's empty pipe."

The relations between the troops and the inhabitants were generally friendly. If a civilian were found to be in communication with a hostile band or concealing ammunition, his house was confiscated or destroyed and he had to seek lodgings with his neighbours. It was in this way that "The Kentish Club" was founded. This was a most select institution, all the members being officers of The Queen's Own or the East Kent Yeomanry. There was no entrance fee or subscription. The premises and furniture were provided free by a certain person whose friends were out on commando. The rules were few. One of them was:— "Ladies, dogs and Dutchmen are not allowed in the vicinity."

The first casualty at Frankfort occurred on October 6, when Private Langley was wounded by a sniper. Three days later Private Ashby was drowned while bathing in the Wilge River, in spite of a gallant attempt by Private Roberts, of D Company, to rescue him.

Several raids were carried out by the garrison. The most successful of these took place on October 10/11. Lieutenant Craig, the District Intelligence Officer, had reported that there was a Boer laager about five miles east of Frankfort. After dark on the 10th the East Kent Yeomanry and C, E, H and the M.I. Companies marched out to a point some two miles south of the laager, which was hidden in a valley between two rocky hills. Native guides then led them to positions to surround it. C and H Companies were able to creep to within 30 yards of the sleeping commando. Colonel Grove's intention was to capture the enemy at dawn without fighting, but at 3.30 a.m. a Boer patrol walked right up to a party of H Company. The alarm was given. Fire was opened into the laager until resistance ceased. Seven Boers lay dead, nine were wounded; 18 prisoners, some 40 rifles and several thousand rounds of ammunition were captured. Sergeant Canty, of H Company, was the only British casualty. He was severely wounded in the body and died on the 16th.

Another notable raid occurred on October 22, when Major Western took out the mounted troops and two companies to burn some farms north-west of Frankfort. The screen of 16 men of the M.I. Company had just crossed a ridge when it suddenly came under fire at close range. Privates Clarke and Sellings were killed and Emmerson was wounded. Colour-Sergeant Grellier dismounted immediately and, with the greatest coolness, returned the fire. He killed one Boer and wounded another, but was himself hit in the shoulder. The remainder of the screen took cover behind the ridge, while D Company (Lieutenant Kitson) put the enemy to flight. The force then went on to burn the farms with but slight opposition.

Four days later the mounted troops raided the farm of Field-Cornet Pretorious. He and his son, who were both in the house, attempted to escape but were made prisoner. This was an important capture, as Pretorious had great influence with the burghers in the Frankfort area.

A brisk action was fought on November 7. The mounted troops, one gun and the equivalent of two companies were returning to camp after burning a farm. The smoke from the fire must have acted as a beacon to the Boers in the district, for small groups closed in from all directions. The column halted and took up a position on a ridge. For a short time the gun was under a heavy fire. Privates Chapman and Hipkins, of F Company, were hit. Sergeant Montague was severely wounded while he was leading his section to a more favourable position. H Company and a section of E then advanced along the ridge. The Boers took refuge in some ditches, from which they were driven by shell fire. When the march was resumed, a score of the enemy harassed the rear of the column and wounded Private Munday. They retired when the gun was trained on them. Both Sergeant Montague and Private Munday died of their wounds. They were buried in the cemetery at Frankfort.

A long-awaited convoy arrived on November 22. It had been escorted from Heilbron by Major-General B. M. Hamilton's column. With it came a draft of 99 men, supplies for 60 days, nine weeks' mail and, what was especially welcome, tobacco. Welcome too was a replenishment of ammunition, for all raids had been suspended because of a lack of it.

The infantry which had escorted the convoy departed with the empty wagons next morning. The remainder of Hamilton's men rode out later to round-up a Boer commando. Before dawn on the 24th Colonel Grove marched with his mounted troops, one gun and three companies to occupy a stop-line to prevent this commando from breaking south. No enemy came in that direction, and Grove's force returned to Frankfort after burning several farms. Hamilton captured 31 prisoners.

Colonel Grove was appointed commandant of the Krugersdorp District on November 25.[1] His departure was delayed because he had injured an ankle while playing polo on a rough piece of ground. It was not until the night of January 3, 1901, that he rode out for Heilbron escorted by 10 troopers of the East Kent Yeomanry. Captain Martyn became his Staff Officer. Major Western assumed command of the Frankfort garrison, and Major Maunsell of the battalion.

During January 1901 — the last month the battalion was in Frankfort — the number of sick increased alarmingly. Enteric fever was the prevalent disease. At one time there were nearly 40 cases, including Captain Woulfe-Flanagan and Lieutenants Kitson, Lister and Belgrave. Civil-Surgeon Turner was himself a patient. Captain Mansfield (R.A.M.C.) carried on single-handed, although he was suffering from dysentery, until Civil-Surgeon Kirkpatrick arrived from Heilbron, the Boers having respected the Red Cross flag. Many measures, such as dividing the camps into smaller enclaves which were easier to keep clean, were taken to combat disease. But the lack of fresh vegetables deprived the men of the necessary vitality. No fewer than 11 died of enteric and six from other maladies during the time that the battalion was defending the town.

* * *

Owing to several aggressive actions by Boer commandos in the early weeks of 1901, Lord Kitchener, who had taken over command from Roberts,[2] decided to evacuate certain perilously placed towns. Frankfort was one of them. The inhabitants as well as the garrison were to be removed. All stores which could not be taken and might be of use to the enemy were to be destroyed.

A column commanded by Lieutenant-Colonel E. C. I. Williams (The Buffs) arrived at Frankfort on January 26 to assist in the evacuation. Williams had with him about 60 wagons, which were to convey the sick, the baggage, the civilians and the supplies to Heilbron.

The preparations for the move occupied three days. Large quantities of oats, mealies, wool and hides were thrown into the Wilge River or burned. Sheds were set alight. The corn mill was blown up. A detachment had to be organised to carry on stretchers a score of the 115 sick, who were too ill to travel on the wagons. Of the 330 civilians, 20 were old men, 80 women and 230 children. The women did not relish the idea of leaving their homes. Several declared that they would not go without their husbands, who were away on commando. Others said that they would make a bolt for it. Ultimately all went with the convoy.

The evacuation started at daybreak on January 29, when the cattle and sheep were driven across the bridge over the Wilge to the south

---

[1] He had been promoted to Brevet-Colonel on August 19.

[2] Lord Roberts had been called back to England to become Commander-in-Chief of the Army.

bank. The civilians, packed with their chattels into 15 wagons, followed. They presented a pathetic sight. Next crossed the supply column, which was not very large. Finally came the hospital wagons and the 20 stretchers. At dusk the usual outposts were mounted so as to deceive the Boers. They were withdrawn after dark, when the garrison crossed the river to come under Colonel Williams' command.

The march began early on the 30th. The road was in a very bad condition after heavy rain. Wagon after wagon stuck in the mud and had to be off-loaded before it could be pulled clear. It took seven hours for the rearguard to move two miles. At this point the Boers began to snipe at the vehicles, which were halted until the mounted troops had cleared the way. About six miles west of Frankfort the enemy were found to be holding a position in strength. The wagons were again halted, while four companies deployed for attack. The Boers did not resist for long, but during the action Private Jupp was hit by a sniper. It was then 4 p.m. and the force bivouacked for the night. When the march was resumed in the morning the Boers were less aggressive. Except for a little sniping and the loss of 20 kits in Krom Spruit, the day was uneventful. The column reached Heilbron soon after noon on February 1. Twenty-five bales of "comforts," sent out by friends at home, were awaiting the battalion.

On the 4th, G, H and the M.I. Companies set out on a six weeks' *trek* with Colonel Williams' Column. Their adventures are described in Annexure 1 at the end of this chapter.

Heilbron was the terminus of a branch of the Kroonstad—Pretoria Railway, and the remainder of the battalion settled down to enjoy full rations and many luxuries which had been unobtainable for several months. Camp routine was much the same as it had been at Frankfort, with outpost duty every other night. On frequent occasions detachments took part in small expeditions to burn farms, to bring in Boer families or to escort supplies to columns. As the weeks passed the health of the men gradually improved. This was chiefly due to better food and to the fact that cricket and football gear was available for recreation.

8. *Railway Protection Duties*

After the British had reached Pretoria in June 1900 they had constructed many protective posts, consisting of trenches and stone sangars, along the railways which they used as lines of communication. Attacks by the Boers had then become frequent, and it had been obvious that more elaborate defences were essential. The type of post that was required was one that was easily portable and took a short time to erect.

A blockhouse which fulfilled these requirements was designed by The Royal Engineers. It was some 13 feet in diameter, and its walls consisted of an inner and an outer "skin" of corrugated iron. The "skins" were some six inches apart, the intervening space being filled with shingle. Each wall was pierced with cross-shaped loopholes measuring six by three inches. The roof, which was either gabled or dome-shaped, was made of one layer of corrugated iron. The door was bullet proof and but two feet square. From it was dug a fire-trench, which surrounded the blockhouse and gave protection to the sentry. At a distance of from 10 to 20 yards round the trench a high wire obstacle was erected.

The blockhouses were at first about one-and-a-half miles apart. These prevented the destruction of the railway tracks and trains, but did not prevent groups of the enemy from crossing the lines at night. The interval was therefore decreased to a half or three-quarters of a mile. Between the blockhouses a trench was dug and a barbed-wire fence with aprons on each side was erected, in order to stop wagons from crossing. On the fences were placed automatic alarms and flares. Fixed rifle-batteries of four or six rifles, which could be fired by one man, were set so that they could sweep the fences along their whole length. Each blockhouse was connected with its neighbours by telephone. Each contained its own water supply and reserves of food and ammunition. The usual garrison was one N.C.O. and 10 men. Native scouts were attached for the purpose of patrolling by night.

The strategy which underlay the blockhouse system on the railways was both defensive and offensive, for it enabled a small number of troops to secure the vulnerable lines of communication, thus increasing the forces available for offensive action.

It was to the role of Railway Protection that the battalion was now gradually assigned. The new duties were assumed in three phases.

First, on March 2, 1901, half of C Company, under Captain Moody, and 50 men of F, under 2nd-Lieutenant Henderson, went by train from Heilbron to Gottenburg and occupied some posts on the railway in relief of a detachment of The Oxfordshire Light Infantry. The other half of C, under 2nd-Lieutenant Twisleton-Wykeham-Fiennes, took over the defence of Riet River Bridge, south of Gottenburg.

Secondly, on May 7, G Company (Lieutenant Luard) moved to Brandfort, north of Bloemfontein, on detachment. One sergeant and 16 rank and file of this company became the guard over No. 2 Armoured Train, which ran from Edenburg to Viljoen's Drift. On the 23rd D Company (Lieutenant Tulloch) went to occupy the blockhouses about Wolvehoek.

Before the next phase was carried out, the 2nd Volunteer Active Service Company joined from Serfontein. It had been defending posts on the railway near there for five weeks. Captain Latter's request for his company to be sent to the 2nd Battalion had then been granted. Having left behind Lieutenant McCracken and 18 other ranks, who were sick or detached, it arrived at Heilbron, two officers and 96 other ranks strong, on May 23.

The third group of railway protection posts was taken over on June 11. Battalion Headquarters, A, E, H, Volunteer and part of

F Companies entrained for Vereeniging, arriving there the same evening. Detachments were dropped at places north of Wolvehoek as follows:—

Somer's Post: 30 of H Company (2nd-Lieutenant Norman).
Steenpan Siding: 13 of H Company.
Taaibosch Kop: 40 of H Company (Captain Pack-Beresford).
Taaibosch Bridge: 30 of F Company (Lieutenant Joslin).
Viljoen's Drift: 70 of Volunteer Company (Captain Latter).

The M.I. Company, which was not suitable for a static role, had become permanently attached to Colonel Williams' (later Western's) Column on April 8 (See Annexure 2).

In July two adjustments were made to the battalion's commitments. On the 1st, G Company moved from Brandfort to Krommellboog. On the 2nd, D Company left Wolvehoek for Vredefort Road. After that, companies and detachments frequently changed over with each other.

The garrisons of the posts on the railway were fully occupied in preventing parties of Boers from crossing the lines at night. Many small engagements occurred. Three of them are recorded below.

Before dawn on March 15 one of the posts near Gottenburg was attacked by about 50 of the enemy. In spite of the darkness their fire was remarkably accurate, but they were repulsed without loss. This success was mainly due to the Post Commander, Sergeant Balding, who, without orders, had strengthened the defences a few days before. A culvert, demolished by the Boers during the raid, was repaired next day.

After dark on June 7 the sentry at a blockhouse on the Wolvehoek—Heilbron line heard a suspicious movement. He gave the alarm. Whereupon four bullets were fired at him at a range of 150 yards. He managed to crawl into the post. Brisk firing was opened by both sides until Sergeant Barden, who was in command of the blockhouse, heard some shouting and ordered "Cease Fire." He found that he was being called upon to surrender. His reply was not in the affirmative. Firing was then resumed till the moon rose, when the enemy retired. Lance-Corporal Bucklow was severely wounded during the action. Referring to this incident the G.O.C. Bloemfontein District wrote:— "' The Lieutenant-General congratulates Sergeant Barden and the men under his command on the able manner in which they performed their duty. If all were like them, less would be heard of surrenders."

The third encounter occurred on the night of June 20. A group of Boers with some wagons tried to cross the railway line near Somer's Post. The garrison of the blockhouse commanded by Sergeant Jasper, by opening rapid fire, forced them to turn back. The following morning, 2nd-Lieutenant Norman captured 15 of their horses.

Brevet-Colonel Grove was placed on half-pay on August 19. Major Western, who had taken over Colonel Williams' Column on April 22, succeeded him to the command of the battalion but remained detached.

Major Maunsell was appointed Second-in-command and continued at the helm at Vereeniging. Lieutenant Isacke became Adjutant.[1]

In September practically the whole battalion, having been relieved of its railway protection duties, assumed a mobile role. Four companies went to join Colonel F. S. Garratt's Column at Meyerton. Four became attached to Brigadier-General G. H. C. Hamilton's Column at Klerksdorp. Battalion Headquarters and the remaining troops (about 130 in all) returned to Heilbron.

9. The Hunt for Louis Botha

At the end of August 1901 Lord Kitchener received reports that Commandant-General Louis Botha, the C.-in-C. of the Boer Army, was about to invade Natal from the north-east. In order to forestall this incursion he ordered several columns, including those commanded by Colonel Garratt and Brigadier-General Hamilton, to concentrate in the Eastern Transvaal.

Colonel Garratt's Column consisted of:—
    The 7th New Zealand Mounted Regiment.
    The 6th Queensland Imperial Bushmen.
    Four field guns and one pom-pom.
    A Company The Queen's Own (Lieutenant Kitson).
    E Company The Queen's Own (2nd-Lieutenant Johnstone).
    H Company The Queen's Own (Captain Lowe and 2nd-Lieutenant Norman).
    Volunteer Company The Queen's Own (Captain Latter and Lieutenant Holcroft).

Major Brock-Hollinshead was in command of The Queen's Own wing.

The composition of Brigadier-General Hamilton's Column was:—
    The 5th Dragoon Guards.
    The 13th Hussars.
    Four field guns, one pom-pom and one Maxim.
    One M.I. Company Royal Engineers.
    C Company The Queen's Own (2nd-Lieutenant Twisleton-Wykeham-Fiennes).
    D Company The Queen's Own (Captain Buckle and Lieutenant Tulloch).
    F Company The Queen's Own (2nd-Lieutenant Tugwell).
    G Company The Queen's Own (Lieutenant Luard and 2nd-Lieutenant Pullman).

The Queen's Own wing with this column was commanded by Captain Moody.

Garratt's Column reached Paardekop on September 7 and reconnoitred across the Elands Berg mountains, through Wakker-

[1] Lieutenant Bonham-Carter actually took over the adjutancy from Captain Buckle in August. But he was replaced by Lieutenant Isacke in November because he received accelerated promotion into the Royal Warwickshires. He was posted back to the Regiment in December 1907.

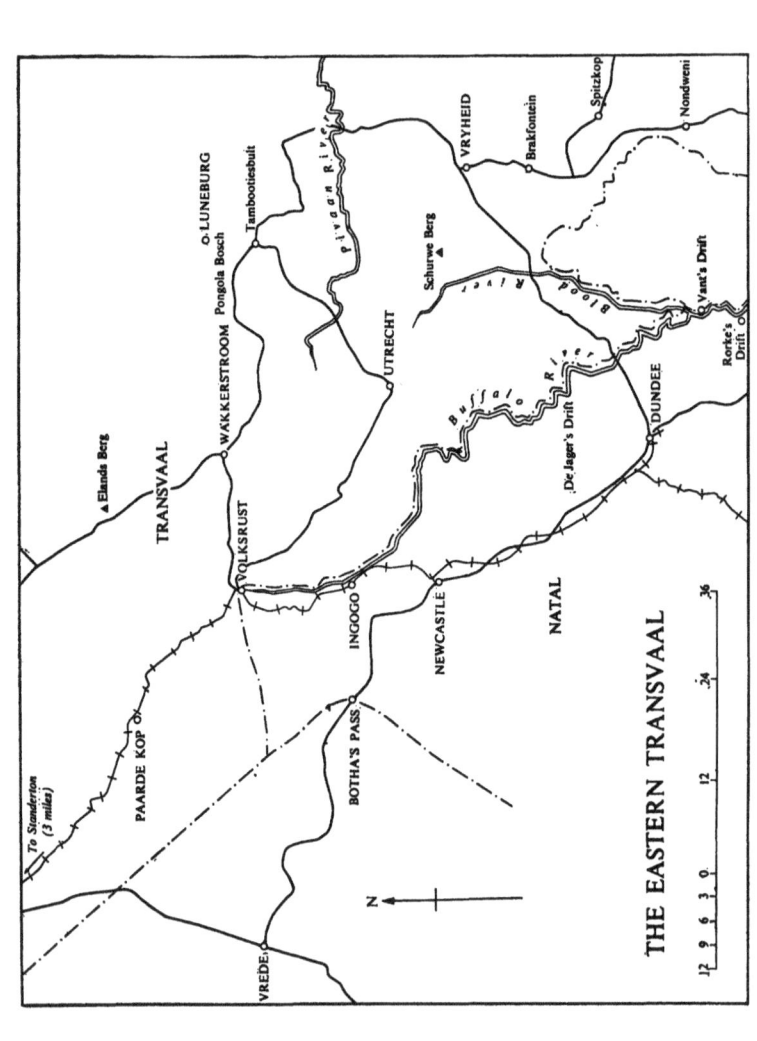

stroom and back to the railway. Two Boers, who were captured, gave almost certain information of the impending incursion. By the time that the column reached Volksrust on the 18th, Botha had been definitely located near Vryheid and other British forces had been extended along the line of the Buffalo River in order to close his path to Natal. Garratt's Column entrained for Newcastle and marched to Utrecht to block his escape route.

Hamilton's Column now came on to the scene. Arriving at Dundee on September 23, it marched to De Jager's Drift and occupied a position east of the Buffalo River. On the 29th it forded the Blood River and stood at Vant's Drift. C Company went on to Rorke's Drift with The 5th Dragoon Guards. No Boers attempted to cross.

Shouldered away from the Natal border, Botha edged back northwards. He was reported to be in the Schurwe Berg area. Garratt marched to Vryheid, whence, on October 2, A and the Volunteer Companies were sent to occupy a pass, while E and H held a hill which commanded it. A dense fog came down and prevented the first party from reaching its position that night. In the morning the advanced-guard suddenly encountered a group of Boers. Private Dix was wounded. Lieutenant Kitson and Private Harold were taken prisoner, but were released when they had been disarmed. The pass was occupied and held until the 7th, while the mounted troops swept the neighbouring hills.

Meanwhile Hamilton's Column had been closing in from the south. It reached Nondweni on the night of the 4th and Spitzkop next day. There the troops took up defensive positions in the mountains, being enveloped the whole time in a thick fog. On the night of the 6th, detachments from D and G Companies surrounded a laager. The Boers escaped, but their families, some ammunition and horses were captured.

Several columns now began to scour the area for Botha's scattered commando. Hamilton first *trekked* through Brakfontein to Vryheid, then west towards Utrecht, and finally by way of a mountainous road north-east to Tambootiesbult. Garratt marched north to Luneburg, where he took up tactical positions while the vicinity was thoroughly searched. Brock-Hollinshead's Wing then joined Hamilton's Column to clear the Pongola Bosch. In thick mist and rain both Queen's Own wings carried out this operation on October 23. Some saddled horses and half-finished breakfasts were found, but the quarry had gone.

As Botha's attempt at invading Natal had failed, the hunt was now called off. Hamilton's Column, which had been on quarter rations for five days, replenished its supplies from a convoy and marched west to Volksrust. Thence it entrained for Standerton. Garratt's Column went to a camp near Utrecht.

*   *   *

Captain Moody's Wing had one more adventure under Brigadier-General Hamilton's command. On October 31 the news reached Standerton that a force commanded by Lieutenant-Colonel G. E. Benson had been attacked and surrounded some 50 miles north. At

3 p.m. the mounted troops of Hamilton's, Allenby's and de Lisle's Columns set off to relieve it. Two hours later Moody's Wing marched after them with the baggage. Soon after the start the convoy was fired at, but the enemy dispersed when D and G Companies deployed for attack. Having marched 38 miles in just over 22 hours, the wing reached the bivouac of the mounted troops, only to find that they had arrived at the scene of the ambush too late to prevent the destruction of Benson's force.

Garratt's Column was employed during November in re-searching the Schurwe Berg area. Using Vryheid as a base, it made several expeditions with varying results. Night marches were also carried out to surprise groups of Boers, but without success. After a refit at Newcastle, the column acted as a covering force to the troops who were building a line of blockhouses from Botha's Pass to Vrede. On December 16 Brock-Hollinshead's Wing was ordered back to the battalion to assume yet another role.

10. *The Heilbron—Frankfort—Tafel Kop Blockhouse Line*

The erection of a network of cross-country blockhouse lines to intersect the whole area of operations had begun in June 1901. The first of these lines in the Orange River Colony was from the Vaal River, near Klerksdorp, to Kroonstad.[1] The connection of Heilbron and Frankfort soon followed. Others erected in the north-east of the Colony were from Kroonstad to Lindley, and from Lindley to Harrismith. The blockhouses were similar to those on the railways, as were the fences and ditches between them.

The 130 all ranks of the battalion, under Major Maunsell, arrived at Heilbron from Vereeniging on September 28, 1901. On October 1 a draft of 169 joined from England. Within a few days most of the local defences and nine blockhouses on the road to Frankfort were taken over. The latter had just been erected. The garrisons were equally divided between the draft and old hands, so that the former could pick up tips on how to live in small groups. Except for occasional half-hearted sniping, the Boers were not aggressive.

C, D, F and G Companies returned from their *trek* with Brigadier-General Hamilton's Column on the morning of November 22. D and F only stayed a few hours, for, having been made up to strength, they departed again at noon with another column.

The battalion, seven officers and 425 other ranks strong, marched for Frankfort on November 23. The Quartermaster with a small staff remained as a base-party at Heilbron. Garrisons were dropped at all posts and blockhouses between Brakvlei and Frankfort, C Company Headquarters being accommodated at Krom Spruit. The defences of Frankfort were taken over from the 1st Battalion The East Lancashire Regiment, which moved out to construct an extension of the blockhouse line to Tafel Kop.

[1] Map "The Southern Transvaal."

After A, E, H and the Volunteer Companies had rejoined from Colonel Garratt's Column on December 18, additional commitments were taken over. These were the defence of Brakvlei and the manning of blockhouses 1 to 10 on the way to Tafel Kop. The remainder of the posts to Tafel Kop were occupied by the East Lancashires.

With the trenches between blockhouses to be completed and the wire fences to be constantly repaired or strengthened, there was plenty of work for the men to do. Otherwise life in the blockhouse line was monotonous. Sentries had to be found both day and night, and there was the routine stand-to at dawn and dusk. Rations were received three times a week. Mails and canteen stores arrived periodically from Heilbron. In this way Christmas came and went without any particular excitement. Every man had his plum pudding and beer, thanks to a canteen grant, but a large consignment of articles subscribed for by friends of the Regiment did not arrive in time.

During the night of January 4, 1902, four posts near Brakvlei were engaged for over two hours with about 60 Boers, who were intent on crossing the line. The brunt of the attack was borne by the garrisons of two blockhouses manned by the Volunteer Company and commanded by Sergeant Spencer and Corporal Muir. After the fight the posts had a number of bullet marks, but none of the defenders was hit. Another attempt to cross the line was made on the night of the 10th. On this occasion the blockhouse commanded by Lance-Corporal Davies was mainly responsible for driving off the enemy.

D and F Companies finally rejoined on January 29. Since their return from the Transvaal they had been attached to Lieutenant-Colonel A. E. Wilson's Column, which had made several attempts to round-up De Wet's Commando. The main operation had been a combined "drive" with five other columns from the Libenberg's Vlei River across the Wolvehoek—Kroonstad Railway. At the Rhenoster River 500 Boers had just managed to escape at a drift. They had been hotly pursued, but night had come on and only 20 men and 150 horses had been caught. When the operation ended on December 14, just over 40 prisoners in all had been taken. After that, Wilson's Column had made night raids and had acted as escorts to various convoys. During one of the raids Private Mott had been mortally wounded by the fire from a blockhouse, the garrison of which had mistaken his party for Boers. In a large-scale sweep to the north of Frankfort, Private Tucker had been killed and Private Sands had been wounded.

The whole battalion, except the M.I. Company, was now in the blockhouse line. As the garrisons of alternate posts had already been reduced from 10 to seven, a number of men were thus available to take over more commitments. The battalion became responsible for all of the blockhouses from Heilbron itself to No. 10 east of Frankfort. This was a total of 70 blockhouses, covering a front of 40 miles, in addition to the posts at Brakvlei, Krom Spruit and Frankfort.

The strategy of the cross-country system, which might have led to an ineffectual dispersion of troops, cannot be considered without the co-ordinated " drives." As the blockhouse lines were erected, so the space in which the Boer commandos could manoeuvre contracted. As this space grew less, so the " drives " had less country to search. Without the blockhouse lines the " drives " would have beaten the air.

While the Heilbron—Tafel Kop blockhouse line was being constructed and occupied, " drives " had been taking place to the north and south of it, mainly in an endeavour to catch De Wet. Lord Kitchener now organised an operation which far outstripped the others in dimensions. Its aim was to herd all the Boers in the eastern portion of the Orange River Colony into a closed funnel formed by the Wilge River, the Klip River and the blockhouse line astride Lindley. In preparation for it many small columns passed east from Heilbron to Frankfort between February 14 and 17. Nearly 800 prisoners were taken besides a large number of animals. But De Wet and President Steyn once more broke through the cordon.

Without delay, Kitchener laid on another large-scale " drive." While it was in progress the battalion manned extra posts between blockhouses, and sentry duty thus became very heavy. The sweep ended with a general advance by 12 columns from the Wilge River to the Wolvehoek—Kroonstad Railway. The main quarry was a commando of some 400 men under Commandant F. Mentz, which boldly charged the Heilbron—Wolvehoek line from the west and got across. It then turned eastwards. In consequence, great vigilance was kept in the Heilbron—Frankfort blockhouses to prevent it from doubling south. The whole operation yielded only 82 prisoners, but a large amount of ammunition and most of De Wet's personal effects were discovered in a cave. The leader himself again escaped.

On March 19 seven columns began a sweep from the line Lindley—Heilbron north-eastwards to the Vaal River. On the 24th some of them came in to Frankfort to replenish their supplies. When the " drive " reached the Wilge it had to halt and await the subsidence of the flooded stream. Some of the troops crossed the bridge at Frankfort on the 31st, while the others waded or swam over next day. For more than a week the battalion, in addition to holding its blockhouse line, manned many intermediate posts and furnished picquets for several miles along the Wilge River. During the operation 10 Boers were killed or wounded and 76 were taken prisoner.

While this sweep was in progress, part of Mentz's Commando made a determined effort to break through the Heilbron—Frankfort line. This incident occurred just east of Heilbron on the night of March 29. Soon after nine o'clock about a hundred Boers approached from the north driving cattle against the wire fence, which was levelled for some 40 yards. Although they were met by heavy fire from two blockhouses held by the Volunteer Company, some of Mentz's men made their way through the gap and rode off southwards. Next morning one dead and one dying Boer, three Lee-Metford rifles and two Mausers were picked up; a number of dead horses and cattle were found. It was learned later that this venture had cost the Boers 18 casualties (five killed and 13 wounded).

The 3rd Volunteer Active Service Company joined the battalion on April 5 in relief of the 2nd, which left for England on the 21st.

During April and May there was little warlike activity. Although no armistice existed, groups of Boers were allowed to cross the blockhouse line on their way to discuss the advisability of surrender. From May 9, two British columns were encamped at Frankfort. Advantage was taken of the lull to play them at polo and football, and to hold gymkhanas and even a race meeting.

The first sign of peace had come on April 10, when the Boer leaders had sent certain proposals to the British Government. This had led to a conference of the elected delegates of the commandos at Vereeniging on May 10. So sure was Lord Kitchener of a peaceful outcome that he forbade any further offensive action south of the Vaal. At 9 a.m. on June 1 this message was received at Frankfort:—

"Peace was signed last night."

11. *The Last Months in South Africa*

Peace had been expected for so long that there was no demonstration when it came. The question was "What happens to us now?" This was soon answered. On June 2 the troops began to dismantle the blockhouse line and take the wire and other material into Heilbron and Frankfort.

Major Brock-Hollinshead, two N.C.O.s and eight men left for England at one hour's notice on June 3 to represent the battalion at the Coronation of King Edward VII. They sailed in the "Bavarian."

On June 25, Headquarters and the companies at and east of Frankfort marched for Heilbron, where the whole battalion concentrated. On the 28th 100 reservists, under Captain Lowe, entrained for Port Elizabeth to embark for Home. This did not bring the strength much below establishment, because a draft of 80 had arrived on May 20. In July the M.I. Company, consisting of Lieutenant Grant and 51 other ranks, rejoined; and two officers and 117 arrived from the 21st Mounted Infantry. With his column broken up, Colonel Western resumed command.

At Heilbron life was comparatively gay. There were two or three dances, a concert, football matches, and an excellent boxing tournament in the Town Hall. Coronation celebrations took place on August 9. They began with a Brigade Church Parade in the Town Square. In the afternoon a Sports Meeting was held on the Heilbron Football Ground, during which three regimental teams and one from a Boer Refugee Camp competed in the Tug-of-War. There was a torchlight procession with fireworks in the evening.

Early in August it became known that the next station was to be Ceylon, and the task of sending home the remaining reservists, the time-expired men and the 3rd Volunteer Active Service Company began. The drafts that departed totalled eight officers and some 380 other ranks.

The much depleted battalion left Heilbron on September 26. After an uneventful four weeks at Kroonstad it entrained for Cape Town, where it was accommodated in a camp at Green Point. On November 5, 16 officers and 574 other ranks strong, it embarked in H.M.T. " Golconda " for passage to Colombo.

All officers and other ranks who served in South Africa during the war received The Queen's South Africa Medal. The King's South Africa Medal was awarded to those who served for 18 months at the front and were still serving on January 1, 1902. Twenty-six clasps were issued. The majority of the battalion received both medals, with the clasps " Wittebergen," " Cape Colony," and " Transvaal."

ANNEXURE 1
COLONEL WILLIAMS' COLUMN

Ferbruary and March 1901

(Map " Orange River Colony ")

Colonel Williams' Column left Heilbron on February 4, 1901. It consisted of: —
    Two field guns.
    Two M.I. companies Royal Irish Rifles.
    M.I. Company The Queen's Own (Captain Woulfe-Flanagan,[1] Lieutenant Bonham-Carter and, later, 2nd-Lieutenant Grant.
    G Company The Queen's Own (2nd-Lieutenants Luard and, at first, Grant).
    H Company The Queen's Own (Captain Pack-Beresford and 2nd-Lieutenants Bennett and Norman).
    Three companies Oxfordshire Light Infantry.

Major Brock-Hollinshead was in command of all five companies of dismounted men.

The object of the expedition was to denude the country round Heilbron, Kroonstad and Ventersburg of inhabitants, food and stock in accordance with Lord Kitchener's " scorched-earth " policy. Only 10 days' rations were taken, but others were picked up from various places during the *trek*. The men fed well as they were allowed to carry away poultry and pigs from the farms that were stripped. Families were given 20 minutes in which to pack their chattels on to the empty wagons which went with the column. The women and children were treated with the greatest kindness, while the men — too old to be on commando — would be given a pipe-full of tobacco at the end of each day's march. When the wagons were full the families were entrained at a station on the railway, whence they were taken to a Refugee Camp.

[1] Captain Woulfe-Flanagan left the M.I. Company on March 2, when he went to join Brigadier-General Alderson's M.I. Brigade in the Eastern Transvaal.

Almost every day the column met with long-range shelling and sniping from the Boers. East of Kroonstad on February 25 Private Bowman, by his plucky and prompt action, enabled the convoy to cross a drift when the rearguard was attacked. Four days later the M.I. Company succeeded in rescuing 13 of Driscoll's Scouts, who were surrounded in a farm. Just before the column entered Virginia Siding on March 6, Private Pocock was severely wounded in an encounter with a party of the enemy.

From Virginia Siding a forced march was made westwards to Bulfontein Drift in order to block it and head off De Wet's commando, which was returning northwards after an incursion into Cape Colony. The distance covered was 36 miles in little more than 24 hours. At the drift a position was occupied and trenches were dug. De Wet broke through the net elsewhere.

When Colonel Williams' Column was re-organised on March 17, The Queen's Own detachment rejoined the battalion at Heilbron. During the *trek* several thousand cattle, sheep and horses had been driven in, and a large tract of country had been cleared. In a complimentary letter, sent by him to the Commanding Officer, Colonel Williams wrote: —

" I never wish to command better officers, N.C.O.s and men. Their marching was excellent; they performed the outpost duties and all other duties in a thoroughly soldierly manner, and the general tone of the detachment merits the highest praise . . . I also wish to bring specially to your notice the good work done by Lieutenant Bonham-Carter and his detachment of M.I. . . .

I have been requested by Lord Kitchener to express to the troops forming my late Column his entire satisfaction of the work done by the column, especially in the Doornberg Mountains, when P. Botha, the Commandant, was killed, and his two sons badly wounded."[1]

ANNEXURE 2
THE M.I. COMPANY WITH COLONEL WESTERN'S COLUMN

April 1901 — July 1902
(Map " Orange River Colony ")

The M.I. Company became permanently detached from the battalion on April 8, 1901, when it joined Western's Column.[2] The composition of this column was: —
Driscoll's Scouts.
Two field guns and one pom-pom.
M.I. Company The Queen's Own (Lieutenants Bonham-Carter and Grant).
Two M.I. Companies Royal Irish Rifles.

[1] The Doornberg Mountains are South of Ventersburg. Philip Botha was the eldest brother of the C.-in-C. of the Boer Army.

[2] Major Western took command of Colonel Williams' Column on April 22, 1901, when Williams went to take over a New South Wales contingent.

Two companies Royal Irish Fusiliers.
Two companies Oxfordshire Light Infantry.
   The Column first operated on both sides of the Vereeniging—Kroonstad Railway in the north of the Orange River Colony. Many sheep and cattle were seized, and an attack was made against a Boer laager north of Heilbron. In a raid on Parys the M.I. Company captured five of the burghers. These prisoners, together with some of the animals which had been rounded up, were taken in to a station on the railway.
   Taking the field again on June 17, Western (now a local lieutenant-colonel) cleared the southern bank of the Rhenoster River to its junction with the Vaal. During this *trek* Lieutenant Bonham-Carter was sent to hospital with jaundice. Captain Pack-Beresford arrived to take command of the company on July 7.
   After several operations in the Klerksdorp district, during which Corporal Saunders was wounded, Colonel Western's Column joined in a co-ordinated " drive " southwards to the Modder River. The object was to sweep the area between the Vereeniging—Bloemfontein and the Vryburg—Kimberley Railways. Passing through Roodewal, the Column reached Cyferfontein on August 7. Next day Captain Pack-Beresford went to search a farm with 17 men. As they approached it they ran into a small laager. In the melee which followed, one man was captured and Private Binder was wounded and subsequently lost an arm. Lieutenant Grant then came up with another party, but the Boers broke out northwards and rode clear. On reaching Bloemfontein Western's Column entrained for Aliwal North.
   The area near the confluence of the Orange and the Caledon Rivers had temporarily become the focal point of the war. Through it Assistant-Commandant-General J. C. Smuts was leading a force to invade Cape Colony. To it seven or eight British Columns were directed in order to forestall Smuts at the crossings over the Orange River. Western's Column held several drifts to the east of Aliwal North. Smuts lay low until the British were exhausted, when he crossed near Herschel on the night of September 3. The M.I. Company followed him for over 50 miles, but he outpaced it and rode on southwards.
   After scouring the country south of the line Dewetsdorp—Edenburg, Colonel Western's Column marched in to Springfontein on December 19. Here the dismounted troops were replaced by some Imperial Yeomanry Sharpshooters and two M.I. companies of The Black Watch. Lieutenant Grant was now the only officer with The Queen's Own M.I., as Captain Pack-Beresford had been sent to hospital on September 28. 2nd-Lieutenant Beamish joined the company on March 20, 1902.
   The Column made its return journey northwards as an all-mounted formation, re-searching the area on the west of the railway as it went. At the Vaal River it joined in a combined " drive " to capture De la Rey. While other columns swept north of the river, Western's combed the south bank from Commando Drift to the Rhenoster River, mainly at night. It rode over 90 miles in 20 hours and entered Klerksdorp with eight prisoners, three of which were taken by the M.I. Company.

After 18 hours' rest, it rode back north of the river and swam across Commando Drift to the south bank. Not a single horse was dropped. This was an outstanding feat of endurance.

On April 15, 1902, the Column made a night march from Bloemhof and surrounded Schweizer Reneke at dawn. The Boers were taken completely by surprise. Fifty-seven of them were captured, including one of De Wet's adjutants. A week later a party of seven men, under Lance-Corporal Hunt, came under fire as it rode out from Bloemhof to act as a cossack post. The two scouts, Privates Conway and Ball, were both hit. Conway died of his wounds.

In May Sir Ian Hamilton organised a great sweep westwards to the fortified Vryburg—Kimberley Railway. Western's Column was part of a force which operated on the left flank. When it reached the Transvaal border on the 7th the Boer leaders were in conference discussing the desirability of continuing the war, and Hamilton was uncertain whether he should continue the pressure. But the Boers removed all doubt by throwing themselves in small groups against the railway. Only one man succeded in breaking out. The troops, now within 15 miles of the line, advanced next day almost shoulder to shoulder. Within a few hours 367 prisoners had been captured. Such was the fortune of war that, of this number, Western's Column accounted for but three.

The march back to Bloemhof began on May 14. Next evening some Boers fired into the bivouac and stampeded the horses. In the morning a patrol of the M.I. Company went out to search the neighbouring bushes. As it was returning to camp, some of the enemy appeared and opened fire. Private Bond was hit and Private Vile's horse was killed. The remainder of the patrol charged through the Boers. Hearing a shout from Vile, Private Ball, now recovered from his wound, turned back, took him on his horse and galloped away. Ball's horse was wounded three times before they rode out of range. An ambulance was sent to bring in Private Bond, but he died almost immediately.

After peace had been signed the M.I. Company entrained at Bloemfontein for Pretoria, where the horses were handed over. It rejoined the 2nd Battalion as B Company on July 17, 1902.

CHAPTER 7

THE HOME FRONT IN ENGLAND AND MALTA

October, 1899—November, 1902

1. *Regimental*

THE disasters in the early months of the South African War caused a surge of patriotism at Home. Nowhere was this emotion greater than in West Kent, where the people of every town and village responded to calls for aid for the wounded and the families of the men at the front. In Maidstone the Mayor opened a South African War Fund, in support of which prominent people organised numerous concerts and entertainments. At many of these functions the chief attraction was the band of either the 3rd Battalion (Militia) or the 1st Volunteer Battalion. All ranks of the Regiment sent generous contributions to local war funds.

Another outcome of this patriotic fervour was the large number of applications which were received at 50th Regimental District Headquarters from ex-soldiers who were eager to return to the Colours. One was from a man of 52, who had been discharged with a pension some 15 years before. As one of his qualifications he claimed that he could "speak the Boer and Kaffir language fairly." The oldest to apply was 54 years of age.

The impact of the war was first seriously felt at the Regimental Depot in December 1899, when Captains Venables and Brown, the Adjutant and the Quartermaster, departed with the 3rd Battalion on its embodiment. Their duties were taken over by Lieutenants Isacke and Nunn, who were serving there at the time. A further interruption in the Depot routine was caused by the calling out of the Regular Army Reserve. Between December 26 and 30 no fewer than 371 Reservists of the Regiment assembled in the barracks. After they had been medically inspected, fitted with clothing, equipped and paid, they were granted short leave. All this meant a great deal of extra work, and the Adjutants of the 1st and 2nd Volunteer Battalions (Captains Umfreville and Wood Martyn) and some of their Sergeant-Instructors were brought in to assist.

After Lieutenants Isacke and Nunn had embarked with the 2nd Battalion for South Africa in March 1900, there were over 600 men in the Depot barracks with very few officers and N.C.O.s to command them. In order to deal with the situation, Captain Umfreville transferred his office from Tonbridge to Maidstone and combined the duties of Adjutant of 50th Regimental District with those of Adjutant of the 1st Volunteer Battalion; Captain Roche was brought back from the Reserve to take on the Quartermaster's task; and several officers of the Volunteer battalions gave their services.

Among those posted to the Depot from the 2nd Battalion were Bandmaster Ingham and the boys who were too young to go on active service. Together with some other boys, who subsequently enlisted into the Regiment, they were formed into a band. The first occasion on which they played in public was at a concert held in the gymnasium on May 24, 1900, to celebrate the Relief of Mafeking. This band made such good progress that it was soon able to fulfil outside engagements.

Soon after the 2nd Battalion had sailed for South Africa, a number of ladies connected with the Regiment began to collect money for " comforts " for the troops. By September 1900 nearly £200 had been received. With half of this sum 30,000 Woodbine cigarettes, 268 pounds of tobacco, 400 pipes and 300 sweaters were bought and despatched. These articles were delivered to the battalion when it arrived at Heilbron in February 1901. The second consignment, consisting of clothing, pipes and tobacco, reached the troops at Vereeniging five months later. Goods costing a further £170 were sent off in the hope that they would arrive in time for Christmas 1901. This time the bales contained a tin of plum pudding for each man, cake and chocolate, as well as pipes, tobacco, cigarettes and clothing. They arrived — too late for Christmas — when the battalion was in the Heilbron-Tafel Kop Blockhouse Line.

A notable innovation was that the troops at the Depot marched to All Saints' Church for their routine Church Parade for the first time on Sunday, April 21, 1901.

With the 1st, 2nd and 3rd Battalions overseas, the part played by the Regiment on the occasion of the funeral of Queen Victoria on February 2, 1901, was necessarily small. A detachment from the Depot, consisting of Lieutenant Nunn (who had returned, sick, from South Africa), three sergeants and 50 rank and file, lined a portion of the processional route at Hamilton Place in Piccadilly. Some men of The Details went by train from Shorncliffe to Charing Cross, marched to Hyde Park Corner and lined the route from Apsley Gate to the Achilles Statue.

The Coronation of King Edward VII was arranged to take place in June 1902. A detachment of the 3rd Battalion, now back in England, was to encamp in Regent's Park and line the route in The

Mall. Major Brock-Hollinshead and 10 men of the 2nd, who had made the voyage from South Africa in 18 days, were to be amongst the first to salute His Majesty as he emerged from Westminster Abbey. The 3rd and each of the Volunteer Battalions was to send its quota to line the streets during the Royal Progress through South London on the day after the King had been crowned. But, owing to the serious illness of His Majesty, all these arrangements had to be postponed. When the Coronation eventually took place on August 9, 1902, it was shorn of much of its pomp. Of the Regiment only a few men of The Details were there to line the route.

2. The Details at Shorncliffe

The Details, which were left at Aldershot when the 2nd Battalion embarked for South Africa, joined the Provisional Battalion at Shorncliffe on April 2, 1900. The purpose of this Provisional unit was to "hold" personnel of regiments, both of whose Line battalions were overseas. It was commanded by Colonel C. H. Kelly, late Royal Scots Fusiliers, and consisted mainly of detachments of The Buffs, The Loyal North Lancashire Regiment and The Queen's Own.

With the arrival of three drafts from the Depot during April and May the strength of The Details of The Queen's Own rose to 600. They were organised into three companies, under Major Daniell. The other officers were Captain Hitchins (2nd Vol. Bn.), Lieutenant Riddle (3rd Vol. Bn.) and two subalterns of the 21st Finsbury Rifle Volunteers, who were attached. Some of the men were sent to construct an extension of the range at Lydd; 20 were employed on permanent range duties at Hythe; the remainder carried out individual and minor tactical training at Shorncliffe.

As the personnel became eligible for posting overseas, they were sent to the 1st, 2nd or 3rd Battalion in Aden, South Africa and Malta respectively. The first, and largest, draft to go to the 2nd embarked at the Royal Albert Docks, Woolwich, on June 30, 1900. It consisted of 2nd-Lieutenant E. H. Norman, who had been commissioned into the Line from the 3rd Battalion, and 150 other ranks.

Early in 1901 a Mounted Infantry Company was formed in the Provisional Battalion. 2nd-Lieutenant G. E. W. Morris, recently commissioned, and 29 other ranks of the Regiment were posted to it. This company embarked for South Africa on May 6 to join the 13th M.I. Battalion. A second company was trained and went out later.

When the 1st Battalion arrived in England towards the end of 1902 to begin its tour of Home service, The Details were posted to it. The Regiment ceased to have any connection with a Provisional unit for the time being.

3. The 3rd Battalion (Militia)

Soon after the outbreak of war a proclamation was issued authorising the embodiment of the Militia. Before the 3rd Battalion was embodied its personnel were asked to volunteer for service overseas. There was an enthusiastic response to this request, and it was placed under orders for garrison duty in Malta. At the time, only one other Militia unit had been selected to go abroad.

All ranks assembled at Maidstone on December 11, 1899. When they arrived at the Depot they were issued with their kit and equipment. They paraded on the square at 2.30 p.m. and, headed by the band of the 1st Volunteer Battalion, marched to the South-Eastern Station. As the column passed down the High Street, the band played " Soldiers of The Queen." There was loud cheering from the onlookers. The enthusiasm reached its height when, to the strains of " Auld Lang Syne," the two special trains moved slowly away. It was dark before the battalion reached Chatham, where it stayed for three weeks.

H.R.H. The Duke of Connaught, the Honorary Colonel, sent the following letter to the Commanding Officer:—

" Osborne, Dec. 30th, '99.

Dear Colonel Bonhote,

Having just heard from Col. Egerton that the 3rd Battalion R.W. Kent Regiment, who were the second Militia Battalion that volunteered for Foreign Service, have been selected to proceed to Malta, I write to congratulate my Regiment and to express my appreciation of their soldierlike and patriotic conduct. I had intended to come to Chatham to see the Regiment, but now that you are under orders to embark at the Albert Docks on the 4th prox. I shall find it impossible to do so.

I wish the Regiment a good passage and a pleasant service at Malta, and I wish you and all ranks a very happy New Year.

Believe me,

Yours sincerely,

Arthur."

The battalion left Chatham Barracks very early in the morning on January 4, 1900, and went by train to the Royal Albert Docks by way of Thames Tunnel and Liverpool Street. It embarked in the hired transport " Golconda," together with the families of five officers and 25 other ranks. When the ship sailed at 2.30 p.m. a large number of friends waved farewell from the quay. The strength on embarkation was 30 officers and 991 other ranks. A list of officers who served with the battalion in Malta is in Appendix CC.

The last few days of the voyage were very stormy. On the night of January 11, off Cape Bon, the steering gear broke down, the chart-house was blown overboard, and the forestay sail had to be carried away with the assistance of some of the troops. The weather was still bad when the " Golconda " entered the Grand Harbour, Malta, on the morning of the 13th. The men went ashore in lighters in Dockyard Creek and marched to Verdala Barracks, where over 700 were quartered. The remaining 280 were accommodated nearby at Zabbar Gate, Zeitun Gate and in the bastions of the Cottonera Lines. It was in this area that part of the 1st Battalion had been stationed for a short time 10 years earlier.

The Governor and Commander-in-Chief of Malta was Lieutenant-General Sir Francis Grenfell. Major-General Lord Congleton commanded the Infantry Brigade, which consisted of five Regular battalions and two of The Royal Malta Regiment of Militia. One of the Regular units left for South Africa within a few weeks.

Training was practically continuous throughout the year. It began in February and March with the annual range courses, which were fired at Pembroke. In April and May half the battalion at a time marched to the north of the island for field work. At the end of July the whole unit went in Government tugs to Mellieha Bay for four weeks' camp. During the autumn, visits were made to Pembroke Camp for range practice and field firing. Frequent tactical exercises were held in different parts of the island during the winter.

News of the Relief of Ladysmith was received on March 1, 1900. In Valetta the people thronged the streets, which were gay with bunting, and followed the local bands to the Palace. When His Excellency the Governor appeared at one of the windows, they cheered enthusiastically. The bands played " God Save The Queen." That evening, as H.E. drove in from his residence to the Opera House, a happy crowd took the horses from his carriage and drew it to the entrance. On the other side of the Grand Harbour there were similar demonstrations. Bands paraded the streets of Vittoriosa and Cospicua amidst the applause of the inhabitants. Ultimately the throng reached Verdala Barracks, where a number of officers of the Royal Malta Regiment of Militia were being entertained. Colonel Bonhote thanked the people from the balcony of the Officers' Mess and called for three cheers for the Queen. The next day was observed as a general holiday. On Saturday the 3rd, Battalion Headquarters and four companies took part in a ceremonial parade to celebrate the occasion This included a march through Valetta with bayonets fixed and Colours flying.

The battalion twice trooped the Colour on the Palace Square, Valetta. On the first occasion, on March 28, 1900, the Regimental Colour of the disbanded 4th Battalion was carried. On the second occasion, on November 21, 1900, the Regimental Colour that was trooped was the one presented to The West Kent Light Infantry Militia exactly 45 years before.

The Queen's Birthday in 1900 was celebrated on May 26. It was marked by an impressive spectacle. At noon a Royal Salute was fired from the ships of the Fleet and by the Royal Artillery. This was followed by a *feu-de-joie,* which began on the east of the Grand Harbour, was taken up by the regiments in Valetta, continued round the walls of the capital, and was brought to a conclusion by the troops at Fort Manoel and Tigne, on the west of Marsamuscetto Harbour. The same procedure was carried out three times. As each round was signalled all the bands played part of the National Anthem. After the third round had been fired, the troops fixed bayonets and presented arms while the bands played the whole of the tune. On a further signal the various units gave three cheers. For this ceremony the battalion lined the ramparts of Corradino Heights, on the east of the Grand Harbour.

Early in December volunteers were invited to train as Mounted Infantry. They were tested at the United Services Sports Club at Marsa. The successful candidates included Lance-Corporal Corrick and 19 men of the 3rd Battalion. These embarked for the front with the Malta Mounted Infantry Company on January 4, 1901. One of the men, Private E. Smith, died during the voyage. Private Cowlard was later accidentally shot at Potgieters Rust.

On January 3, 1901, Colonel Bonhote was asked whether the battalion would volunteer for service in South Africa. As he had already expressed personally and by letter the desire of his officers and men to go, he sent a prompt reply in the affirmative. Nothing came of this.

On the day of Queen Victoria's funeral, the battalion attended a Memorial Service in the Garrison Chapel, Marguerita Hill. At retreat the band played the National Anthem on Verdala parade ground, and the buglers sounded the Last Post.

When their Royal Highnesses the Duke and Duchess of Cornwall and York landed from the Royal Yacht "Ophir" on March 25 on an official visit, the troops of the garrison lined the route from the quay to the Palace, Valetta. The battalion was in position close to the Customs House.

In May the battalion was ordered to hold itself in readiness to return home on relief by the 1st Royal Garrison Regiment. On the 20th Sir Francis Grenfell and his Staff dined in the Officers' Mess. On the 29th a farewell ceremony of Trooping the Colour was carried out on the Floriana Parade Ground, at the conclusion of which Colonel J. Spence, the Chief Staff Officer, wished the men "God Speed" in the name of H.E. The Governor and Commander-in-Chief.

The battalion (less two and a half companies) embarked in the hired transport "Formosa" on May 31. The ship left the Grand Harbour at 8 a.m. next day. B and K Companies and part of E, under Captain Neve, sailed in the "Dilwara" on June 2. The "Formosa" berthed at Southampton at dawn on June 9 after a splendid voyage. Those companies on board arrived at Maidstone in the evening, and were played to barracks by the bands of the 1st and 2nd Volunteer Battalions. Having handed in their equipment, the men left for their homes that night. The detachment in the "Dilwara" arrived at Maidstone and dispersed on the 10th.

His Majesty King Edward VII was graciously pleased to approve the grant of the Mediterranean Medal to all officers and other ranks, including the Permanent Staff, who were on garrison duty with Militia units in Gibraltar, Malta and Egypt during the South African War.

* * *

Those men who were unable to go with the battalion to Malta carried out their annual training with The Details at Shorncliffe in 1900 and 1901.

In 1902 the annual camp was at Colchester from June 9 till July 5. The battalion was under canvas with the 1st Militia Brigade (Colonel C. W. Hill) at Middlewick. On June 13 the brigade went by train to Aldershot for the Royal Review, which, owing to the illness of King Edward, was taken by Her Majesty Queen Alexandra on the 16th. The battalion returned to Colchester next day.

Their Mediterranean Medals were presented to those who were entitled to them on June 23 by Lieutenant-Colonel E. W. G. Bailey, who was now commanding.

4. *The Volunteer Battalions*

The surge of patriotism caused a spate of enlistments into the Volunteer battalions in 1900. Over 500 recruits joined the 1st, and new companies or detachments were formed at Sevenoaks, Southborough and Orpington. In the 2nd an additional company was established at Beckenham.

There was some anxiety in England because of the lack of Regular troops for home defence. This had a marked effect on the training of the Volunteers, which was carried out with renewed verve. The most notable feature was that the annual camp of the 2nd Volunteer Battalion in 1900, which took place at Hythe, lasted for a month instead of the usual week. During it, three companies went to Chattenden, near Chatham, to take part in a test mobilization exercise in connection with the defence of the Thames Estuary. In August 1901 the 1st, 2nd and 3rd were all in camp at Aldershot at the same time, the 1st and 3rd being brigaded with the Sussex Volunteers. In 1902 the battalions trained at Shorncliffe from August 2—9 as the West Kent Volunteer Brigade.

A Cyclist Company was included in the establishment of the Volunteer battalions in 1900. That of the 1st was a new company, with its Headquarters at Maidstone and detachments at Tonbridge, Tunbridge Wells and Sevenoaks. In both the 2nd and 3rd one of the existing companies was issued with bicycles.

* * *

The decision to send Volunteer Active Service Companies to South Africa was warmly supported by the Regiment. Preparations to muster the first company began in February 1900. The conditions of service were that volunteers must be unmarried, between 20 and 34 years of age, and first-class shots. They must also have been returned as efficient during 1898 and 1899. Every man in the 1st and 2nd Volunteer Battalions, who was eligible, was sent a post-card to find out whether he was able to go. Another card brought him to his Battalion Headquarters for medical inspection and attestation by a Justice of the Peace. As each man was sworn in he was presented with a new 1900 shilling. He was then given leave to return to his home, where he was treated by the local people as a hero.

The 1st Volunteer Active Service Company assembled at the Depot on February 24. It consisted of Captain Watney (who went out as a subaltern) and 57 N.C.O.s and men from the 1st Volunteer Battalion; and Captain Morphew, Lieutenant W. G. Morris and 56 other ranks from the 2nd. It remained at Maidstone for three weeks, during which it trained for operations in the field. A subscription list was opened locally, and a banquet was provided for the members of the company in the Corn Exchange on March 13. Many of the leading citizens were present, the tables being set for 250. Each of the departing " gentlemen in khaki " was presented with a packet of tobacco and cigars, while each Maidstone man received in addition a Service knife as a souvenir.

The company left the Depot for South Africa early on March 16. On the way to the West Station the streets were lined with cheering crowds. In the station yard the men had to force their way in single file through hundreds of people, while the officers were carried shoulder high. At Southampton Captain Morphew and his men embarked in the " Tagus." As she steamed out she passed the " Bavarian," with the 2nd Battalion on board. The voyage was marred by the death of Private Helmer, who succumbed to tuberculosis. The company disembarked at Port Elizabeth and went by train to Springfontein, whence it escorted a convoy to Edenburg. While waiting there to move up to the front, guards were furnished for vulnerable points on the line of communications. The contingent was under orders to join the King's Royal Rifle Corps, but this plan was now changed. It left Edenburg on May 30 and went to the 2nd Battalion at Hammonia.

A reinforcement draft, consisting of Lieutenant Marchant (2nd Vol. Bn.) and 20 more Volunteers, joined the 2nd Battalion at Ficksburg on July 6.

The 2nd Volunteer Active Service Company assembled at the Depot early in March 1901. It was composed of detachments from the 1st, 2nd and 3rd Volunteer Battalions, and was about 115 strong. Its officers were Captain Latter (2nd Vol. Bn.), Lieutenant Holcroft (1st Vol. Bn.) and Lieutenant McCracken (3rd Vol. Bn.). It sailed from Southampton on March 16 in the " Kildonan Castle," and disembarked at East London on April 7. The rail journey was slow because no trains ran after dark north of Cape Colony. At Pretoria Captain Latter received orders to return to Serfontein, 20 miles north of Kroonstad. Two more days of uncomfortable travelling brought the somewhat bewildered troops to that place on April 17. The company eventually joined the 2nd Battalion at Heilbron on May 23.

The 3rd Volunteer Active Service Company, comprising Lieutenant Sawers (2nd Vol. Bn.), Lieutenant Wyllie (4th Vol. Bn.) and 56 other ranks, left England in March 1902, when the war was near its close. It joined the 2nd Battalion in the Heilbron-Tafel Kop Blockhouse Line on April 5.

* * *

On its return from South Africa the 1st Volunteer Active Service Company received a tremendous welcome. It arrived at Southampton in the " Tagus " on April 28, 1901, and went by train to Maidstone. There it was met by the bands of the Depot and the 1st Volunteer Battalion. After a short Thanksgiving Service in All Saints' Church, His Worship the Mayor addressed the men from the steps of the Town

Hall. In the evening they were entertained in the Corn Exchange. When they returned to their homes, they were lavishly treated in their various towns and villages. All the officers and men re-assembled at the Depot on Saturday October 5 to be presented with their Queen's South Africa Medals by Earl Stanhope, Lord Lieutenant of Kent, at a special parade. Most of the company were awarded the clasps "Wittebergen," "Cape Colony" and "South Africa, 1901."

The 2nd Volunteer Active Service Company did not receive so enthusiastic a welcome on its return. However, all its members were presented with their Queen's South Africa Medals on impressive parades. Those from the 1st Volunteer Battalion were handed their medals by Earl Stanhope in the grounds of Tonbridge Castle on June 22, 1902; the contingent from the 2nd received theirs from Colonel Satterthwaite, their Commanding Officer, on the Bromley Recreation Ground on June 23; the medals of the active service men from the 3rd were presented by Major-General Sir Frederick Maurice at the conclusion of a Church Parade at Woolwich, also on June 23. Most of the company were awarded the clasps "Cape Colony," "Orange Free State" (another name for the Orange River Colony), "Transvaal," "South Africa, 1901," and "South Africa, 1902."

The return of the 3rd Volunteer Active Service Company in the autumn of 1902 appears to have been "unhonoured and unsung." Nor were their medals presented at special parades. They were awarded the clasps "Cape Colony," "Orange Free State" and "South Africa, 1902."

5. *The Formation of the 4th Volunteer Battalion*

Authority was issued from the War Office on May 17, 1900, for the formation of the 4th Volunteer Battalion of the Regiment. It was recruited from Chatham, Strood, Rochester and New Brompton. The Headquarters were established at 21 Victoria Street, Rochester. Charles James, formerly Lieutenant 1st Buckinghamshire Volunteer Rifle Corps, of "The Mount," Frinsbury-by-Rochester, was appointed to command. Captain Parsons, The West Riding Regiment, was the first Adjutant. Honorary Lieutenant Hayman, late 1st London Volunteer Artillery, was the Quartermaster. As both Regular battalions were overseas, no N.C.O.s of the Regiment were available to act as Sergeant-Instructors. Consequently, several N.C.O.s of the Royal Marine Light Infantry were posted in. There was no difficulty in getting together the nucleus of a battalion, and during May and June 12 officers were appointed.

The first Annual Inspection was made on Chatham Lines in October 1900 by Colonel Brock, Officer Commanding 50th Regimental District. There were some 650 all ranks on parade, including both band and drums and a strong Cyclist Company. The Mayors of Chatham and Rochester and many spectators were present. In the evening the officers attended their first Mess dinner at the Bull Hotel, Rochester; the N.C.O.s held their first annual dinner in the Queen's Hall, Military Road.

―――――― CHAPTER 8 ――――――

MODERNISATION

November, 1902—December, 1908

1. *Regimental*

B Y the end of 1902 the Regiment was back to normal. One Line battalion (the 1st) was at Home and the other overseas. The 3rd Battalion had resumed its routine of assembling once a year for annual training. The men of the 3rd Volunteer Active Service Company had returned from South Africa to their units.

As soon as the War in South Africa was over, a fund was opened for a Memorial to the two officers and 114 other ranks of the Regiment, who had lost their lives during the campaign. Donations amounting to nearly £370 were received from all seven battalions, the Depot and men who had been discharged. The Memorial, a Window and Plaque, was unveiled in All Saints' Church on Saturday June 20, 1903. In the absence through illness of General Sir Fowler Burton, K.C.B., the Colonel of the Regiment, the unveiling ceremony was performed by Colonel Grove.[1] The Memorial was dedicated by the Right Reverend Bishop J. Taylor Smith, Chaplain-General to the Forces. Charge of it was accepted by the Vicar, Canon P. Joy. Earl Stanhope, Lord Lieutenant of Kent, was present. The Mayor and Corporation of Maidstone attended in state. The Guard of Honour was provided by the 1st Battalion. A number of former members of the Regiment were there, besides detachments from all battalions except the 2nd.

A Mural Tablet to the memory of the nine other ranks of the 2nd Volunteer Battalion, who died while on active service, was unveiled in St. Alfege's Church, Greenwich, on October 10, 1903, by Colonel Brock, Officer Commanding 50th Regimental District. Seven of the nine were members of the Volunteer Active Service Companies.[2]

―――――――――――――――
[1] General Burton was awarded his K.C.B. in June 1903. At this time Colonel Grove was Assistant-Adjutant-General, Scottish Command.

[2] The seven were :— Sgt. Eveleigh, Lance-Corporal White and Privates H. Barnes, Creasey, Helmer, Lucock and Turpin.

A Tablet of alabaster marble was unveiled in Rochester Cathedral by Dean Hole on January 16, 1904, " in memory of all the soldiers of the County of Kent who gave their lives in their country's cause during the War in South Africa." It is on the wall of the Lady Chapel in the south aisle of the nave.

The following Battle Honours were approved by His Majesty King Edward VII in December 1904: —

1st and 2nd Battalions.	" South Africa,	1900-02."
3rd Battalion (Militia).	" Mediterranean,	1900-01."
1st Volunteer Battalion.	" South Africa,	1900-02."
2nd Volunteer Battalion.	" South Africa,	1900-02."
3rd Volunteer Battalion.	" South Africa,	1901-02."
4th Volunteer Battalion.	" South Africa,	1902."

" South Africa, 1900-02 " was emblazoned on the Regimental Colour of each of the Line battalions; " Mediterranean 1900-01 " on that of the 3rd Battalion

The campaign in South Africa had shown the importance of accurate and rapid snap-shooting. During the war Lord Roberts had telegraphed Home pressing for a shorter rifle. What was required was a weapon about five inches shorter than the existing Lee-Enfield and Lee-Metford.[1] Trials proved that such a rifle could be produced, and during the years 1903-1908 the Short Magazine Lee-Enfield, Mark 1, gradually became the standard rifle of the British Army. It was clip-loading (five rounds in a clip); the magazine held 10 rounds. The 1st Battalion was issued with this weapon at Dover in January 1907, the 2nd at Singapore in May, and the Depot in October of the same year. The programme for the Militia and Volunteers was completed in 1908. Brown leather equipment was issued with the short rifle.

Another important decision was that the Regular troops should work and train in the dress which they would wear in war, " Red " being kept for ceremonial and walking-out. The uniform selected was of khaki serge, of a pattern similar to that worn in South Africa. The headdress provided some difficulty, for the pith helmet of South African days was unsuitable in the United Kingdom. The peakless Brodrick cap, which was first issued, was unpopular and ugly. A peaked cap was produced in 1904. The 1st Battalion was issued with this Service Dress at Shorncliffe in January 1903, khaki greatcoats a year later, and the peaked cap in December 1905. The 2nd Battalion was already in possession of khaki serge, having worn it in South Africa. Overseas, in warm climates or in hot weather, the troops worked and trained in khaki drill.

The years 1903 to 1908 saw great changes in infantry tactics. During training no unit was allowed to be in close order within 3,000 yards of the objective. Great attention was paid to the use of ground and cover. Volley firing was entirely abolished; slow and rapid fire — the latter up to 15 rounds a minute — were alone used. Field firing

---

[1] In the Regiment only the 1st Battalion had been issued with the Long Lee-Enfield. The other battalions retained the Lee-Metford until they received the Short Lee-Enfield

ranges were made wherever possible. Rifle firing was constantly practised; in the Line battalions of the Regiment several trophies were presented by officers to encourage shooting.

The *entente* with France, which was cemented in April 1904, led to an agreement that Britain would go to the aid of the French if Germany should move against them. For this purpose it was necessary to create an Expeditionary Force in the British Isles, and to re-organise the Auxiliary Forces into a second line for Home defence and expansion. Much of the re-casting was carried out in 1908 by Mr. R. B. Haldane, who was then Secretary of State for War. In that year the Militia was replaced by a Special Reserve for the Regular Army, and the Volunteers were re-formed into a Territorial Force. Details of these changes are set out in the appropriate sections of this chapter.

Regimentally there were two important events during this period. The first was that a Compassionate Fund was opened by Colonel Brock to assist ex-members of, and families connected with, the Regiment. It was inaugurated in May 1903 by a gift of £30 from the Lord Lieutenant's County Fund for Kentish Soldiers. The second donation was £50 from the Regimental Institutes of the 1st Battalion. To these was added the balance, about £46, which was left in the Memorial Fund. Before long nearly all the officers, both past and present, were subscribing annually.

The second Regimental innovation was the formation of The Association of Sergeants. Membership included all warrant officers and sergeants, past and present, of the Line, Militia and Volunteer battalions. The first annual dinner took place at the Corn Exchange, Maidstone, in March 1904. About 130 members attended out of the 257 who had enrolled. From 1905 till 1908 the dinner was held in the drill halls of the 3rd and 4th Volunteer Battalions or in the gymnasium at the Depot. Subsequently it was usually at a restaurant in London.

The Annual Regimental Dinner for the officers of the Line battalions, which had not taken place during the War in South Africa, was resumed. Normally, as before, it was held at the Grand Hotel, Trafalgar Square.

Sir Fowler Burton died of heart failure on April 3, 1904. He was buried at Pennycross, near Devonport, on April 9. Major-General E. Leach, C.B., replaced him as Colonel of the Regiment and became Patron of the Regimental Compassionate Fund and of The Association of Sergeants.

The Union Jack Club, near Waterloo Station, was opened on July 1, 1907, by King Edward VII. A sum of £202 was collected to provide two bedrooms, which were dedicated to The Queen's Own and to which men of the Regiment had prior claim.

Notable achievements at sport by members of the Regiment during this period were: —

    1908. Lance-Corporal A. Baker (1st Bn.) won the Army and Navy Light Weight Boxing Championship.

    1908. Lance-Corporal R. Darley (1st Bn.) won the Army and Navy Feather Weight Boxing Championship.

2. The Regimental Depot

When Colonel Brock vacated command of 50th Regimental District on his retirement on July 11, 1904, a successor was not appointed. The responsibility devolved temporarily on Major Style, the senior officer at the Depot. By an Army Order of January 1905 the appointment of "Officer Commanding Regimental District" was abolished, and Regimental Districts were grouped geographically, each group being commanded by a brigadier-general. This officer was to inspect all depots and Militia battalions in his Group once a year. 50th Regimental District was in the Home Counties Group, the headquarters of which were at Guildford.[1]

Depot Commanders were gazetted from January 1, 1905, on which date Major Style became the first Officer Commanding The Depot The Queen's Own (Royal West Kent Regiment). He left Maidstone to be Second-in-Command of the 1st Battalion on July 28, 1905. Major Lowe succeeded him. A roll of Depot Commanders is in Appendix B.

Great care was taken over the comfort and messing of the recruits at the Regimental Depot. Their cleanliness and smartness on parade were outstanding. Major Lowe began the custom of presenting a medal to the best man in each squad at gymnastics and miniature range shooting, two of the essential parts of recruit training. Early in 1908 the height standard for the Regiment was raised to five feet seven, one inch above that laid down by recruiting regulations.

Boxing tournaments were frequently held in the drill-shed. The spectators included many of the prominent people and tradesmen of Maidstone. Some of the best known boxers in the district as well as Depot personnel competed. The band of the 3rd Battalion or that of the Maidstone Volunteer Companies played during the interval. Displays of ju-jutsu and fencing were often included in the programme.

Each year a Depot Shooting Team went in a brake to Benenden, near Cranbrook, to try conclusions with the Benenden Rifle Club. After the contest, the team adjourned for refreshments to the residence of Major Neve (now retired from the 3rd Battalion). An annual shooting match was also held against the School of Musketry, Hythe.

The 1907-08 football season was a successful one for the Depot. The team reached the third round of the Army Cup, and was beaten only in extra time by the eventual winners, the Depot Battalion Royal Engineers. In the following season it won the Maidstone and District Football League.

For a number of years the annual drill inspection of St. Paul's Boys' School (the school attended by the children of the Depot personnel) had been held on the Back Field or on the Square. In July 1907 the display was particularly impressive. After the inspection had been carried out by Major Lowe, the 300 boys marched past and then performed physical training exercises. The presentation of prizes

---

[1] The Home Counties Grouped Regimental District consisted of the 2nd (The Queen's), the 3rd (The Buffs), the 7th (Royal Fusiliers), the 31st (East Surrey), the 35th (Royal Sussex) and the 50th (The Queen's Own) Regimental Districts. It was re-named "No 10 (Home Counties) District" in the autumn of 1907.

by the Mayoress of Maidstone ended the ceremony. Some 2,000 spectators were present.

3. The Details at Dover

The 1st Battalion went to Malta in April 1904. This meant that both Line battalions of the Regiment were once more overseas, and that The Details again had to be "held" by a Provisional unit. At that time there was only one Provisional Battalion. It was in Grand Shaft Barracks, Dover, and was commanded by Lieutenant-Colonel W. C. Ross, formerly The Durham Light Infantry. Other Details held by this unit were those of The Royal Sussex Regiment, The Essex Regiment and The Royal Munster Fusiliers.

In the early autumn of 1904 a draft of 102 other ranks was sent from Dover to Malta to join the 1st Battalion, and another of 83 other ranks embarked for Ceylon to join the 2nd. In November The Details were formed into two companies, a recent draft from the Depot forming No. 2 Company.

At the end of November both companies moved to Lydd for work on the ranges. While they were there they fired their annual course. They returned to Dover in the spring of 1905. Further drafts were sent overseas during the next trooping season.

Leaving the Queen's Own Details in Grand Shaft Barracks, the Provisional Battalion moved to Tidworth in December 1906. A few days later the 1st Battalion arrived at Dover and marched into the barracks. The Details were posted to it.

4. The 1st Battalion at Shorncliffe, Malta and Dover

The 1st Battalion arrived at Southampton from its overseas tour on December 13, 1902. Two troop-trains took it to Shorncliffe. Night had fallen before the main body marched into Napier Barracks. An advanced-party had organised things so well that next day half the battalion was able to go on leave.

Colonel Harrison arrived from hospital in Malta in March 1903, but was granted nine months' sick leave. On March 24, Major Brock-Hollinshead took over temporary command from Major Rowe, who was posted to the 2nd Battalion.

Company training, with the troops wearing the new khaki serge Service Dress, began on February 1. This was followed by the firing of the annual range course at Hythe. Brigade training took place in July. In mid-August the battalion marched to West Down Camp on Salisbury Plain for divisional exercises, after which Army Manoeuvres were held between Corsham and Hungerford.

The 3rd Battalion (Militia) was at Shorncliffe for annual training in June, and the four Volunteer battalions were there in camp during the first week in August. There was much liaison between the Regulars and the Auxiliaries in the various messes. Several inter-unit cricket games and shooting matches were held. For the latter the teams drove to and from the range at Hythe in brakes.

In October some officers and a party of recruits went to Eastbourne for three weeks to fire a rifle course. The officers lived in lodgings, and the other ranks were accommodated in an old redoubt on the sea front. The reason why this detachment did not fire on a range closer to Shorncliffe is not recorded.

Colonel Harrison was placed on half-pay on March 21, 1904. Major G. W. Maunsell came from the 2nd Battalion to succeed him.

Early in January 1904 a telegram was received from the War Office ordering the battalion to be prepared to embark on or about March 18 for Malta — the station it had left only 14 months before. This was a great disappointment to all ranks, who had looked forward to a full tour in Kent. It was small comfort to them that the departure was postponed for three weeks.

The voyage to Malta was made in the troopship "Soudan." Disembarkation took place in the Grand Harbour on April 16. At first the battalion was accommodated in tents at Pembroke in order to fire the annual range course. Early in May it marched to Mellieha, in the north of the island, for field firing. Quarters were then taken up in Casemates and Notre Dame Barracks at Floriana, just outside Valetta. The officers were accommodated in Montgomery House.

Various inspections, the Malta Command Rifle Meeting, battalion cricket games at the Marsa, shooting matches, an inter-company water polo competition, and a Battalion Aquatics Meeting occupied the summer months.

On October 6 nearly the whole battalion went to Pembroke Ranges to compete for the Regimental Bowl, the Rowe Cup and the Harrison Cup. The last was a new trophy which had been presented by Colonel Harrison when he left the battalion.[1] The Maxim gun teams fired their course on the same day. During the autumn, four companies at a time went to camp at Mellieha for training. The whole battalion was back in barracks for Christmas.

The King's Birthday Parade was held at the Marsa on November 9. Every unit in the garrison took part. After the Royal Salute, the troops marched past His Excellency The Governor, General Sir Charles Mansfield Clarke. A *feu-de-joie* was then fired.

With only slight variations the same round of shooting and training was carried out during the years 1905 and 1906. Two events only need be recorded. While the battalion was in camp in the north of the island in March 1905, it was inspected on parade and at training by H.R.H. The Duke of Connaught, who was then Inspector-General of the Forces. When Her Majesty Queen Alexandra visited Malta from May 11 to 15, 1905, the battalion furnished a Guard of Honour on the Palace Square, Valetta, on her arrival.

[1] The Rowe Cup had been presented by Major Rowe in 1892 when he was a Captain.

A Boxing Club was started in the battalion by Captain Grant in the spring of 1905. It brought immediate results. In a contest between the Malta Garrison and the Navy, held in the Valetta Gymnasium, Privates Baker, Darley and Smith fought for the Garrison. The fight of the evening was that in which Baker lost on points after an extra round to a champion of the Mediterranean Fleet. Lance-Corporal Andrews won several bouts at other meetings. Baker and Darley were to become outstanding boxers.

Four silver statuettes were presented to the Officers' Mess by General Leach in the summer of 1906. They represented a private, a drummer and two officers of The 50th Foot at different periods.

Two companies were moved to huts on Manoel Island in July 1906 so as to give them some relief from the heat and sandflies of Floriana.

Before the battalion left Malta, a painting of St. Luke and a plaque were unveiled by Colonel Maunsell in the Barracca Garrison Church, Castille Square, in memory of the 12 other ranks who died while the unit was quartered on the island in 1902 and 1904-06.[1] The picture of St. Luke was painted by Professor Cali, the Maltese artist.

After he had inspected the battalion on the Floriana Parade Ground on December 14, 1906, Sir Charles Mansfield Clarke bade it farewell. Brigadier-General F. S. F. Stokes, who was commanding the infantry brigade, spoke to the men when they paraded for embarkation. In the course of his address, he said:—

"Most of the duties of the garrison have fallen on you, but they have been done in a most cheerful and satisfactory manner and without any fuss. In addition to this, your barracks being so close to Valetta, you have always been under the eyes of those in authority, so that any little thing going wrong would have been noticed ... "

The battalion embarked in the "Braemar Castle" on December 18. Christmas Day was spent on board and, except for heavy seas off Ushant, the voyage was pleasant. At Southampton there was snow on the ground when the troops went ashore on December 27. General Leach met them on the platform at Dover.

The satisfaction of being back in Kent was somewhat offset by the discomfort of Grand Shaft Barracks. Situated in the dingy western part of the town, they were old-fashioned, inconvenient and lacked many amenities. Nor was Dover to be commended as a military station. There was no range close at hand of over 200 yards in length, no drill ground on which garrison parades could be held, and no adequate playing field. Consequently the annual courses were fired at Lydd, the King's Birthday Parades were held on the sea front, and all Home battalion football matches had to be played on the ground of Dover Town Football Club at Crabble.

The first party to use the new Short Lee-Enfield Rifle on the range was a squad of recruits, who went to Lydd for two weeks in February 1907 to fire their course. They were followed by the remainder of the battalion, two companies at a time. Concurrently, company training

[1] The Barracca Church was de-dedicated in 1953, and this memorial is now in St. Luke's Garrison Church, Tigne Barracks.

was carried out on areas near West Hougham and Fort Burgoyne. The competitions for the shooting trophies were held at Hythe on July 18. In August the battalion was in camp at Ringwood in the New Forest for brigade training. Divisional manoeuvres were held near South Damerham.

Twice in 1907 — on February 2 and on March 4 — King Edward VII passed through Dover on his way to France. On each occasion a detachment of the battalion, some 50 strong, was on duty on the pier as His Majesty passed from the train to the ship. When the French President paid a return visit on May 25, 1908, The Queen's Own furnished a Guard of Honour at the Priory Station. Another ceremonial event was the arrival of His Imperial Highness Prince Fushimi of Japan on May 6, 1907. The Guard of Honour was found by the battalion, and the band played the Japanese Anthem as the Prince came ashore.

Colonel Maunsell was placed on retired pay in March 1908, on completion of his four years in command. Major R. C. Style was promoted to succeed him.

By the summer of 1908 Haldane's Expeditionary Force was taking shape. That year the battalion trained as part of the 12th Brigade of 4th Division. In July it went to Barossa Camp, Camberley, for two weeks' brigade training. It then marched on through Alton and Winchester to Rockford Common Camp, Ringwood, for divisional exercises. Manoeuvres on Salisbury Plain were cancelled owing to stormy weather.

Handicapped by the lack of a Home ground, the football team performed only moderately. Its one success was to win the Dover Charity Cup in 1908. Boxing had now caught the interest of the battalion, and several mammoth tournaments were held in Dover Town Hall. Baker and Darley, now Lance-Corporals, were still the stars. In October 1908 they both won their weights in the Army and Navy Championships at Aldershot.

5. *The 2nd Battalion in Ceylon, China and Singapore*

The " Golconda," with the 2nd Battalion aboard, reached Colombo at dawn on November 22, 1902. All that day was spent in conveying the heavy baggage ashore in lighters and loading it into trains. Next morning headquarters and six companies disembarked, G Company going to Kandy and the remainder to Diyatalawa. A and F Companies went round in the " Golconda " to the naval base at Trincomalee.

At Diyatalawa the battalion (less three companies) relieved the 1st Battalion The Duke of Cornwall's Light Infantry as the guard over Boer prisoners of war. The accommodation consisted of wooden hutments. The country round the camp was mainly grassy hills and deep valleys, which provided suitable areas for training. There was a rifle range nearby. The Boers gave remarkably little trouble, probably because they knew that they were soon to be repatriated. By Christmas most of them had returned to South Africa. In the middle of January only 20 remained, and they were sent to a jail in Colombo. The detachment at Trincomalee was accommodated in comfortable bungalows close to the harbour. The training area was restricted by dense jungle, and the main occupation of the troops was to find guards over the military prison. The Kandy detachment lived on the fringe of the ancient town in a two-storey building, which overlooked a grass parade and football ground.

The married families re-joined the battalion on December 14, after nearly three years' separation. They had come from the Depot with Bandmaster McKelvey and the band boys in the "Dunera." The ship also brought 250 other ranks from the 1st Battalion. This draft had been picked up at Malta on November 26.

During January and February 1903, Battalion Headquarters, the band and drums and three companies moved from Diyatalawa to Echelon Barracks, Colombo. Thereafter Diyatalawa was used as a training and musketry camp, to which all companies went in turn. The whole battalion wore khaki drill uniform for normal duties throughout the year.

Echelon Barracks were close to the sea and were spacious and cool. There was an excellent hall for concerts and theatrical entertainments. Cricket and hockey were played on the Square, which was grass. The football ground was on the Galle Face, with only a road between it and the beach. The band was kept busy, as it played at most of the social functions in Colombo. On these occasions it wore white drill uniform with white helmets.

The South African Medals were presented on September 28, 1903, to the companies then in Echelon Barracks by Brigadier-General G. L. C. Money, who was commanding the troops in Ceylon. The remainder of the battalion received their medals from him in November.

Owing to the wide dispersal of the companies, the Battalion Rifle Meetings were held under difficulties. Firing took place on three ranges — at Hunupitiya (near Colombo), Diyatalawa and Trincomalee. Besides the Officers' Cup, the Company Shield and the Eccle's Cup, there were two new trophies to be competed for in 1904. These were the Western Cup and the Long Cup — one presented by the Commanding Officer; the other by Lieutenant Long on his transfer to The Irish Guards.

Each July the Ceylon Volunteers assembled for their annual training at Diyatalawa. The companies which were there at the time joined in their field days.

During the last few weeks in Ceylon there was a spate of farewell concerts and farewell football and hockey matches. On November 5, 1904, leaving some time-expired men in Colombo to await a passage to England, the bulk of the battalion embarked in the transport "Avoca." Next day the ship steamed round to pick up the detachment at Trincomalee. Thence it turned eastwards for China.

When the "Avoca" arrived at Hong Kong on November 18, Battalion Headquarters, the band and A, D, E and G Companies disembarked. The remainder, under Major Rowe, continued the voyage on the 20th to North China. Major Rowe's headquarters, two companies and the drums were stationed at Tientsin; two companies went inland to Peking. The distance between these two detachments was 80 miles. They interchanged every six months by march route.

Peking, the capital of China, was enclosed by a high wall some 40 feet wide. About a square mile of the city had been appropriated by the Foreign Legations. Each nation (there were 10 of them) had its own small walled-in concession and its own troops. Generally speaking the soldiers of all these countries got on well together. The principal duty of the British contingent — two companies of infantry and 50 men of the Royal Garrison Artillery — was to find the British Legation Guard. Except for the annual rifle course, which was fired on a range just outside Peking, training was limited to route-marching on the city wall. The chief recreation was football.

Tientsin was very different from Peking. It was an open straggling city, intersected by canals. In the European quarter were the enclaves of the various nations which had business interests in the area. The quarters occupied by the British troops were in a very old two-storey building. The main duty was to provide a guard over the military prison. Recreations included skating on a frozen pond in winter.

In Hong Kong, Battalion Headquarters and three companies were accommodated in Murray Barracks. These were in Victoria, the capital, and consisted of two main blocks connected by a covered way. On the ground floors were the offices and institutes. The troops occupied the two upper storeys. The Officers' Mess overlooked Queen's Road, the principal thoroughfare. The fourth company lived at the top of Mount Austin, known as the Peak. It was quartered in a building which had once been a hotel, and some of the rooms had tiled fireplaces and large mirrors. There was no rifle range on the island; two companies at a time went into camp at Kowloon, on the mainland, to fire the annual course and to carry out field training. In Victoria the troops had a Soldiers' Club and a Sailors' and Soldiers' Home. They could bathe at Stonecutter's Island. There were facilities for boating in the harbour. At the Happy Valley, a reclaimed swamp two miles east of Victoria, several football, cricket and hockey grounds were available.

At first the battalion found the change from the equable warmth of Ceylon to the variable temperature of China very trying. In Peking and Tientsin some nights were so cold that the sentries wore special fur-lined coats; and in these places khaki serge uniform was worn for routine duty all the year round. In Hong Kong the dress was khaki serge in winter and khaki drill in summer.

The Russo-Japanese War was being waged at this time. For some days a Russian Fleet was cruising in the vicinity of Hong Kong, and a naval battle seemed to be imminent. One of the duties of the troops in Hong Kong was to guard three officers and 90 sailors from the Russian cruiser " Burnei," which had been run aground and scuttled near Chefoo.

There was a lighter side. In August 1905 Prince Arisugawa of Japan visited Hong Kong, and The Queen's Own provided a Guard of Honour. While the Prince was inspecting the guard, the band played "The Men of Kent." The following morning a local paper described this tune as "a weird Japanese naval air."

Brevet-Colonel W. G. B. Western, C.B., relinquished command of the battalion on August 18, 1905. He was succeeded by Brevet-Lieutenant-Colonel H. G. Fitton, D.S.O., who had been transferred from The Royal Warwickshire Regiment in February 1904.[1]

A typhoon struck Hong Kong on September 18, 1906. It came suddenly at about 9 a.m. and lasted for two hours. During that time large steamers as well as native junks were torn from their moorings and flung up on the Kowloon shore. When the typhoon was signalled, half of G Company was on the quay waiting to embark in a launch. This party immediately marched back to Murray Barracks, which were soon surrounded by branches blown from trees, and by verandahs, sheds and telephone poles, which had been uprooted. In the town trams were overturned and the roads were blocked by debris. Five thousand Chinese lost their lives. On the 19th, and for several days afterwards, large numbers of The Queen's Own were employed in clearing wreckage and recovering bodies. A letter of thanks for this assistance was received from Sir Matthew Nathan, the Governor of Hong Kong.

The 3rd Battalion The Middlesex Regiment arrived at Hong Kong on October 30, 1906, and encamped on the parade ground at Murray Barracks. A few days later four of its companies embarked for North China to relieve the detachments at Tientsin and Peking. These detachments reached Hong Kong on November 19, and on the 28th the 2nd Battalion The Queen's Own sailed in the troopship "Soudan" for Singapore.

Having disembarked on December 5, the battalion marched through the town of Singapore to Tanglin Barracks. Each company had its own bungalow surrounded by a garden. In the centre were the Orderly Room, Guard Room and Quartermaster's Stores. Nearby were the Canteen, two swimming baths, a gymnasium, and a large hall which was used as a theatre and library. To the north of the bungalows was the Sergeants' Mess. The Officers' Mess was half a mile away to the east. Between it and the bungalows was the Garrison Church. Cricket and hockey were played on the parade ground, and football on a level field near the Church. The town of Singapore could be reached by rickshaw in half an hour.

The annual courses were fired on Normanton Range, which was three miles from Tanglin. Each company in turn encamped near the range for the duration of the courses. Training was mainly carried out from barracks; but for one week each year one company at a time crossed to Blakang-Mati island, where it went under canvas and was shown how the Royal Garrison Artillery handled the guns in the forts.

[1] Fitton had been Second-in-command of the 1st Battalion since February 20, 1904.

The annual mobilization of the garrison took place in August. During it the defences of Singapore Island were tested.

On account of the climate — the temperature rarely fell below 90 degrees during the day and 80 at night — all outside routine work was finished if possible by 8 a.m. Khaki drill was worn throughout the year, and the order that topees must be worn when out of doors between 8 a.m. and 4 p.m. was strictly enforced.

In February 1907 H.R.H. The Duke of Connaught, as Inspector-General of the Forces, passed through Singapore on his way to Hong Kong. He was received at Johnstone's Pier by a Guard of Honour provided by The Queen's Own. When he returned to Singapore 12 days later, he inspected the battalion at Tanglin and lunched in the Officers' Mess. Before he left the island, a review of the Straits Settlements' Garrison was held on the Racecourse. On the left of the line was a contingent of Malays under the Sultan of Johore.

The competitions for the shooting trophies, which had not been held during the tour in China, were resumed. There was now yet another trophy to be competed for. This was the Maunsell Cup, presented by Major Maunsell when he left to take command of the 1st Battalion.

A Boxing Club was started in March 1907. The first meeting was a Novices' Competition. After that a series of bouts was fought to produce the champion at each weight. This laid the foundation for a battalion team.

In the spring of 1908 the officers challenged the sergeants to contest nine events. These were: — shooting, cricket, hockey, football (Association and Rugby), bayonet fighting, attack practice, tug-of-war and a relay race. The officers won. The sergeants then threw down the gauntlet, and the tournament became an annual affair. A challenge cup for it was presented by Colonel Fitton.

At the end of the battalion's stay on the island a brass plaque was placed in the Garrison Church in memory of Lieutenant Leir and six other ranks who died in Singapore.

The battalion marched out of Tanglin Barracks for the last time on November 29, 1908, and embarked in the transport "Dufferin." Next day many friends assembled on the quay to wave farewell as the ship sailed for India.

6. *The Last Years of the Militia*

The annual training of the 3rd Battalion (Militia) in 1903, 1905, 1906 and 1907 was held as usual at Shorncliffe. In 1904 the recruits assembled at the Depot on June 27 and went to Gravesend. They were accommodated in Milton Barracks, where preliminary drills were carried out. Firing took place on Milton Ranges. The remainder of the battalion assembled at Maidstone on July 11. The right half (six companies) went to Gravesend to fire the annual course; the left half went to the Isle of Grain for company training. On July 23 the half-battalions changed over. From July 30 until August 6 the whole unit was together on the Isle of Grain for field days and the annual inspection.

Since the South African War it had been difficult to keep the Militia up to strength because so many of the young men transferred into the Line.[1] This, and the rudimentary nature of its training, made the force of little value as a fighting organisation for Home defence. So, at the end of 1907, it was decided that the historic Militia, with its ancient traditions, should cease to exist. Simultaneously an entirely new organisation, known as the Special Reserve, would come into being. Henceforth the Regular Army Reserve would be divided into two classes of men: those of the old style who went to the Reserve after a period of colour service, and those of the new style — the Special Reservists — who would enlist direct into the Reserve and undergo a period of training each year. The Special Reservists would not draw Reserve Pay but would receive an Annual Bounty. They would be carried on the strength of Reserve Battalions, of which there would normally be one to each infantry regiment. These battalions would be based upon the Regimental Depots. For Annual Training they would assemble as units under their own officers. On mobilization they would provide first reinforcements for the Line battalions.

At Maidstone recruits were enlisted for the Special Reserve from January 16, 1908. They were drilled at the Depot for six months, their rifle course being fired at Gravesend. Their syllabus was similar to that of the Line recruits, but they were placed in separate squads. By May, 190 Special Reservists had enlisted, the barrack rooms were full, and the more advanced squads were living in tents on the Back Field.

The 3rd Battalion (Militia) attended its last annual camp from July 13 to August 7, 1908, at Shorncliffe. It returned to the Depot on August 8. Next day all the officers and 466 other ranks accepted the invitation to transfer to the Special Reserve. One hundred other ranks elected to take a free discharge. Thirty-five decided to serve out the term of their Militia engagements.

The 3rd Battalion (Reserve) The Queen's Own (Royal West Kent Regiment) was formed on August 9, 1908. Recruits continued to come in steadily until September 30, by which date the establishment had been exceeded. Recruiting was closed temporarily.

7. *The Volunteers are Re-formed*

On January 1, 1903, new conditions were laid down for the enrolment and training of the Volunteers. The enlistment of men, who were unable to give adequate time for training beyond elementary drill, was not permitted. Recruits had to do 40 drills, and trained men 10.

---

[1] In the Regiment about 400 Militia recruits joined the Line each year.

Camp for six days was obligatory every other year. The rifle course was to be fired at week-ends.

The four Volunteer battalions of the Regiment had now been formed into The West Kent Volunteer Brigade. In 1903 this brigade, over 2,500 strong, was in camp at Shorncliffe under the command of Colonel Brock. In 1904 and 1905 the camps were at Dover and in Arundel Park, respectively. Lieutenant-Colonel Satterthwaite (2nd Vol. Bn.) acted as brigade commander. On June 1, 1906, having relinquished command of his battalion, he was promoted to Colonel and was appointed to command the brigade. In 1906 the brigade camp was at Sheerness; in 1907 at Worthing.

During 1903 a drill hall for the headquarters and the eight companies of the 4th Volunteer Battalion was erected on War Department land on the Chatham Recreation Ground. The building was taken into use early in 1904.

By 1907 Mr. Haldane had perfected his plans for a second line Volunteer formation. It was to be known as the Territorial Force and was to be an Army complete in itself, with a Staff, Artillery and Services. It would be enlisted for Home defence. If the Regular Expeditionary Force were sent overseas to fight, the Territorials would be embodied and would train for six months. At the end of that time it was expected that the Force would be efficient and that units would volunteer to go to the theatre of war. To administer the Force, but not to train it, County Territorial Associations were formed.[1]

The Territorial Force included 14 infantry divisions. There were 10 cyclist and 204 infantry battalions in all; some of the old Volunteer units disappeared. Two London divisions were created, and in order to form them 27 battalions changed their titles. Whereas in the past they had been Volunteer units of The Queen's Royal Regiment, The Royal Fusiliers, The Middlesex Regiment, The East Surrey Regiment, The Queen's Own (Royal West Kent Regiment), The King's Royal Rifle Corps or The Rifle Brigade, they now became battalions of a new corps — The London Regiment.

The creation of the Territorial Force affected The Queen's Own as follows:—

1st Volunteer Battalion	Became the 4th Battalion The Queen's Own (T.F.)
2nd Volunteer Battalion	The Bromley, Beckenham, and Dartford detachments formed the nucleus of the 5th Battalion The Queen's Own (T.F.)
	The other companies became the right half of The 20th Battalion The London Regiment.
3rd Volunteer Battalion	Became the headquarters and left half of The 20th Battalion The London Regiment.

[1] Major A. Wood Martyn (reserve of officers) was Secretary of the Kent Territorial Association. Colonel Satterthwaite was a member.

4th Volunteer Battalion	Disbanded on March 31, 1908.
The 6th (Cyclist) Battalion The Queen's Own (T.F.)	This was a new unit which replaced the numerous cyclist detachments of the Volunteer battalions in Kent. Major C. E. Warner (1st Vol. Bn.) was promoted to command it.

From this it will be seen that the whole of the 3rd Volunteer Battalion and the Lee, Blackheath, Deptford, St. John's, Greenwich, Charlton and Goldsmith's College Companies of the 2nd were replaced by a new unit, the full title of which was the 20th (County of London) Battalion The London Regiment (Blackheath and Woolwich). The headquarters were at Holly Hedge House, Blackheath. The outlying drill halls were at Woolwich (Beresford Street) and the Armoury of Goldsmith's College at New Cross.[1] The battalion was authorised to wear the West Kent cap badge and buttons, to play " A Hundred Pipers " as its Quick March, and to retain the black facings of the 2nd Volunteer Battalion. The majority of the Permanent Staff was supplied by the Line battalions of The Queen's Own.

The 4th and 5th Battalions The Queen's Own (T.F.) and the 20th Battalion the London Regiment all inherited the Battle Honour " South Africa, 1900-02 " from the 1st and 2nd Volunteer Battalions. The property of the 1st Volunteer Battalion was divided between the 4th and 5th Battalions The Queen's Own; that of the 2nd and 3rd was taken over by the 20th London.

As there was no official affiliation between the 20th London and The Queen's Own until 1920, a record of the activities of the former has not been included in this volume. A roll of its commanding officers can however be found in Appendix B. See also Appendix E.

The 2nd Volunteer Battalion held its last parade on March 29, 1908. It assembled at Holly Hedge House, 800 strong, and marched to St. Alfege's Church, Greenwich, for divine service. Before the battalion was dismissed, Lieutenant-Colonel E. J. Heward bade farewell and expressed the hope that all would join the " New Army." His wish was not fulfilled, for many of the personnel declined to do so.

The day appointed for the start of the Territorial Force was April 1, 1908. All Volunteers then serving were invited to re-enlist into the new force for one, two, three or four years. They were given up to June 30 to decide whether they would accept the terms of service. The response was barely satisfactory. That August the Kent Territorial Infantry Brigade, consisting of the 4th and 5th Buffs and the 4th and 5th Queen's Own and commanded by Colonel Satterthwaite, went to camp at Walmer very much under strength. Nevertheless, a beginning had been made.

[1] Woolwich, New Cross and the Blackheath area were within the County of London.

CHAPTER 9

ON THE VERGE
January, 1909—August, 1914

1. Regimental

BY 1909 the Expeditionary Force in the British Isles had been created, and the second line for Home defence was in being. During the next five years the Army at Home steadily prepared for the major conflict which loomed on the Continent. Behind the war clouds the affairs of The Queen's Own took their normal course.

The first Regimental event of importance was the laying-up of the Old Colours of the Line battalions in All Saints' Church. This took place on November 3, 1909. The Colours concerned were those which had been carried by the 1st Battalion until three months back, and the pair which had been borne by the 2nd until June 1891. They were carried to the church by Lieutenants Stevenson and Brock (1st) and 2nd Lieutenants Hardy and B. H. Bonham-Carter (2nd). The escort and the band were provided by the 1st Battalion. On parade were the Permanent Staff of the Depot; detachments from all battalions of the Regiment except the 2nd; and contingents from several local Territorial units. The Mayor and Corporation of Maidstone were present. Major-General Sir Edmund Leach, K.C.B., the Colonel of the Regiment, handed the Old Colours to the Vicar, the Rev. E. H. Hardcastle, at the altar rails. Having accepted them for safe-keeping, the Vicar addressed the congregation. The buglers then sounded "The Last Post." As the troops filed out, the band played "Auld Lang Syne."

On the death of King Edward VII, which occurred on May 6, 1910, the Colonel of the Regiment sent a letter of sympathy to Queen Alexandra through her Private Secretary, the Honourable Sidney Greville. In her reply the Queen requested that her thanks should be conveyed to all ranks. For the King's funeral on May 20 the 1st Battalion lined both sides of Piccadilly from Bolton Street to

Clarges Street. During the period of mourning, no official functions were held. Among those cancelled were the Annual Dinner of the officers of the Line battalions and that of The Association of Sergeants, which had been arranged for June 14 and 25 respectively.

On the occasion of the Coronation of King George V and Queen Mary, which took place on June 22, 1911, a detachment of three officers and 50 other ranks of the 1st Battalion under Captain Twisleton-Wykeham-Fiennes was in position in Parliament Square. 2nd-Lieutenant Kent-Lemon and 25 N.C.O.s and men of the 3rd Battalion (Reserve) lined a portion of the route in Whitehall. One officer and 25 other ranks from each of the Territorial units were in Trafalgar Square with the 23rd Provisional Infantry Brigade. At Maidstone the troops from the Depot and part of the 4th Battalion (T.F.) attended a service in All Saints' Church.

On July 22, 1911, a committee, consisting of past and present senior officers and other ranks, met at the Golden Cross Hotel, London, to draw up rules for an Old Comrades' Association. The committee decided that membership should be open to all past members of the Line battalions; to all serving Regulars with seven or more years' service;[1] and to all ranks of the Auxiliary units who had been on active service with the Regiment. The annual subscription would be 1s. (5s. for officers). A dinner would be held each year in London on Cup Final Day. The committee would be empowered to make grants to the Regimental Compassionate Fund, which, till then, had been supported solely by the officers. The Colonel of the Regiment would be asked to be President, and the Adjutant of the Depot would be Secretary and Treasurer.

By the end of the year 250 members had been enrolled for the Old Comrades' Association, and a badge and membership card had been decided on. The first Annual Dinner was held at Victoria Mansions Restaurant in Victoria Street on April 20, 1912; over 120 were there. The second dinner, on April 19, 1913, was at Cannon Street Hotel. One hundred and sixty members attended out of the 517 who had now joined. In April 1914 the dinner was at the Horseshoe Hotel in Tottenham Court Road.

At the dinner of The Association of Sergeants at Alderton's Hotel, Fleet Street, in December 1912, the Colonel of the Regiment announced that the Governor of New Zealand had asked whether the 1st (Canterbury) Regiment could be allied to The Queen's Own. General Leach added that this would be an excellent thing, as The 50th Foot had served in New Zealand. The Alliance began on January 30, 1913, on which date the following letter was sent from the War Office to the Colonel of the Regiment:—

" Sir,
I am commanded by the Army Council to inform you that His Majesty The King has been graciously pleased to approve of the 1st (Canterbury) Regiment, New Zealand, being shewn

[1] In January 1913 membership was extended to include all Regular serving soldiers.

in the War Office Army List as allied to The Queen's Own (Royal West Kent Regiment).

A copy of this letter has been sent to the Officers Commanding the 1st, 2nd and 3rd Battalions, and to the Officer in Charge of Infantry Records, Hounslow.

I am,
Sir,
Your obedient servant,
(sgd.) E. W. D. Ward."

During this period flying machines, in small numbers, were used on manoeuvres to follow the movements of bodies of troops. In the infantry, equipment of webbing material replaced the heavy leather equipment. It was issued to the 1st Battalion at Bordon on October 1, 1909; to recruits at the Depot from December 1910; and to the 2nd Battalion in India on February 17, 1913. The Territorial units received this new equipment before August 1914.

In the summer of 1914 it became clear that Germany was about to risk all on an adventure for world domination. Her army was stronger than it had ever been, and the Kiel Canal had recently been enlarged to allow the passage of her "Dreadnoughts." The cause of war between her and Great Britain was the German violation of the neutrality of Belgium, which had been guaranteed by Britain and France. When war was declared at midnight on August 4, the Expeditionary Force was ready. Behind it the Special Reserve was prepared to provide the necessary reinforcements. Behind that again stood the 14 divisions of the Territorial Force.

Between January 1909 and August 1914 the following members of the Regiment distinguished themselves at sport:—

1909. Corporal A. Baker (1st Bn.) won the Army and Navy Light Weight Boxing Championship.

1909. Corporal R. Darley (1st Bn.) won the Army and Navy Feather Weight Boxing Championship.

1910. Private W. Smith (1st Bn.) won the Army and Navy Light-heavy Weight Boxing Championship.

1910. Private A. Holding (1st Bn.) played Association Football for the Army against the Royal Navy.

1911. Lance-Sergeant A. Baker (1st Bn.) won the Army and Navy Welter Weight Boxing Championship.

1911. Corporal J. Sheppard (2nd Bn.) won the Army (in India) Light Weight Boxing Championship.

1911. Corporal J. Powell (1st Bn.) played Association Football for the Army against the Royal Navy.

1911. Sergeant W. Keeble (1st Bn.) played Association Football for Kent.

1913- Sergeant W. Keeble (Depot) played Association Football for
1914. Kent on six occasions and was awarded his County Cap.

2. *The Regimental Depot*

After the 3rd Battalion (Reserve) was formed, the Permanent Staff of the Regimental Depot as well as that of the Militia were posted to it. These Staffs became "The Regular Establishment of the Special Reserve." When the 3rd Battalion was called out for annual training, nearly all of the Regular Establishment went with it, only a skeleton staff being left behind to administer the Depot and drill the Line recruits. Should the 3rd Battalion be mobilized for war, none of the Regular Establishment would remain at Maidstone. A retired Regular officer, already earmarked, would take over the command of the Depot; his first duty would be to improvise a new staff from the personnel who returned to the Colours from the ordinary Reserve.

In actual fact, life at the Depot went on as before, except that there were usually more recruits to be trained. For, when the Special Reservists had completed six months' service, they were allowed to transfer to the Line. Many of them did so. Consequently recruiting for the 3rd Battalion, which had closed in the autumn of 1908, was re-opened. The vacancies were immediately filled. And so it went on. Normal wastage was also quickly replaced. In May 1914 the barracks were more crowded than they had been for five years. Some 230 Special Reserve and over 30 Line recruits were under training. The dining hall was being used as accommodation; meals were served in the drill-shed.

The Married Quarters at the Depot were re-built and modernised in 1911.

The first cross-country race for recruits ever held at the Depot was run in February 1913. Although it was only 4½ miles in length, it was called a "Marathon."

3. *The 1st Battalion at Dover, Bordon and Dublin*

For the 1st Battalion the most memorable event of its last year at Dover was the presentation of New Colours by the Marchioness of Camden, wife of the Lord Lieutenant of Kent. This took place in the grounds of Dover College on the afternoon of August 6, 1909. Owing to the number of her engagements, Her Majesty Queen Alexandra was unable to perform the ceremony. The Colours were consecrated by the Right Reverend Bishop J. Taylor Smith, Chaplain-General to the Forces. Lieutenant Stevenson received the King's Colour, and Lieutenant Phillips the Regimental. The R.S.M. was Sergeant-Major Rogers. When the Colours had been presented, the Marquess of Camden addressed the battalion. Colonel Style replied. Afterwards, a reception was held in the Officers' Mess, and the sergeants were At Home to the many old soldiers who had watched the parade. That night the officers gave a Colour Ball in Dover Town Hall. These New Colours replaced the pair which had been presented to The 50th Foot in 1863. The Old Colours were laid up in All Saints' Church in November; this ceremony has already been described in Section 1.

At the Battalion Rifle Meeting which was held at Hythe in August 1909, 2nd-Lieutenant Palmer won all three trophies — the Rowe Cup for officers, the Harrison Cup for officers and sergeants, and the Regimental Bowl for marksmen and first-class shots. This was the first time that the Harrison Cup had been won by an officer. To appease the sergeants, Colonel Style presented a cup for annual competition by members of their Mess.

That year divisional training and manoeuvres were carried out in Berkshire. On September 23, without returning to Dover, the battalion entrained at Shrivenham and arrived after midnight at Bordon Station. Thence it marched to Quebec Barracks.

At Bordon, which was in the Aldershot Command, all the requirements of a military station were at hand. There was an adequate range within three miles (at Longmoor); training areas were but a short distance away; and grounds for all games were close to barracks. The troops were accommodated in brick bungalows, which had recently been built. Within the camp were a Church of England Hall and a Wesleyan Institute. The return railway fare to London was 3/10, and to Aldershot 1/-.

The battalion was now in the 3rd Brigade (Major-General F. Hammersley) of 1st Division (Lieutenant-General J. M. Grierson). Training was practically continuous throughout the spring and summer. It began in March with company exercises amongst the heather and sand of the Bordon areas. Battalion schemes followed. Then the troops went to Rushmoor Camp, Aldershot, for brigade training, and to other camps for divisional manoeuvres. After a welcome 10 days' leave, they marched out again in September for Army Manoeuvres on Salisbury Plain. In addition, there was the Aldershot Command Rifle Meeting on Ash Ranges in August; and all companies entered teams for the arduous competition for the Evelyn Wood Cup, which entailed a forced march followed by a shoot on the range.

For Army Manoeuvres in 1910 the Reserve was called out, and units were reinforced by their Special Reservists. During the training season of 1911 the battalion tried out a new travelling cooker.

In May 1911 all Regiments, whose titles referred to "The Queen," provided detachments at the unveiling of the Memorial to Her Majesty Queen Victoria at the western end of The Mall. The Queen's Own detachment consisted of Colonel Style, Captain Twisleton-Wykeham-Fiennes, Lieutenant Legard and 50 rank and file, and a Colour Party of 2nd-Lieutenants Palmer and Newton and three colour-sergeants. They went to London on Sunday the 14th and were accommodated in Chelsea Barracks. Next day a rehearsal in Service Dress was held. On the 16th, while the statue was being unveiled by King George V, the Queen's Own detachment was drawn up in The Mall. After the unveiling, it marched round the Memorial past the King and the German Emperor, Wilhelm II. It returned to Bordon in the evening.

On June 22, 1911, the day of the Coronation of King George V, the battalion (less three officers and 50 other ranks already in London[1])

---

[1] This was the detachment mentioned in Section 1. While in London it was accommodated in a camp in Regent's Park. For the Royal Progress through South London on June 23, it lined a portion of Pall Mall to the east of the Haymarket.

went by train to Waterloo Station and thence to a camp in Hyde Park. Early on the 23rd it marched to Southwark to line a portion of the route for the Royal Progress through South London. By 8.30 it was in position in Westminster Bridge Road, between St. George's Road and St. George's Circus. During the long wait the band and drums played selections. At about 1.30 p.m., after the procession had passed, the battalion marched back to Hyde Park, where it spent a very wet night. It returned to Bordon next day.

Five days later, on June 29, the whole battalion was in London for the Drive of His Majesty through the northern suburbs. On this occasion it lined part of St. John Street and the City Road near "The Angel," Islington.

. Divisional and Army Manoeuvres were cancelled that year because of a Railway Strike and a drought. The Strike occurred in August. On the 10th the troops at Bordon were placed at six hours' notice. Soon after midnight on the 17th the 3rd Brigade left barracks and arrived in a camp in Kensington Gardens early on the 18th. On the afternoon of the 19th the battalion was sent in motor buses to various points to protect public property. One company went to Neasden Power Station; one to Camden Goods Depot; and one to each of Euston, Paddington, St. Pancras and King's Cross Railway Stations. B Company provided patrols at several underground stations, while H found a guard over the magazine in Hyde Park. The Strike ended that night, and the companies returned to Kensington Gardens. Next day the battalion was confined to camp while a mass meeting of strikers took place in Hyde Park. On the 22nd the 3rd Brigade was relieved by the 1st. The Queen's Own arrived back in barracks at midnight.

Soon after the battalion moved to Bordon from Dover, a series of cross-country races was started in order to find runners to compete in the Brigade and Command Inter-Unit Competitions. Quick results were not to be expected. In fact the best the team did was to finish eighth in the Aldershot Command Race in the spring of 1911. The football team had no outstanding success either, although several of the players were above the average. At boxing, Corporals Baker and Darley won their weights in the Army and Navy Championships in 1909. In 1910 they were both incapacitated by injuries, and Private Smith was the only Queen's Own boxer to win a championship.

The battalion moved to Dublin on October 2—3, 1911. The crossing from Holyhead was made in the "Anglia." Having disembarked at North Wall, The Queen's Own marched to Richmond Barracks led by the band and drums of the 1st Battalion The Buffs.

Richmond Barracks were situated in an insalubrious suburb of Dublin, about 20 minutes' ride by tram from the centre of the city. One part of the barracks was occupied by the personnel of a Cavalry Depot, with whom the square, the institutes and the playing field were shared. Every fourth day the battalion provided the garrison guards. The most important of these was the scarlet pomp of Dublin Castle, where, when the Lord Lieutenant was in residence, an Officers' Guard with the King's Colour was mounted.

Colonel Style was placed on half-pay in March 1912 at the end of his period of command. He was succeeded by Major A. Martyn.

Each year in the late winter and early spring company training was carried out on areas close to Dublin. When that was finished, a considerable period was devoted to Company Marches. During these, the men lived for a week under active service conditions. Range courses and rifle meetings were fired at Kilbride. There, the troops were accommodated in tents; the Institutes and Messes were in tin huts. The most important practice in the course was the 15 rounds rapid in 60 seconds. The men called this "The Mad Minute," although their instructors told them to "keep cool, calm and collected" while firing it. In 1912 battalion training was at Trim, on the River Boyne. In 1913 it was at Wicklow.

Higher training was carried out with the 13th Brigade (Brigadier-General T. Capper) of 5th Division (Major-General W. P. Campbell)[1]. In 1912, after a few brigade exercises at the Curragh, further training was cancelled because of an outbreak of foot-and-mouth disease. In 1913 manoeuvres were at Roscrea and near Shillelagh, 50 miles south of Dublin; an aeroplane co-operated in the divisional exercises.

At the beginning of the winter of 1912-13 the battalion held a practice mobilization. Kits were packed, stores were issued, and all measures except sharpening bayonets and calling out the Reserve were taken. Embarkation was rehearsed at North Wall.

Labour unrest fermented by James Larkin, a leading spirit in the Irish Transport Workers' Union, broke out in Dublin in August 1913. At Richmond Barracks inlying picquets stood by. The Royal Irish Constabulary were for the most part masters of the situation. But on one occasion there was street fighting on a large scale. Stones and bottles were thrown at the police, and one company of the battalion was sent out. The rioters were dispersed. Disturbances continued until after Christmas.

All training in 1913 had been carried out in double-companies. By an Army Order of September 16 the organisation of a Regular battalion at Home was changed from eight companies to four, each of which was sub-divided into four platoons. On October 1, A and G Companies were amalgamated to form A Company; B and C to form B; D and E to form C; and F and H to form D Company. Platoons were numbered throughout the battalion from 1 to 16. When the re-organisation was complete, each of the four companies had a sergeant-major and a quartermaster-sergeant instead of two colour-sergeants.

The principal recreation in Dublin was football, and teams were entered for the Army Cup, the Irish Army Cup and the Dublin and Mullingar League. Boxing was still a major interest. In the Irish Army Inter-Unit Competition in 1912 The Queen's Own was second by a margin of two points; Baker, back to his old form, won both the Welter and the Middle Weights. In this competition in 1913 the battalion was again second; Baker won the Middles. In 1914 The Queen's Own was third, three points behind the winners; Darley,

[1] In August 1914 the 13th Brigade was commanded by Brigadier-General G. J. Cuthbert, and 5th Division by Major-General Sir Charles Fergusson.

now recovered from the effects of a broken arm, won the Light Weight. Baker had been discharged.[1] That year the battalion was seventh in the All-Ireland Military Cross-Country Competition.

1914 began with the usual routine of company training and range courses. Battalion training was due to start on July 27. But on that day the measures laid down for a precautionary period were put into operation. Large detachments were sent forthwith to guard various vulnerable points in Dublin. The order to mobilize was received on August 5. By the third day of mobilization nearly 600 Reservists had arrived from Maidstone. The battalion was up to strength when, on the 13th, it embarked in the "Gloucestershire" for active service in France.

4. The 2nd Battalion at Lebong, Peshawar and Multan

The 2nd Battalion disembarked at Calcutta on December 7, 1908. One company went by rail to Barrackpore, 22 miles north. Another company and the families entrained for Lebong. The remainder marched to a camp on the *maidan* outside Fort William.

Headquarters and six companies stayed in Calcutta for 10 weeks for winter drills and training. They also took part in several ceremonial parades, including the traditional Proclamation Parade on January 1. They then set out for Lebong. The first stage of the journey, 300 miles to Jalpaiguri, was by rail; the crossing of the River Ganges was made by ferry. At Jalpaiguri two training exercises were carried out in co-operation with The North Bengal Mounted Rifles, a Volunteer corps. The journey was resumed by march route, the 95 miles being covered in seven days. The road wound uphill through the foothills of the Himalayas to Lebong, which was 6,500 feet above sea level.

There was little for the troops to do at Lebong. The surrounding country was mainly unsuitable for field training, since it was a series of ridges covered with tea plantations or jungle. The rifle range was very small. As for entertainment, Darjeeling, the nearest town, was half an hour's walk from camp and had nothing to offer. In camp The Queen's Own Dramatic Club gave several concerts and plays in the tiny theatre; the Boxing Club organised frequent tournaments; and there were good clay football and hockey grounds for inter-company games. A small detachment was stationed at Jalapahar to guard a Convalescent Depot.

For the detachment at Barrackpore life was equally uneventful. In the hot weather it was very uncomfortable. The company there was relieved every three months.

Brevet-Colonel Fitton relinquished command in August, 1909[2]. His

---

[1] After the 1914-18 War Baker, as a civilian, was employed as Boxing Instructor at the Depot.

[2] Fitton became Assistant-Adjutant-General, Eastern Command. In September 1913 he was appointed Director of Recruiting and Organisation at the War Office with the temporary rank of brigadier-general.

successor, Lieutenant-Colonel N. H. S. Lowe, did not arrive at Lebong until November 10. In the meantime command devolved on Major Pedley.

On January 15, 1910, the battalion (less the detachments at Jalapahar and Barrackpore) entrained at Darjeeling for Calcutta, where it again went under canvas on the *maidan*. Training, including a physical endurance exercise called " Kitchener's Test," was carried out until the end of February. Then the seven companies went by train from Calcutta to Jalpaiguri for manoeuvres. These lasted for two weeks. The troops arrived back at Lebong on March 21.

In November 1910 five of the seven companies at Lebong and Battalion Headquarters went to Calcutta, and one moved with the families to Peshawar, which was to be the next station. The seventh company remained at Lebong and Jalapahar until December 4, when it moved, on relief by another unit, to Peshawar.

During the third stay in Calcutta, Headquarters and five companies took part in two impressive ceremonial parades. The first was for the outgoing Viceroy, the Earl of Minto. The second was to welcome Lord Hardinge of Penshurst, the new Viceroy.[1] Early in December Lord Hardinge visited The Queen's Own in their camp on the *maidan*. He was particularly pleased with the Quarter Guard which was composed of Penshurst men. On December 10 disturbances, known as the Bakr-Id Riots, broke out in the streets. For five days and nights two companies at a time were in the town on duties in aid of the civil power. They slept on the pavements or other unsuitable places, and their meals were taken out to them.

Headquarters and five companies left Calcutta in two trains on December 19 and arrived at Peshawar on the 23rd. The detachment at Barrackpore was picked up on the way. The whole battalion and the families were thus again united.

At Peshawar the battalion was quartered in Roberts' Barracks. Surrounding the cantonment was the Circular Road, on which robbers prowled at night. These " Loose Wallahs " were mainly after firearms, and the men's rifles, with the bolts removed, were securely locked in racks in the barrack rooms. Periodically one company occupied a fort two miles from the cantonment. On at least two occasions a detachment was sent for a tour of duty to Jamrud Fort, near the Khyber Pass. Courses were fired on a range close to Peshawar. Tactical training and field firing were usually carried out from a camp at Dag, 27 miles away.

Each year, at the end of April, four companies with their families went up to the hill station at Cherat for the hot weather. The other families went to Khanspur. At Cherat, which was 50 miles from Peshawar, the troops were accommodated in stone bungalows. Within the camp was an adequate recreation ground. Nearby were some large rocks, in which had been cut the crests and badges of the regiments that had been stationed at Cherat. The crest of The Queen's Own was added.

[1] Lord Hardinge was the son of Viscount Hardinge, who had been the C.O. and Honorary Colonel of the 1st Volunteer Battalion..

At the end of November 1911 the battalion boxing team, having won the Peshawar Division Tournament earlier in the year, went to Delhi to compete for the Coronation Durbar Cup, presented by the King Emperor. Boxing went on for 16 nights. The first four teams were: —

    2nd Battalion The Queen's Own - - - - - 15 points
    4th Battalion The King's Royal Rifle Corps - - 11 points
    2nd Battalion The Royal Welch Fusiliers - - - 11 points
    2nd Battalion The Black Watch - - - - - - 10 points

The battalion team, which was trained by Private E. McCarthy and Sergeant H. Childs, was: —

Corporal J. Sheppard	Lance-Corporal C. Russell
Lance-Corporal G. Andrews	Private D. Brown
Private J. Harris	Private H. Ott
Private C. G. Briselden	Private F. Barnes

Corporal Sheppard, who won the Light Weight and the Locke-Elliott Belt, received the cup from the Queen Empress on the afternoon of December 15.

During the Durbar holiday which, at Peshawar, was from December 6 to 13, regimentally the chief event was the Battalion Rifle Meeting. This included the competitions for the Officers', Eccles, Long, Western and Maunsell Cups, which had not been held at Lebong.

On March 7, 1912, a number of buildings in Peshawar caught fire, or were set alight by hooligans. The flames spread quickly, and for four days the battalion provided picquets and cordons. The main task was to prevent looting. For these extra duties the G.O.C., Lieutenant-General Sir John Nixon, presented 500 rupees to the funds of the Regimental Institutes.

Lieutenant-Colonel Lowe was placed on half-pay on account of ill-health in March 1912. Major S. H. Pedley was promoted in his stead.

Lord Hardinge of Penshurst paid another visit to the battalion in April 1912. He was received by a Guard of Honour and lunched in the Officers' Mess.

The boxing team again won the Peshawar Division Tournament in 1912 and 1913. The football team, after practising for several weeks at Cherat, made the tedious journey to Simla in September 1912 to play in the Durand Tournament, the premier competition in India. It lost to the 1st Battalion The Connaught Rangers in the third round, after a replay.

The tour at Peshawar ended on November 19, 1913, when the battalion moved in two troop-trains to Multan. The barracks had already been taken over by a draft from the 1st Battalion. They consisted of two-storey buildings which stood on the edge of a sandy plain. During the hot weather the temperature rose to 120 degrees by day and rarely fell below 100 at night. Military duty was reduced to a minimum.

In April 1914 Headquarters and four companies went up to Dalhousie for the summer. The troops occupied wooden bungalows, while the officers lived in Stiffle's Hotel, where they rented a room as a Mess. As was usual at hill stations, little training was done. Much time was devoted to recuperation and entertainment. The Dramatic Club presented "An Englishman's Home" for four nights. The last performance was on August 4. Next day England was at war. Within a short time the battalion was ordered to assume the role of Internal Security Troops.

5. The 3rd Battalion (Reserve)

The 3rd Battalion (Reserve) assembled at Maidstone for its first annual training on July 12, 1909. A special train took the personnel to Shorncliffe. The camp on St. Martin's Plain had been prepared by an advanced-party. The 20 days' training began with instruction in the short rifle, which had recently been issued. Firing on Hythe ranges started on Monday the 19th. On the following Sunday the Right Reverend Bishop J. Taylor Smith conducted a Church Service on Sir John Moore's Plain for all the troops at Shorncliffe. During the last few days some tactical exercises were carried out. The personnel returned to Maidstone and were dispersed on July 31.

In 1910 the battalion went to Bisley on September 5 and camped on the ground of the National Rifle Association. The courses were fired on the N.R.A. ranges. On the 17th nearly 300 all ranks joined the 1st Battalion at Bordon for Army Manoeuvres. The remainder stayed at Bisley till the 24th, when they returned to the Depot for dismissal. The personnel who had attended manoeuvres were dismissed at Maidstone on the 25th.

The annual camps for 1911, 1912 and 1913 were at Shorncliffe. The period of training had now been extended to 27 days. On August 17, 1911, the last day but one in camp, the battalion was ordered to be ready to move in two hours' time for strike duty. All preparations were made, but the order was cancelled.

Colours were presented to the battalion on St. Martin's Plain, Shorncliffe, on August 19, 1913, by the Marchioness of Camden. They were consecrated by the Venerable A. T. Scott, Archdeacon of Tonbridge. Lieutenant Furber received the King's Colour, and Lieutenant Snelgrove the Regimental. The R.S.M. was Sergeant-Major Grellier. After the Colours had been presented, the Marquess of Camden addressed the parade. The Commanding Officer, Lieutenant-Colonel Sir Arthur Griffith-Boscawen, Knt., M.P., replied and read a letter from Field-Marshal H.R.H. The Duke of Connaught, the Honorary Colonel. The battalion then marched past to "The Low-backed Car." Afterwards, the officers and the sergeants entertained their guests to lunch in marquees on the ground. These Colours were similar to those of the Line battalions, and bore the same Battle Honours.

Until these Colours were received, the battalion had carried the pair presented to the 2nd Battalion The West Kent Light Infantry

Militia in 1877.[1] The latter were laid up in All Saints' Church on Sunday November 23, 1913, after the morning service. The Colour Party consisted of Lieutenants D. C. C. Sewell and Whitehouse and three colour-sergeants. The Mayor and Corporation were present, as were many of the officers and other ranks of the battalion, who had made the journey to Maidstone to be there. Lieutenant-Colonel Griffith-Boscawen handed the Colours at the altar rails to the Vicar, the Rev. E. H. Hardcastle, who delivered an address. The buglers sounded "The Last Post." The organist played "The Men of Kent" as the troops filed out.

On July 27, 1914, the personnel assembled at Maidstone for annual training and went to Shorncliffe. On August 3 the training was ended by the imminence of war. In the mobilization scheme the battalion was allotted the duty of manning a section of the Thames defences. Within a few days it arrived at Chattenden, near Chatham, to take up its wartime role.

6. *The Territorial Battalions*

Towards the end of 1908 recruiting for the Territorial Force received a powerful stimulus from the Press. The numbers increased rapidly. By January 1909 the three Territorial units of The Queen's Own had taken shape as follows: —
4th Battalion:
Headquarters in the Corn Exchange, Tonbridge.
Uniform: as for the Line battalions.
Range: at Shoreham in Kent.
Companies: A and B at Maidstone; C at Tonbridge; D and E at Tunbridge Wells; F at Orpington; G at Sevenoaks; H at Westerham and Edenbridge.
5th Battalion:
Headquarters at the Drill Hall, East Street, Bromley.
Uniform: as for the Line battalions.
Range: at Milton, near Gravesend.
Companies: A and B at Bromley; C at Dartford; D at Beckenham and Penge; E at Sidcup; F and G at Chatham; H at Horton Kirby.
6th (Cyclist) Battalion:
Headquarters at Tonbridge.
Uniform: as for the Line battalions, with some modifications.
Companies: at Ashford, Bromley, Canterbury, Chatham, Folkestone, Maidstone, Ramsgate, Tonbridge and Tunbridge Wells.

In February 1909 the 6th (Cyclist) Battalion was removed from the corps of The Queen's Own. It was re-named The Kent Cyclist

[1] The Colours presented to The West Kent Light Infantry Militia in 1855 were carried by the 3rd Battalion (Militia) until 1905. Some years later they were lodged in St. Peter's Church at Ightham. They were laid up in All Saints' Church on July 21, 1929.

Battalion and became Army Troops attached to the Home Counties Division (T.F.). The Regiment continued to provide the Permanent Staff.

Another Territorial unit closely connected with The Queen's Own was The Kent Brigade Company Army Service Corps, which belonged to the Home Counties Division Transport and Supply Column. It was formed by Captain Lattimer (1st Vol. Bn.) from the Transport Section of the West Kent Volunteer Brigade. Nearly all the personnel were members of the Maidstone Church Institute, where its headquarters were located.

The 4th and 5th Battalions received their Colours from His Majesty King Edward VII at Windsor Castle on June 19, 1909. It was a mass presentation of Guidons and Colours to 108 yeomanry and infantry units of the Territorial Force, which had attained 75 per cent. of their establishment. Each battalion was represented by a detachment, 20 strong, and a Colour Party. The detachment of the 4th Battalion was commanded by Captain Garrard; that of the 5th by R.S.M. Spooner. The officers for the Colours were Lieutenants Henson and L. Smithers (4th), and Lieutenants Neame and Hills (5th). The parade was drawn up on the East Lawn so that the representative detachments formed three sides of a hollow square. In front of the saluting base, which was the fourth side, were the Colour Parties in order of precedence, with the massed bands of the Brigade of Guards behind them. Many important personages were present. On the arrival of His Majesty, the Royal Salute was given. The ceremony began with the consecration of the Guidons and Colours by the Right Reverend Bishop J. Taylor Smith. A short service followed. Each Colour Party then advanced in turn. The title of the unit was read out, and the Colours were drooped in front of the King by two officers of the Brigade of Guards. His Majesty touched the Colours with his right hand. The subalterns took them, and the Colour Party marched to the front of its own detachment in the hollow square. When all the presentations had been made, the parade presented arms and the Guidons and Colours were dipped in a Royal Salute. The ceremony ended with three cheers for His Majesty the King. Emblazoned on the Regimental Colour of both the 4th and 5th Battalions was the Battle Honour " South Africa, 1900-02."

When the representative detachment of the 5th Battalion arrived at Bromley from Windsor that night, nearly the whole of the unit, wearing ceremonial dress, was drawn up at the South Station to received its Colours. The column then marched to the Municipal Buildings, where the Colours were placed in the Council Chamber for temporary safe-custody. The Colours of the 4th Battalion were uncased for the first time, in the presence of the troops, at Tonbridge on October 16th. As heavy rain had made the Angel Ground unfit, the parade was held at Battalion Headquarters in the Corn Exchange. Colonel C. S. Williams, the Honorary Colonel, told the men that the ladies of Kent had subscribed towards the cost of the Colours.

A drill hall, for Headquarters and C Company of the 4th Battalion and other local Territorials, was opened at Tonbridge by the Earl of Cranbrook on February 5, 1910. The building was in Bank Street and contained offices, armouries, a Recreation Room for the rank and file, and Messes for the officers and sergeants. A drill hall for the Maidstone Territorials was opened by the Marquess of Camden on December 6, 1911. It stood in Union Street, on the site of the Militia Barracks.

G and H Companies of the 4th Battalion were present at the unveiling of the statue of General James Wolfe on the Green at Westerham on January 2, 1911. The ceremony was performed by Field-Marshal Earl Roberts.

The system of training in the Territorial Force was practically the same as that of the Volunteers. Drills took place locally once or twice a week; the range courses were fired at week-ends; and camps, attendance at which was compulsory, were held once a year. The main differences were that more week-end exercises were organised for the training of specialists, such as signallers and scouts, and the period of annual training was for two weeks instead of one.

The 4th and 5th Battalions trained with the 4th and 5th Buffs in the Kent Territorial Infantry Brigade of the Home Counties Division. This brigade was commanded by Colonel E. Satterthwaite until June 1911, when Colonel V. T. Bunbury (late The Leicestershire Regiment) took over. The annual camps in 1909 and 1910 were at Dover. In 1911 the camp was inland at Crowborough. In 1912 the brigade went to Worthing and in 1913 to Seaford. The first week of training was devoted to minor tactical schemes and route marching. During the second week, one or two brigade exercises were usually held.

On July 26, 1914, the Home Counties Division went by train to Longmoor and Bordon. Four days later it started to march across Hampshire to Salisbury Plain. The column had reached the eastern edge of the Plain by August 3, when the units were ordered back to their headquarters because war was imminent. After waiting for 24 hours on the roadside, the 4th and 5th Battalions entrained at Amesbury and Andover respectively and reached their drill stations in the early hours of the 5th. That night they went by rail to Dover, where they took up their pre-arranged battle positions.

7. Conclusion

Since 1881 we have seen how The 50th and The 97th Foot became united as the Line battalions of The Queen's Own (Royal West Kent Regiment), and how this new Regiment set out harmoniously to establish traditions of its own. We have observed how the two Militia battalions of The Queen's Own were reduced to one, and how this battalion, having loyally served in Malta during the South African War, became outmoded and was replaced by a Special Reserve unit. And we have watched the Volunteers develop from separate, independent rifle corps into well-equipped battalions of an organised force.

Now, at the outset of the greatest conflict which had till then been fought, we leave The Queen's Own, with the 1st Battalion marching through Northern France to a position on the Mons-Condé Canal; the 2nd about to assume internal security duties in Western India; the 3rd guarding vulnerable points near Chatham; and the 4th and 5th defending Dover. The story of how the Regiment fared in the war is told in "The Queen's Own Royal West Kent Regiment, 1914-1919." It is an epic of fortitude, resolution and courage.

ROLL OF HONOUR 1881—1913

A list of Members of

The Queen's Own

who were killed in action or died of wounds, accident, or disease contracted on active service

EGYPT AND THE SUDAN, 1882 — 1886

Adams, J., 2323, Sgt.	Polymedia	23	10	1882	Disease
Anderson, A. J., Lieut.	Tani	16	5	1885	Enteric
Atkins, W., 2820, Pte.	Akasheh	14	7	1885	Enteric
Baker, J., 2223, Pte.	Tani	26	3	1885	Enteric
Ballard, J., 56, Pte.	Kurot	17	5	1885	Enteric
Birch, A. L., Capt.	Tani	2	5	1885	Enteric
Bonfield, W., 50, Pte.	Wadi Halfa	12	1	1885	Enteric
Bridgett, F., Pte.	Polymedia	12	1	1884	Pneumonia
Brown, H. J., 654, Pte.	Wadi Halfa	13	8	1885	Enteric
Brown, J., 510, Sgt.	Ramleh	23	6	1886	Enteric
Burdett, E., 985, L/Cpl.	Ramleh	13	6	1886	Drowned
Burr, A., 1799, Pte.	Tanjour	23	12	1884	Enteric
Bush, R., 819, Pte.	Wadi Halfa	19	12	1885	Enteric
Camber, W., 2886, Cpl.	Wadi Halfa	9	1	1885	Enteric
Campbell, J., 1766, Sgt.	Gibraltar	8	8	1886	Disease
Carpenter, C., Pte.	Egypt	Autumn		1882	Dysentery
Carr, E. H. Major	Wadi Halfa	19	1	1886	Enteric
Chapman, J., 265, Pte.	Tani	19	4	1885	Enteric
Chown, S. H., 1988, Cpl.	Abu Fatmeh	18	4	1885	Enteric

141

Name	Place	Date	Cause
[1]Clissold, G., 2280, Cpl.	Sudan	Spring 1885	Disease
Collins, J., 2943, Pte.	Egypt	Autumn 1882	Disease
Cotterell, M., 2676, Pte.	Egypt	Autumn 1882	Disease
Crocker, J., 750, Pte.	Akasheh	18 12 1885	Dysentery
Crookenden, C., 2890, Pte.	Tani	11 4 1885	Enteric
Davis, C., 2255, Pte.	Alexandria	22 10 1882	Enteric
Earley, G., 2873, Pte.	Egypt	Spring 1886	Disease
Farrow, T., 2358, Cpl.	Cairo	12 1882	Typhoid
Gibbons, P., 2845, Pte.	Tani	1 5 1885	Enteric
Golding, F., 100, Pte.	Tani	18 3 1885	Enteric
Golding, H., 1402, Pte.	S.S. "Nevada"	8 10 1882	Dysentery
Gowers, J., 917, Pte.	Ramleh	17 6 1886	Enteric
Green, F., 1299, C/Sgt.	Cairo	12 1882	Typhoid
Gurr, H., 2939, Pte.	Absarat	11 2 1885	Dysentery
Hale, W., 556, L/Cpl.	Tani	12 5 1885	Enteric
Harris, J., 1721, Pte.	Alexandria	24 3 1883	Disease
Hayes, W., 2953, Pte.	Ramleh	24 2 1886	Disease
Hayward, G., 2487, Pte.	Alexandria	20 10 1882	Enteric
Hilling, J., 2797, Pte.	Gibraltar	6 8 1886	Enteric
Holland, J., 812, Pte.	Wadi Halfa	17 12 1884	Enteric
Howard, G., 1496, Sgt.	Nefisha	24 8 1882	Sunstroke
Ingram, F., 914, Pte.	Ramleh	6 6 1886	Enteric
Jarrett, J., 934, Pte.	Gibraltar	10 7 1886	Enteric
Mansfield, A., 617, L/Cpl.	Wadi Halfa	8 7 1885	Heart
[1]Miles, G., 2611, Cpl.	Abu Klea	17 1 1885	Killed
Miller, J., 771, Pte.	Tani	9 5 1885	Enteric
Mizon, E. H., 289, Pte.	Wadi Halfa	9 8 1885	Enteric
Morrison, A., 2031, Pte.	Egypt	Autumn 1882	Disease
Moules, G., 916, Pte.	Ramleh	10 6 1886	Enteric

[1] 2nd Battalion Contingent of M.I.

ROLL OF HONOUR 1881-1913

Name	Place	Date	Cause
Murray, G., 2032, Pte.	Egypt	9 1882	Disease
Newport, J., 549, Pte.	Abri	10 7 1885	Enteric
Patterson, R., 2554, Pte.	Koyekeh	9 6 1885	Enteric
Pearson, R., L/Cpl.	Egypt	Autumn 1882	Disease
Potts, T. N., 515, C/Sgt.	Sudan	Spring 1885	Disease
Ransome, G., Sgt.	Alexandria	26 3 1883	Disease
Ransome, W., 836, Pte.	Wadi Halfa	28 12 1885	Dysentery
Richardson, F., 953, Pte.	Semneh	21 12 1884	Drowned
Rix, E., Pte.	Sudan	1 1885	Disease
Robinson, E. J., Major	Wadi Halfa	29 12 1884	Enteric
Roe, W., 2930, Pte.	Egypt	10 1882	Disease
Rolfe, W., 2778, Pte.	Korosko	2 6 1885	Disease
Ryder, J., 593, Pte.	Wadi Halfa	21 9 1885	Disease
Simpson, E., Bdsm.	Alexandria	3 9 1884	Accident
Smith, A., 669, Pte.	Wadi Halfa	26 12 1885	Enteric
Smith, G., Pte.	Egypt	Autumn 1882	Disease
Smith, H. F., 776, Pte.	Tani	29 4 1885	Enteric
Smith, W., 234, Pte.	Portsmouth	10 11 1885	Debility
Smith, W. H., 872, Pte.	Ramleh	1 7 1886	Enteric
¹Stacey, J., 2610, Pte.	Sudan	12 1884	Disease
Stone, F., 2215, L/Cpl.	Wadi Halfa	27 7 1885	Enteric
Sullivan, J., 2942, Pte.	Dongola	16 6 1885	Enteric
¹Swinbourne, S., 2604, Pte.	Mettemmeh	27 1 1885	Of Wounds
Tuck, W., 2508, Pte.		Spring 1883	Disease
Waghorne, S., 2952, Pte.	Wadi Halfa	23 7 1885	Enteric
Warren, G., 2004, Pte.	Ramleh	13 2 1886	Disease
Williams, E. M., Lieut.	Tani	20 4 1885	Enteric
Williamson, G., 552, Pte.	Sudan	4 1885	Disease
Wilson, W., 249, Pte.	Tani	18 3 1885	Pneumonia

¹ 2nd Battalion Contingent of M.I.

L

144   THE QUEEN'S OWN ROYAL WEST KENT REGIMENT

Woods, E., 2612, Pte.	Minieh	11 9 1885	Drowned
Wormleighton, S., Pte.	Egypt	Spring 1886	Disease

THE PUNJAB FRONTIER, 1897—98

Berry, F., 3357, Drm.	Agrah	30 9 1897	Killed
Browne-Clayton, W. C., Lieut.	Agrah	30 9 1897	Killed
Cooper, W., 4168, Pte.	On march	8 1897	Sunstroke
Courteney, P., 4051, Pte.	Dum Dum	11 2 1898	Disease
Golding, J., Lieut.	At Home	22 6 1898	Disease
Halsey, W., 1581, Sgt.	Nowshera	12 11 1897	Disease
Hutson, T. C., 3393, Pte.	Agrah	30 9 1897	Killed
Jones, G., 3998, Pte.	Agrah	30 9 1897	Killed
Knox, E., 2970, Pte.	Nowshera	11 12 1897	Disease
Moore, W., 3577, Pte.	Peshawar	3 11 1897	Disease
Ramsey, W., 3918, Pte.			Disease
Smith, F., 3153, Pte.			Disease
Stockham, P., 2941, Pte.	Peshawar	9 1 1898	Disease
Stuart, C., 3108, Pte.	Chakdara	3 10 1897	Disease
Tollman, J., 3097, Sgt.	On march	8 1897	Sunstroke
Warner, J., 1341, Sgt.			Of Wounds
Watts, C., 2758, Pte.	Jalala	15 11 1897	Disease

THE ADEN EXPEDITION, 1901

Edwards, C. P., 4377, Pte.	Camp Wahat	16 7 1901	Sunstroke
Hoy, G., 3765, Pte.	Ad Daraijah	26 7 1901	Killed
Wood, F., 4864, L-Cpl.	Nobat Dakim	20 7 1901	Sunstroke

ROLL OF HONOUR 1881-1913 145

THE WAR IN SOUTH AFRICA, 1900 — 1902

Name	Place	Date	Cause
Abbey, F., 4329, Pte.	Heilbron	5 3 1901	Enteric
Allen, J., 2522, Pte.	Frankfort	23 12 1900	Heart
[7]Ansell, G., 5648, Pte.	Elandsfontein	4 11 1901	Pneumonia
Ashby, J., 5108, Pte.	Frankfort	9 10 1900	Drowned
Ashton, E., 2435, Pte.	Frankfort	24 1 1901	Enteric
Auty, W., 7058, Pte.	Heilbron	29 4 1902	Enteric
Bailey, A., 4483, Pte.	Frankfort	22 1 1901	Enteric
Balding, J., 3006, Sgt.	Heilbron	2 6 1901	Enteric
Ball, R., 4136, Pte.	Heilbron	11 3 1901	Dysentery
[2]Barnes, H. 6910, Pte.	Norvals Pont	18 1 1901	Enteric
Barnes, W., 5514, Pte.	Frankfort	17 12 1900	Disease
Barwick, C., 5398, Pte.	Winburg	13 2 1901	Enteric
Bennett, E., 4209, Sgt.	Harrismith	27 1 1901	Enteric
Bird, A., 5293, L/Cpl.	Heilbron	18 2 1901	Dysentery
Bish, A., 4705, Pte.	Uitkijk	8 2 1901	Dysentery
Bridges, W., 3798, Pte.	Deelfontein	13 7 1900	Enteric
Brightman, W., 5279, Pte.	At Sea	27 3 1900	Disease
Bond, W., 5334, Pte.	Vergenoed	16 5 1902	Of Wounds
Brown, H., 5912, Pte.	Norvals Pont	30 1 1902	Enteric
Burgess, W., 1458, Sgt.	Elandsfontein	28 7 1901	Pneumonia
Canty, W., 3766, Sgt.	Frankfort	16 10 1900	Of Wounds
Capon, W., 3664, Pte.	Harrismith	23 11 1900	Dysentery
Chandler, H. 2480, Pte.	Springfontein	2 4 1901	Enteric
Chaplin, J., 2775, Pte.	Heilbron	2 2 1902	Enteric
Christie, M., 5168, Pte.	Frankfort	23 2 1901	Enteric
Clarke, J., 2660, Pte.	Frankfort	22 10 1900	Killed
Collins, W., 4659, Pte.		8 1 1901	Enteric

[7] 21st Mounted Infantry. [2] 1st Volunteer Active Service Company.

146 THE QUEEN'S OWN ROYAL WEST KENT REGIMENT

Name	Place	Date	Cause
Collison, W., 5142, Pte.	Springfontein	5 2 1902	Enteric
Conway, C., 4818, Pte.	Bloemhof	22 4 1902	Of Wounds
Court, E., 4461, Sgt.	Kroonstad	19 12 1900	Dysentery
Cousins, J., 3878, Pte.	Winburg	3 6 1900	Enteric
¹Cowlard, S., 1616, Pte.	Potgieters Rust	11 8 1901	Accid. shot
³Creasey, H. E., 7003, Pte.	Heilbron	9 5 1902	Dysentery
Daley, W., 5250, Pte.	Winburg	19 5 1901	Enteric
Davis, J., 5185, Pte.	Ficksburg	26 8 1900	Enteric
Dornan, S., 4376, Pte.	At Sea	30 3 1900	Disease
Edwards, W., 2567, Pte.	Heilbron	2 6 1901	Enteric
²Eveleigh, E., 6948, Sgt.	Norvals Pont	22 11 1900	Enteric
Fincham, T., 2516, Pte.	Heilbron	20 6 1901	Enteric
Fricker, A., 2957, Pte.	Frankfort	20 12 1900	Enteric
Frisby, J., 5428, Pte.	Springfontein	25 12 1901	Enteric
Galpin, F., 3387, Pte.	Harrismith	26 12 1900	Enteric
Gordon, F., 4332, Pte.	Kroonstad	1 4 1901	Enteric
Green, H., 5799, Pte.	Heilbron	20 3 1902	Enteric
Greenwood, J., 4035, Pte.	Frankfort	8 1 1901	Dysentery
⁷Griffin, T., 5657, Pte.	Johannesburg	15 11 1901	Enteric
Harland, T., 2907, Pte.	Heilbron	13 6 1902	Enteric
¹Harman H., 5705, Pte.	Ventersdorp	17 7 1901	Enteric
²Helmer, F. A., 6878, Pte.	At Sea	3 1900	Disease
Hills, W., 3888, Pte.	Heilbron	1 7 1901	Enteric
Horsnell, R., 1168, L/Cpl.	Bloemfontein	18 7 1900	Enteric
Hudson, C., 5688, Pte.	Bloemfontein	3 4 1900	Disease
⁷Huggins, T., 5919, Pte.	Johannesburg	28 12 1901	Enteric
Humphreys, J., 4987, Pte.	Naauwpoort	28 7 1900	Enteric
Huntley, C., 5487, Pte.	Harrismith	30 4 1901	Enteric
Jones, W., 5812, Pte.	Heilbron	2 1 1902	Enteric

¹ 3rd Battalion. ³ 2nd Volunteer Active Service Company. ² 1st Volunteer Active Service Company. ⁷ 21st Mounted Infantry.

ROLL OF HONOUR 1881-1913 147

Name	Location	Date	Cause
Kehone, J., 2589, Pte.	Heilbron	27 5 1901	Enteric
Kew, G., 2538, Pte.	Dewetsdorp	26 4 1900	Accid. shot
King, T., 889, Pte.	Cape Town	1 3 1901	Pneumonia
King, T., 7042, Pte.	Pretoria	2 4 1902	Enteric
Lawrence, R., 2586, Pte.	Heidelberg	15 7 1901	Killed
Lee, W., 4565, L/Cpl.	Norvals Pont	30 12 1901	Enteric
Lewis, J., 4498, L/Sgt.	Heilbron	7 2 1902	Accid. shot
Lines, E., 3282, Pte.	Bloemfontein	11 7 1900	Enteric
Littlefield, J., 5841, Pte.	Norvals Pont	1 1 1902	Enteric
Long, W., 5059, Pte.	Heilbron	12 5 1901	Enteric
[3] Lucock, A. F., 7013, Pte.	Kroonstad	12 12 1901	Enteric
Macey, J., 5507, Pte.	Harrismith	31 3 1901	Enteric
Malvern, A., 2424, Pte.	Ficksburg	13 7 1900	Gangrene
Manser, H., 5527, L/Cpl.	Norvais Pont	7 1 1902	Enteric
Marchant, I., 2587, Pte.	Ficksburg	12 7 1900	Enteric
[2] Marchant, H., 6868, Cpl.	Norvals Pont	18 12 1900	Enteric
Matthews, T., 5341, Pte.	Heilbron	9 5 1901	Abscess
McBride, G., 7053, Pte.	Norvals Pont	22 1 1902	Enteric
McCoy, E., 2826, Pte.	Vryheid	2 12 1901	Accid. shot
Mills, S., 4649, Pte.	Harrismith	12 3 1901	Enteric
Montague, W., 3431, Sgt.	Frankfort	29 11 1900	Of wounds
[6] Morris, G. E. W., Lieut.	Near Ermelo	28 1 1902	Of wounds
Mott, G., 5420, Pte.	Heilbron	31 12 1901	Of wounds
Mulloy, C. C., Lieut.	Kroonstad	14 3 1901	Abscess
Munday, J., 1745, Pte.	Frankfort	18 11 1900	Of wounds
[7] Murgatroyd, C., 5622, Pte.	Elandsfontein	20 12 1901	Enteric
Olds, J., 5190, Pte.	Frankfort	28 12 1900	Disease
Orange, J. G., 5898, Pte.	Heilbron	30 7 1902	Pneumonia
Page, F., 4060, Cpl.	Bloemfontein	2 6 1900	Enteric

[3] 2nd Volunteer Active Service Company.   [2] 1st Volunteer Active Service Company.   [6] 13th Mounted Infantry.   [7] 21st Mounted Infantry.

Name	Date	Place	Cause
Parker, E. J., 5913, Pte.	18 11 1901	Heilbron	Enteric
Parker, W., 4137, Sgt.	15 1 1902	Brakvlei	Drowned
Parry, R., 3763, Pte.	4 12 1901	Leeuw Spruit	Drowned
Pike, H., 3082, Pte.	4 12 1900	Frankfort	Enteric
Reed, E., 3098, Pte.	1 4 1900	At Sea	Disease
Richardson, J., 3817, Pte.	16 1 1901	Harrismith	Enteric
Roff, T., 4681, Pte.	7 2 1901	Kroonstad	Enteric
Rolfe, C., 5288, Pte.	23 5 1901	Bloemfontein	Enteric
Roots, E., 5155, Pte.	31 5 1901	Heilbron	Enteric
Rowe, T., 5600, Pte.	11 2 1901	Heilbron	Enteric
Sansom, A., 3855, Pte.	10 4 1902	Standerton	Enteric
Sellings, W., 2566, Pte.	22 10 1900	Frankfort	Killed
Shoebridge, G., 4304, Pte.	3 12 1900	Frankfort	Enteric
Simmonds, W., 6976, Pte.	21 12 1901	Heilbron	Enteric
Smith, A., 5720, Pte.	30 5 1902	Elandsfontein	Dysentery
¹Smith, E., 2777, Pte.	16 1 1901	At Sea	Disease
Smith, W., 4844, Pte.	5 12 1900	Frankfort	Enteric
Soper, A., 2323, Pte.	29 12 1900	Harrismith	Disease
Stevenson, J., 5999, Pte.	5 1 1902	Heilbron	Enteric
⁷Tanner, P. A., 5859, Pte.	8 4 1902	Pretoria	Enteric
Taylor, G., 1204, Sgt.	3 5 1901	Kroonstad	Dysentery
Taylor, W., 2418, Pte.	4 10 1901	Cape Town	Drowned
Thorne, A., 1298, C/Sgt.	7 2 1901	Mooi River	Dysentery
Tucker, J., 5318, Pte.	29 1 1902	Near Frankfort	Killed
²Turpin, H., 6884, Pte.	10 12 1900	Norvals Pont	Enteric
²Twort, H., 6845, Pte.	17 4 1901	At Sea	Rem. fever
Wharam, T., 5687, Pte.	27 5 1902	Heilbron	Disease
³White, E., 7050, L/Cpl.	1 4 1902	Heilbron	Enteric
⁵Whitebread, W., 5968, Pte.	31 12 1901	Pretoria	Enteric

1 3rd Battalion. 7 21st Mounted Infantry. 2 1st Volunteer Active Service Company. 3 2nd Volunteer Active Service Company. 5 4th Mounted Infantry

²Wilcox, F., 6865, Pte.	Norvals Pont	15 12 1900	Enteric
Wood, C. W., 2659, Sgt.	Dewetsdorp	3 5 1900	Dysentery

EAST & WEST AFRICA, 1900 — 1904

Luard, E. D., Lieut.	Garrero, Somaliland	13 11 1903	Enteric
Marsh, F. C., Brev.-Major	Burmi, N. Nigeria	27 7 1903	Of wounds
Marshall, G., Capt.	Edubia, Gold Coast	28 6 1900	Of wounds
Mendham, W. B., Sgt.	Oricha Alona, S. Nigeria	28 1 1904	Killed

² 1st Volunteer Active Service Company.

BIBLIOGRAPHY

1875-1914. "The Queen's Own Gazette." Published monthly at Maidstone by the *Kent Messenger*.

1895. Colonel A. E. Fyler. "The History of The 50th or The Queen's Own Regiment."

1903. John Stirling. Chapter on the 2nd Battalion in "Our Regiments in South Africa, 1899-1902."

1909. Colonel J. Bonhote. "Historical Records of the West Kent Militia."

1924. C. T. Atkinson. "The Queen's Own Royal West Kent Regiment, 1914-19."

1930. Anon. "A Short History of The Queen's Own Royal West Kent Regiment."

1933. Captain H. N. Edwards. Medal Roll Part 2, 1882-1902. Published in "The Queen's Own Gazette."

1933. Captain H. N. Edwards. "A Short Record of the Colours of The Queen's Own Royal West Kent Regiment." Reprinted from "The Queen's Own Gazette."

1937-1938. Captain H. N. Edwards. Articles on "The Clothing, Equipment and Arms of The Queen's Own, 1756-1936." Printed in "The Queen's Own Gazette"

1956. Lieutenant-Colonel H. D. Chaplin. "The Queen's Own Royal West Kent Regiment, a Short Account of its Origins, Service and Campaigns, 1756-1956."

APPENDIX A

BADGES AND DEVICES ADOPTED BY THE REGIMENT IN 1881

HELMET PLATE

Made of gilt metal. A star surmounted by a crown. On the star, a laurel wreath. Within the wreath, a Garter inscribed *Honi soit qui mal y pense.* Within the Garter, in silver on a black velvet ground, the White Horse of Kent with *Invicta.* Above the Horse, a scroll with the motto *Quo Fas et Gloria Ducunt.*

On the officers' plate was another scroll at the bottom of the wreath bearing the title " The Royal West Kent Regiment."

GLENGARRY CAP BADGE

Made of gilt metal. A Garter with motto, surmounted by a crown. Badge and ground as for the helmet plate.

FORAGE CAP BADGE

Made of silver metal. The White Horse of Kent with *Invicta.* Beneath it, a blue silk gold embroidered scroll " The Queen's Own Royal West Kent Regiment."[1]

BELT PLATE

In silver metal, on a frosted gilt centre, the Royal Crest (a Lion and Crown). On a circle surrounding it, " The Queen's Own Regiment."

COLLAR BADGES

The Royal Crest. For the officers, in gold embroidery. For the other ranks, of cut brass.

BUTTONS

The buttons of the officers bore the Royal Crest.

SHOULDER STRAPS

The shoulder straps of the rank and file bore the title " W. Kent " in white letters on a red ground.

[1] In February 1895 Kentish grey was approved as the regimental colour of the 1st and 2nd Battalions, and that colour was allowed as trimmings to the Field Service Cap.

ROLL OF COLONELS, HONORARY COLONELS AND COMMANDING OFFICERS

July, 1881—August, 1914

COLONELS OF THE REGIMENT

General Sir E. W. Forestier Walker, K.C.B. (1st Bn.)	July 1, 1881[1]
General The Hon. Sir F. Colborne, K.C.B. (1st Bn).	July 28, 1881
General J. M. Perceval, C.B. (2nd Bn.)	July 1, 1881[2]
General J. M. Perceval, C.B.	July 18, 1885
General W. R. Preston	Feb. 28, 1888
General Sir Fowler Burton, K.C.B.	Oct. 5, 1890
Major-General Sir Edmund Leach, K.C.B.	Apr. 3, 1904

OFFICERS COMMANDING 50th REGIMENTAL DISTRICT AND THE REGIMENTAL DEPOT

Brevet-Colonel Hales Wilkie	1 7 81[3]— 30 12 81
Brevet-Colonel D. R. Barnes	31 12 81 — 13 3 83
Colonel W. J. Chads, C.B.	14 3 83 — 7 6 87
Colonel R. A. Manners	8 6 87 — 11 7 89
Colonel D. J. D. Safford	12 7 89 — 11 7 94
Colonel W. H. Bayly	12 7 94 — 11 7 99
Colonel T. H. Brock	12 7 99 — 11 7 04
Major R. C. Style (Acting)	12 7 04 — 31 12 04

[1] General Walker had been Colonel of The 50th since March 1872.
[2] General Perceval had been Colonel of The 97th since March 1874.
[3] Wilkie had been in command of No. 46 Sub-district since March 1878.

(The appointment of "Officer Commanding Regimental District" lapsed. From January 1, 1905, a major was gazetted to command the Regimental Depot only).

Major R. C. Style	1	1 05 — 27 7 05
Major N. H. S. Lowe	28	7 05 — 24 7 08
Major A. Martyn	25	7 08 — 7 11
Major C. G. Pack-Beresford		7 11 — 17 7 14
Major P. M. Robinson, C.M.G.	18	7 14 — 4 8 14
Colonel G. W. Maunsell	5	8 14[1]—

COMMANDING OFFICERS OF THE LINE BATTALIONS

1st Battalion

Lieut.-Col. A. E. Fyler	1	7 81[2]— 16 11 83
Colonel E. Leach, C.B.	17	11 83 — 22 12 85
Lieut.-Col. J. L. Tweedie, D.S.O.	23	12 85 — 22 12 89
Lieut.-Col. W. H. Bayly	23	12 89 — 22 12 92
Brevet-Col. T. H. Brock	23	12 92 — 22 12 98
Lieut.-Col. C. W. H. Evans, D.S.O.	23	12 98 — 20 3 00
Lieut.-Col. C. E. C. B. Harrison	21	3 00 — 20 3 04
Lieut.-Col. G. W. Maunsell	21	3 04 — 20 3 08
Lieut.-Col. R. C. Style	21	3 08 — 20 3 12
Lieut.-Col .A. Martyn	21	3 12 —

2nd Battalion

Colonel C. H. Browne	1	7 81[3]— 8 9 84
Lieut.-Col. D. J. D. Safford	9	9 84 — 30 6 87
Lieut.-Col. J. A. Murray	1	7 87 — 18 3 90
Lieut.-Col. C. E. Partridge	19	3 90 — 18 3 94
Lieut.-Col. J. C. Cautley	19	3 94 — 18 8 96
Brevet-Col. E A. W. S. Grove, C.B.	19	8 96 — 18 8 01
Brevet-Col. W. G. B. Western, C.B.	19	8 01 — 18 8 05
Brevet-Col. H. G. Fitton, D.S.O., A.D.C.	19	8 05 — 18 8 09
Lieut.-Col. N. H. S. Lowe	19	8 09 — 13 3 12
Lieut.-Col. S. H. Pedley	14	3 12 —

THE MILITIA AND SPECIAL RESERVE

Honorary Colonels

George Byng, Viscount Torrington	July 1, 1881[4]
H.R.H. The Duke of Connaught	Aug. 23 1884

[1] Maunsell rejoined from the Reserve on the outbreak of war.

[2] Fyler had commanded the unit since August 31, 1880, when it was known as The 50th Foot.

[3] Browne had commanded the unit since September 9, 1879, when it was known as The 97th Foot. He became a colonel in December 1882.

[4] Viscount Torrington had been Honorary Colonel of the West Kent Light Infantry Militia since May 1869

COMMANDING OFFICERS

3rd Battalion (Militia)

Lieut.-Col. Cmdt. M. D. Treherne	1 7 81[1]—	13 4 89
Lieut.-Col. Cmdt. (Hon. Col.) E. E. Larking	4 5 89 —	30 12 91
Lieut.-Col. Cmdt. (Hon. Col.) E. T. Luck	9 1 92 —	31 3 94

(On April 1, 1894, the six companies of the 4th Battalion (Militia) were posted in. Thereafter the battalion comprised 12 companies).

Lieut-Col. Cmdt. (Hon. Col.) E. T. Luck	1 4 94 —	20 5 96
Lieut.-Col. (Hon. Col.) J. Bonhote	30 5 96 —	29 5 01
Lieut.-Col. E. W. G. Bailey	30 5 01 —	30 5 06
Lieut.-Col. C. H. Farquharson	16 6 06 —	8 8 08

(On August 9, 1908, the bulk of the battalion transferred to the Special Reserve).

↓

3rd Battalion (Reserve)

Lieut.-Col. C. H. Farquharson	9 8 08 —	2 9 10
Lt.-Col. Sir A. S. T. Griffith-Boscawen, Knt., M.P.	3 9 10 —	

4th Battalion (Militia)

Lieut.-Col. C. Larking	1 7 81[2]—	20 5 87
Lieut.-Col. (Hon. Col.) E. E. Larking	21 5 87 —	3 5 89
Lieut.-Col. (Hon. Col.) E. T. Luck	4 5 89 —	8 1 92
Lieut.-Col. (Hon. Col.) C. W. Hume	6 2 92 —	31 3 94

(Amalgamated with the 3rd Battalion (Militia) on April 1, 1894).

THE VOLUNTEERS AND TERRITORIALS

1st Volunteer Battalion

HONORARY COLONELS

Colonel Viscount Hardinge, V.D., A.D.C.	Nov. 14, 1891 till his death on Jul. 28, 1894
Colonel G. Henderson, V.D.	Dec. 19. 1902
Colonel C. S. Williams, V.D.	Dec. 20, 1906

COMMANDING OFFICERS

Colonel Viscount Hardinge, V.D., A.D.C.	1 2 83[3]—	13 11 91
Lieut.-Col. (Hon. Col.) G. Henderson, V.D.	19 12 91 —	18 12 02

[1] Treherne had commanded the unit since March 1877, when it was known as the 1st Bn. West Kent Light Infantry Militia.

[2] C. Larking had commanded the unit since March 1877, when it was known as the 2nd Bn. West Kent Light Infantry Militia.

[3] Viscount Hardinge had commanded the unit since July 1860, when it was known as the 2nd Administrative Battalion Kent Rifle Volunteers.

ROLL OF COLONELS   155

Lieut.-Col. (Hon. Col.) C. S. Williams, V.D.   19 12 02 — 18 12 06
Lieut.-Col. (Hon. Col.) A. T. F. Simpson, V.D.   19 12 06 — 31 3 08
   (On April 1, 1908, this unit became the 4th (Territorial) Battalion
The Queen's Own).

↓

4th Battalion (T.F.)

HONORARY COLONEL

Colonel C. S. Williams, V.D.   Apr. 1, 1908

COMMANDING OFFICERS

Lieut.-Col. (Hon. Col.) A. T. F. Simpson, V.D.   1 4 08 — 19 12 10
Lieut.-Col. C. N. Watney, T.D.   4 1 11 —

2nd Volunteer Battalion

HONORARY COLONELS

Colonel E. H. Lenon, V.C.   Dec. 15, 1883
                                                       till Aug., 1886
Captain Sir I. H. Benn, Bt., C.B., D.S.O.[1]   May 26, 1906

COMMANDING OFFICERS

Lieut.-Col. E. H. Lenon, V.C.   1 2 83[2]— 14 12 83
Lieut.-Col. Cmdt. (Hon. Col.) W. H. Bristow, V.D. 15 12 83 — 23 5 96
Lt.-Col.-Cmdt. (Hon. Col.) E. Satterthwaite, V.D. 17 6 96 — 26 4 06
Lt.-Col. Cmdt. (Hon. Col.) E. J. Heward, V.D.   27 4 06 — 31 3 08
   (On April 1, 1908, part of this unit became the nucleus of the
5th (Territorial) Battalion The Queen's Own. The remainder became
the right half of the 20th Battalion The London Regiment).

5th Battalion (T.F.)

COMMANDING OFFICERS

Lieut.-Col. (Hon. Col.) A. S. Daniell, V.D.[3]   1 4 08 — 24 5 12
Lieut.-Col. H. M. Twynam, D.S.O.[4]   25 5 12 — 8 4 13
Lieut.-Col. F. A. Frazer   9 4 13 —

   [1] Sir Ion Benn was a captain in the R.N.V.R.
   [2] Lenon had commanded the unit since November 1871, when it was the
1st Administrative Battalion Kent Rifle Volunteers.
   [3] Daniell had commanded the 4th (West London) Volunteer Battalion The
King's Royal Rifle Corps from 1898 till 1905. He was a member of the Surrey
Territorial Association.
   [4] Twynam had been a Regular officer in The East Lancashire Regiment.

3rd Volunteer Battalion

HONORARY COLONEL

Lieutenant-General Sir J. M. Adye, G.C.B.   Feb. 1, 1883[1] till Aug., 1900

COMMANDING OFFICERS

Lieut.-Col. (Hon. Col.) J. D. C. Farrell, V.D.	1 2 83[2]— 26	9 93
Lieut.-Col. C. D. Davies, V.D	6 1 94 — 24	5 98
Lieut.-Col. W. Hunt, V.D.	25 5 98 — 15	3 01
Lieut.-Col. (Hon. Col.) E. J. Moore, V.D.	16 3 01 — 31	3 08

(On April 1, 1908, this unit became the headquarters and left half of the 20th Battalion The London Regiment).

20th (County of London) Battalion The London Regiment
(Blackheath and Woolwich)

HONORARY COLONEL

Captain Sir I. H. Benn, Bt., C.B., D.S.O.   Apr. 1, 1908

COMMANDING OFFICERS

Lieut.-Col. (Hon. Col.) E. J. Moore, V.D.	1 4 08 — 7	4 11
Lieut.-Col. H. A. Christmas	8 4 11 —	

4th Volunteer Battalion

HONORARY COLONEL

The Earl of Darnley   Jul. 16, 1902

COMMANDING OFFICERS

Lieut.-Col. C. James	17 5 00 — 31	1 02
Lieut.-Col. F. A. Newington	1 2 02 — 10	10 03
Lieut.-Col. R. J. Passby	11 10 03 — 31	3 08

(Disbanded on March 31, 1908)

---

[1] General Adye had been Honorary Colonel of the unit since May 1870, when it was known as the 26th Kent Rifle Volunteer Corps.

[2] Farrell had commanded the unit since March 1880, when it was known as the 4th Kent Volunteer Corps.

APPENDIX C

LISTS OF OFFICERS IN CAMPAIGNS

WITH 1st BATTALION, EGYPT, 1882

Comd. Offr.	Lieut.-Colonel	A. E. Fyler
2nd-in-Command	Lieut.-Colonel	R. H. P. Doran
	Bt.-Lieut.-Colonel	E. Leach
Comd. B Coy.	Major	W. H. Bayly
	Captain	J. C. Cautley
Adjutant	Captain	M. Wynyard
Comd. A Coy.	Captain	E. H. Carr
	Captain	H. Cummings
	Captain	E. B. L. Bevan
Comd. D Coy.	Captain	H. D. Armstrong
Comd. E Coy.	Captain	J. W. Jones
	Lieutenant	H. W. Ozanne
	Lieutenant	C. W. H. Evans
	Lieutenant	F. A. M. Arnold
	Lieutenant	C. E. C. B. Harrison
Transport Offr.	Lieutenant	A. T. Morse
	Lieutenant	O. J. Daniell
	Lieutenant	G. W. Maunsell
	Lieutenant	L. Brock-Hollinshead
With M.I.	Lieutenant	E. A. H. Alderson
	Lieutenant	W. E. Rowe
	Lieutenant	F. Wintour
	Lieutenant	C. H. M. Arrowsmith
	Lieutenant	T. A. G. Sangster
	Lieutenant	A. Pressey
	Lieutenant	W. R. Minchin
Quartermaster	Hon. Lieutenant	R. J. Roche
Paymaster	Hon. Captain	J. H. Vander-Meulen
Medical Officer	Surgeon-Major	W. Alexander

WITH 1st BATTALION, SUDAN, 1884-86
Left Cairo With The Battalion

Comd. Offr.	Colonel	E. Leach
2nd-in-Command	Lieutenant-Colonel	J. L. Tweedie
Comd. B Coy.	Major	W. H. Bayly
Comd. C Coy.	Major	E. J. Robinson
Comd. A Coy.	Major	E. H. Carr
Comd. D Coy.	Captain	H. D. Armstrong
Comd. E Coy.	Captain	J. W. Jones
Comd. G Coy.	Captain	C. W. H. Evans

158   THE QUEEN'S OWN ROYAL WEST KENT REGIMENT

Comd. H Coy.	Captain	A. L. Birch
	Lieutenant	W. G. B. Western
Comd. F Coy.	Lieutenant	L. Brock-Hollinshead
	Lieutenant	W. E. Rowe
Adjutant	Lieutenant	F. Wintour
	Lieutenant	T. A. G. Sangster
	Lieutenant	W. R. Minchin
	Lieutenant	H. Mann
	Lieutenant	J. P. Dalison
	Lieutenant	J. M. Maxwell
	Lieutenant	A. J. Anderson
	Lieutenant	K. H. Eddis
Quartermaster	Hon. Lieutenant	R. J. Roche
Paymaster	Hon. Captain	R. R. B. Ternan
Medical Officer	Surgeon-Major	G. Laffan

Joined at Korti, Feb., 1885

Lieutenant	E. M. Williams
Lieutenant	J. H. Kennedy

Joined at Wadi Halfa, Aug.-Dec., 1885

Major	D. T. C. Belgrave
Captain	G. W. Maunsell
Lieutenant	W. R. N. Annesley
Lieutenant	A. G. Eckford
Lieutenant	F. Hodges
Lieutenant	E. C. H. Beldam
Lieutenant	A. Wood Martyn
Lieutenant	R. C. Style
Lieutenant	H. E. C. B. Nepean
Lieutenant	E. V. O. Hewett

WITH 1st BATTALION, PUNJAB FRONTIER, 1897-98
Left Peshawar With The Battalion

Acting Comd. Offr.	Major	C. W. H. Evans
Comd. C Coy.	Captain	J. P. Dalison
Bde. Signal Offr.	Captain	E. V. O. Hewett
Adjutant	Lieutenant	C. G. Pack-Beresford
	Lieutenant	H. Isacke
	Lieutenant	R. B. Hope
	Lieutenant	W. C. Browne-Clayton
	2nd Lieutenant	V. E. Muspratt
	2nd Lieutenant	W. S. Leslie
	2nd Lieutenant	F. A. Jackson

Rejoined at Amandarra, Aug., 1897

	Captain	S. H. Pedley
Transport Offr.	Lieutenant	O. B. Simpson
Acting Paymaster	Lieutenant	J. Golding
	Lieutenant	T. P. C. Smith
	Lieutenant	P. M. Robinson
	Lieutenant	P. Hastings
Quartermaster	Hon. Captain	A. E. Mansfield

Rejoined at the Malakand, Sep., 1897

2nd-in-Command	Major	W. G. B. Western
Comd. A Coy.	Captain	R. C. Style
	Captain	N. H. S. Lowe
	Captain	F. H. Hotham
	Captain	E. F. Venables
Signal Offr.	Lieutenant	J. W. O'Dowda
	Lieutenant	H. S. Bush
	Lieutenant	T. R. C. Price

Joined on First Appointment at Kunda, Dec., 1897

2nd Lieutenant   L. H. Hickson

WITH 2nd BATTALION, SOUTH AFRICA, 1900-02
Embarked With The Battalion

Comd. Offr.	Lieut.-Colonel	E. A. W. S. Grove
2nd-in-Command	Major	O. E. C. B. Harrison
Adjutant	Captain	M. P. Buckle
Quartermaster	Hon. Lieut.	J. Couch
R.S.M.	Sgt.-Major	W. E. Turner
R.Q.M.S.	Q.M.-Sgt.	G. Barnes
Ord. Rm. Sgt.	Q.M.-Sgt.	J. R. Wood

A Company

Coy. Comd.	Captain	A. Montgomery-Campbell
	2nd Lieut.	G. Elgood
	2nd Lieut.	J. H. Bennett
Col.-Sgt.	Col.-Sgt.	A. Thorne

M.I. Company

Coy. Comd.	Captain	R. J. Woulfe-Flanagan
	Lieutenant	T. H. C. Nunn
	Lieutenant	C. Bonham-Carter
	Lieutenant	G. D. Lister
Col.-Sgt.	Col.-Sgt.	B. H. Grellier

C Company

Coy. Comd.	Captain	H. L. C. Moody
	2nd Lieut.	J. T. Twisleton-Wykeham-Fiennes
Col.-Sgt.	Col.-Sgt.	R. W. Silver

D Company

Coy. Comd.	Captain	J. P. Dalison
I/c. Maxim Gun	Lieutenant	R. M. G. Tulloch
	2nd Lieut.	K. D. Henderson
Col.-Sgt.	Col.-Sgt.	E. J. A. Bullock

E Company

Coy. Comd.	Major	L. Brock-Hollinshead
	Lieutenant	C. C. Mulloy
	2nd Lieut.	T. E. Hulbert
Col.-Sgt.	Col.-Sgt.	L. F. A. Redderson

F Company

Coy. Comd.	Captain	A. Martyn
	Lieutenant	F. J. Joslin
Col.-Sgt.	Col.-Sgt.	A. G. Wood

G Company

Coy. Comd.	Major	G. W. Maunsell
	2nd Lieut.	E. D. Luard
	2nd Lieut.	A. K. Grant
Col.-Sgt.	Col.-Sgt.	J. H. Outten

H Company

Coy. Comd.	Captain	N. H. S. Lowe
	Lieutenant	H. Isacke
	Lieutenant	C. Druce
Col.-Sgt.	Col.-Sgt.	H. Evans

Joined in South Africa

Rank	Name	Place	Date
Captain	¹G. Morphew	Hammonia	9 Jun. 1900
Lieutenant	¹C. N. Watney	Hammonia	9 Jun. 1900
Lieutenant	¹W. G. Morris	Hammonia	9 Jun. 1900
Lieutenant	¹C. S. Marchant	Ficksburg	6 Jul. 1900
Major	W. G. B. Western	Vrede	3 Sep. 1900
Captain	C. G. Pack-Beresford	Vrede	3 Sep. 1900
Lieutenant	C. E. Kitson	Bethlehem	25 Sep. 1900
Captain	²B. H. Latter	Heilbron	23 May 1901
Lieutenant	²C. Holcroft	Heilbron	23 May 1901
Captain	E. F. Venables	Frankfort	16 Jan. 1902
Lieutenant	³J. Sawers	Frankfort	5 Apr. 1902
Lieutenant	P. S. Hall	Frankfort	23 Apr. 1902
Captain	J. Lees	Heilbron	3 Aug. 1902

Joined on First Appointment

Rank	Name	Place	Date
2nd Lieut.	⁴H. D. Belgrave	Ficksburg	6 Jul. 1900
2nd Lieut.	⁴E. H. Norman	Bethlehem	25 Sep. 1900
2nd Lieut.	W. B. P. Tugwell	Heilbron	18 Mar. 1901
2nd Lieut.	⁴A. H. Pullman	Heilbron	25 Apr. 1901
2nd Lieut.	B. Johnstone	Vereeniging	24 Jul. 1901
2nd Lieut.	⁴G. S. T. Fenning	Heilbron	1 Nov. 1901
2nd Lieut.	A. Lowry-Corry	Frankfort	11 Jan. 1902
2nd Lieut.	J. F. S. Tulloh	Frankfort	5 Feb. 1902
2nd Lieut.	M. J. Dinwiddy	Frankfort	5 Feb. 1902
2nd Lieut.	A. S. Hewitt	Frankfort	13 Mar. 1902
2nd Lieut.	F. C. Beamish	Nr. Hoopstad	20 Mar. 1902
2nd Lieut.	C. E. de St. C. Stevenson	Frankfort	7 Apr. 1902
2nd Lieut.	O. Y. Hibbert	Frankfort	15 Apr. 1902
2nd Lieut.	⁴C. W. Case-Morris	Frankfort	20 May 1902

1 1st Volunteer Active Service Company.

2 2nd Vclunteer Active Service Company.

3 3rd Volunteer Active Service Company.

4 From the 3rd Battalion (Militia).

APPENDIX CC

OFFICERS WITH 3rd BATTALION IN MALTA

1900—1901

EMBARKED WITH THE BATTALION

Colonel	J. Bonhote
Lieutenant-Colonel	E. W. G. Bailey
Major	C. H. Farquharson
Captain	J. H. Kennedy
Captain	E. Fleming
Captain	A. J. P. Annesley
Captain	F. W. Burbury
Captain	G. Wilson
Captain	A. S. T. Griffith-Boscawen
Captain	H. Neve
Captain	A. C. Pine
Lieutenant	R. W. Grant
Lieutenant	C. D. Barrow
Lieutenant	E. M. A. Wakefield
2nd-Lieutenant	E. C. Norman
2nd-Lieutenant	E. P. Mainwaring-White
2nd-Lieutenant	A. K. Grant
2nd-Lieutenant	A. H. Hooper
2nd-Lieutenant	W. D. O'Brien
2nd-Lieutenant	E. H. Norman
2nd-Lieutenant	J. Bazley-White
2nd-Lieutenant	H. D. Belgrave
2nd-Lieutenant	A. C. Beeman
2nd-Lieutenant	K. L. Cameron
2nd-Lieutenant	A. Blair
2nd-Lieutenant	A. H. Pullman
2nd-Lieutenant	S. S. Hayne
Captain and Adjutant	E. F. Venables
Captain and Q.M.	E. W. Brown

JOINED IN MALTA

Captain	A. C. Edwards
Lieutenant	G. S. T. Fenning
2nd-Lieutenant	H. T. Thornhill

JOINED IN MALTA ON FIRST APPOINTMENT

2nd-Lieutenant	A. P. Stone
2nd-Lieutenant	C. M. Allfrey
2nd-Lieutenant	C. W. Case-Morris
2nd-Lieutenant	A. I. Irons
2nd-Lieutenant	A. C. K. T. Clarke
2nd-Lieutenant	H. A. Waring

―――― APPENDIX D ――――

HONOURS AND AWARDS
1881—1913

EGYPT, 1882

THE DISTINQUISHED CONDUCT MEDAL

Saddler, M., Quartermaster-Sergeant

BREVET PROMOTION

Grove, E. A. W. S.   Captain to Brevet-Major

TURKISH DECORATIONS

Carr, E. H., Captain	—	4th Class Medjidie
Fyler, A. E., Lieut.-Colonel	—	3rd Class Medjidie
Johnson, F. F., Lieutenant	—	4th Class Medjidie
Leach, E., Bt.-Lieut.-Col.	—	4th Class Osmanieh
Maunsell, G. W., Lieutenant	—	5th Class Medjidie

THE NILE EXPEDITION, 1884-85

COMPANION OF THE ORDER OF THE BATH

Leach, E., Colonel

BREVET PROMOTIONS

Armstrong, H. D.   Captain to Brevet-Major
Wintour, F.   Captain to Brevet-Major

OPERATIONS SOUTH OF WADI HALFA, 1885-86

THE DISTINGUISHED SERVICE ORDER

Annesley, W. R. N.   Lieutenant
Tweedie, J. L.   Lieutenant-Colonel

The Distinguished Conduct Medal

Harridine, R.	Private
Ralph, T.	Private
Simpkins, H.	Private

Mentioned In Despatches

Martyn, A. Wood	Lieutenant

1886 — 1897

Companion Of The Order Of The Bath

Browne, C. H. (May 1886)	Colonel

Brevet Promotions

Alderson E. A. H.   Major to Brevet-Lieutenant-Colonel
(For service with the Mounted Infantry in Matabeleland, 1896-1897).
Brock, T. H.   Lieutenant-Colonel to Brevet-Colonel
(Dec. 23, 1896. After four years in command)

PUNJAB FRONTIER, 1897-98

The Distinguished Service Order

Evans, C. W. H.	Major

The Distinguished Conduct Medal

Collins, C.	Private
McGee, J.	Lance-Corporal
Willis, W. J.	Colour-Sergeant

Mentioned In Despatches

Evans, C. W. H.	Major
Hewett, E. V. O.	Captain
Jackson, F. A.	2nd-Lieutenant
Western, W. G. B.	Major

SUDAN CAMPAIGN, 1898

The Distinguished Conduct Medal

Sheppard, H.	Colour-Sergeant

SOUTH AFRICA, 1900 — 1902

Companion Of The Order Of The Bath

Alderson, E. A. H.	Brevet-Lieutenant-Colonel
Grove, E. A. W. S.	Brevet-Colonel
Western, W. G. B.	Lieutenant-Colonel

The Distinquished Service Order

Buckle, M. P.	Captain
Nunn, T. H. C.	Captain

The Distinquished Conduct Medal

Bullock, E. J. A.	Colour-Sergeant
Dorrell, T. C.	Corporal
Grellier, B. H.	Colour-Sergeant
Grey, F.	Colour-Sergeant
Humphreys, E. F.	Lance-Corporal
Huntley, G. J.	Lance-Corporal
Jupp, F. W.	Private
Redderson, L. F. A.	Colour-Sergeant
Wood, A. G.	Colour-Sergeant

Brevet Promotions

Alderson, E. A. H.	Brevet-Lieutenant-Colonel to Brevet-Colonel
Grove, E. A. W. S.	Lieutenant-Colonel to Brevet-Colonel
Isacke, H.	Captain and Adjutant to Brevet-Major
Marsh, F. C.	Captain to Brevet-Major
Martyn, A.	Captain to Brevet-Major
Western, W. G. B.	Major to Brevet-Lieutenant-Colonel
Wintour, F.	Major to Brevet-Lieutenent-Colonel

Promotions

Bowman, J.	Private to Corporal
Couch, J.	Hon. Lieutenant to Hon. Captain
Dorrell, T. C.	Corporal to Sergeant

Mentioned In Despatches

Twice

Croucher, F. W.	Sergeant
Isacke, H.	Lieutenant
Western, W. G. B.	Major

Once

Alderson, E. A. H.	Brevet-Lieutenant-Colonel
Allen, J.	Private
Bowman, J.	Lance-Sergeant
Boxell, E.	Lance-Sergeant
Buckle, M. P.	Captain
Couch, J.	Hon. Lieutenant
Druce, C.	Lieutenant

French, G. R.	Lance-Corporal
George, J.	Private
Grant, A. K.	Lieutenant
Grey, F.	Colour-Sergeant
Hanlon, J.	Sergeant
Harrison, C. E. C. B.	Lieutenant-Colonel
Hickson, L. H.	Lieutenant
Hughes, G.	Private
James, E. L. H.	Lieutenant
Joslin, F. J.	Lieutenant
Marsh, F. C.	Captain
Martyn, A.	Captain
Maunsell, G. W.	Major
Mitchell, C. B.	Sergeant-Major
Nunn, T. H. C.	Lieutenant
Outten, J. H.	Colour-Sergeant
Pack-Beresford, C. G.	Captain
Sheppard, H.	Sergeant, D.C.M.
Silver, R. W.	Colour-Sergeant
Taylor, G.	Sergeant
Thorne, R.	Sergeant
Wood, A. G.	Colour-Sergeant
Woulfe-Flanagan, R. J.	Captain

BROUGHT TO NOTICE OF G.O.C.

Barden, G. W.	Sergeant
Bishop, H.	Private
Bond, W.	Private
Court, R.	Sergeant
Crisp, J.	Private
Dadd, W.	Corporal
Guest, E.	Corporal
Grellier, B. H.	Colour-Sergeant
Styles, G.	Private
Thorne, A.	Colour-Sergeant

1903 — 1913

KNIGHT COMMANDER OF THE ORDER OF THE BATH

Burton, Fowler (June 1903)	General, C.B.
Leach, E. (June 1907)	Major-General, C.B.

THE HONOUR OF KNIGHTHOOD

Griffith-Boscawen, A. S. T.   Lieutenant-Colonel, M.P.
(Coronation Honours List, June 1911)

Companion Of The Order Of The Bath

Fitton, H. G.   Brevet-Colonel, D.S.O., A.D.C.
(Coronation Honours List, June 1911)

Companion Of St. Michael And St. George

Robinson, P. M.   Major
(For service with the West African Frontier Force, 1912)

Brevet Promotions

Fitton, H. G., D.S.O.   Lieutenant-Colonel to Brevet-Colonel
(14th February, 1907)

Western, W. G. B., C.B.   Lieutenant-Colonel to Brevet-Colonel
(9th April, 1904)

Gold Liakat Of Macedonia

Martyn, A.   Major
(For service with the Macedonian Gendarmerie, 1908)

Mentioned In Despatches

Twice

Robinson, P. M.   Captain
(For service with the West African Frontier Force, 1903 and 1906)

MISCELLANEOUS

4th Class Osmanieh

Montgomery-Campbell, A   Captain
(For service with the Egyptian Army, Sudan, 1888)

Mentioned in Despatches

Marsh, F. C.   Lieutenant
(For service in West Africa, 1897)

Wintour, F.   Brevet-Major
(For service with the Tochi Field Force, 1897)

APPENDIX E

PRESENTATION OF COLOURS TO THE 20th (COUNTY OF LONDON) BATTALION THE LONDON REGIMENT (BLACKHEATH AND WOOLWICH)

A FUND to provide Colours for the 20th (County of London) Battalion The London Regiment (Blackheath and Woolwich) was opened by Mr. Alfred Dent, of Lee Park, Blackheath, in May 1909. The Colours were not presented before the start of the Great War of 1914-18 because the battalion did not attain 75 per cent. of its establishment.

During the 1914-18 War the 20th London expanded to three battalions. The 1/20th went to France and took part in many of the great battles. The 2/20th also went overseas and fought in Palestine. The 3/20th remained in England as a draft-finding unit for the other two battalions.

The Colours were presented by Major-General Sir William Thwaites, Director of Military Intelligence, on the Ranger's Field in Greenwich Park on Saturday, June 28, 1919. They were consecrated by the Bishop of Woolwich. Lieutenant Hallett received the King's Colour, and Lieutenant Andrews the Regimental. The parade was commanded by Brigadier-General A. B. Hubback, C.M.G., D.S.O., a former officer of the 20th London. After the Colours had been presented, the troops marched past to "A Hundred Pipers" and returned to Holly Hedge House, Blackheath, their headquarters. Emblazoned on the Regimental Colour was the Battle Honour "South Africa, 1900-02."

* * *

A King's Colour was presented to the 2/20th by His Royal Highness Prince Albert (later King George VI) at Holly Hedge House on April 10, 1920. At the same ceremony the Prince unveiled a Memorial to those of the 20th London who had fallen during the Great War. Lieutenant-Colonel E. Ball was in command of the parade. The Colour was consecrated by the Bishop of Woolwich and was received by 2nd-Lieutenant Batty. This Colour now hangs in St. Mary's Church, Lewisham.

APPENDIX F

ERRATA IN OTHER WORKS CONCERNING THE HISTORY OF THE REGIMENT

A Short Record of The Colours

Page 21—The 1880-1891 Colours of The 97th were carried until 23rd June, 1891; NOT 25th June, 1891.

Page 27—The 1891-1931 Colours of the 2nd Battalion were presented on 23rd June, 1891; NOT 25th June, 1891.

Page 28—Colours were presented to the 4th and 5th Battalions (T.F.) on 19th June, 1909; NOT in 1908.

A Short Account of the Origins, Service and Campaigns, 1756-1956

Page 6—The Sutlej Campaign. 1st para. Delete " Private Hale."

Page 7—The Sutlej Campaign. 2nd para. For " Sergeant-Major Cantwell " put " Private L. Hale."

Page 10 The Indian Mutiny. 2nd para. For " the Residency " put " the Alam Bagh."

Page 14—2nd Battalion. 1st para. For " June 25th " put " June 23rd."

Page 15—The War in South Africa. 3rd para. For " May 28th " put " May 29th."

Page 23—Afghanistan. For " May 26th " put " May 27th."

Page 24—20th London. 2nd para. For "April 20th " put "April 10th."

The Queen's Own Royal West Kent Regiment, 1920-1950

Page 52—1st para. For the last sentence substitute : " This was the start of The Queen's Own Tent Club."

Page 61—Last para. For the first sentence substitute : " In 1922 the custom began of laying a wreath at the foot of Nelson's Column in London on October 21 each year, in memory of the period in 1794 when The 50th Regiment served with Nelson in Corsica."

Page 62—3rd para. For " In July, 1928 " put " On July 21, 1929."

Page 68—Last para. For " In July " put " On July 19."

Page 111—Last para. 1st line. For " in May " put " on May 17."

Page 422—1st Para. 11th line. For " 3rd Battalion West Kent Rifle Volunteers " put " 3rd (West Kent) Volunteer Corps."

Page 422—1st para. 12th line. For " the autumn of 1881 " put " February, 1883."

Page 422—3rd para. 5th line. For " headquarter companies " put " whole."

Page 429—27th line. For " May 24, 1940 " put " July 26, 1940."

Page 437—16th line. For " 1882 " put " 1884."

Page 478 4th Battalion, Burma. Put " (Gen. List) " after " J. C. Breaden."

INDEX OF PERSONS

Abercrombie, Sir R., Gen., 2
Adams, J., Sgt., 25, 141
Ahmed, M. (The Mahdi), 30, 35, 37, 39
Ailwood, F., Cpl., 47; Sgt., 70
Albert, H.R.H. Prince of Wales (later King Edward VII), 45, 67, 72, 97, 103, 104, 107, 108, 112, 113, 118, 126, 138
Albert, H.R.H., Prince (later King George VI), 167
Alderson, E. A. H., Lieut., 14, 15, 25, 28, 31, 34-36, 41, 48, 157; Capt., 49; Maj., 163; Brev.-Lieut.-Col., 76, 85, 164; C.B., 163; Brev.-Col., 164; Brig.-Gen., 98.
Alexandra, H.M. Queen, 108, 116, 126, 129
Alison, Sir A., Lieut.-Gen., 28
Allenby, E. H. H., Maj., 94
Anderson, A. J., Lieut., 37, 141, 158
Andrews, G., L/Cpl., 117, 135
Andrews, W., Pte., 81
Andrews, W. T., Lieut., 167
Annesley, W. R. N., Lieut., 39, 158, 162
Arabi, Col., 20, 21, 25-28, 30
Ardrey, H., Pte., 81
Arisugawa, Prince, 121
Armstrong, H. D., Capt., 25, 157 (twice), 162
Ashby, G., Sgt., 62
Ashby, J., Pte., 86, 145
Baker, A., Pte., 117; L/Cpl., 113, 118; Cpl., 128, 131; L/Sgt., 128, 132, 133
Bailey, E. W. G., Lieut.-Col., 108, 154, 161
Baines, E. H., Lieut., 18
Balding, J., Sgt., 91
Ball, E., Lieut.-Col., 167
Ball, H., Pte., 101
Ball, J., Mus., 51
Barden, G. W., Sgt., 91, 165
Barnes, A., Pte., 85
Barnes, D. R., Brev.-Col., 12, 152
Barnes, F., Pte., 135
Barnes, G., Q-M.-Sgt., 76, 159
Barnes, H., Pte., 111, 145
Barton, S. J., Sgt.-Maj., 57

Bass, W. E., Sgt., 44, 51
Batty, J., 2/Lieut., 167
Bayly, W. H., Maj., 25, 28, 33, 38, 157 (twice); Lieut.-Col., 18, 45-47, 153; Col., 152
Beale, F. G., Sgt.-Maj., 49
Beamish, F. C., 2/Lieut., 100, 160
Belgrave, H. D., 2/Lieut., 88, 160, 161
Bennett, J. H., 2/Lieut., 98, 159
Benson, G. E., Lieut.-Col., 93, 94
Berry, F., Drm., 62, 144
Biddulph, Sir R., Maj.-Gen., 29
Binder, B., Pte., 100
Birch, A. L., Capt., 37, 141, 158
Bishop, H., Pte., 81, 165
Blood, Sir B., Maj.-Gen., 57-59, 62, 63
Bond, W., Pte., 81, 101, 145, 165
Bonham-Carter, B. H., 2/Lieut., 126
Bonham-Carter, C., Lieut., 73, 78, 79, 92, 98-100, 159
Bonhote, J., Lieut.-Col. (Hon. Col.), 105-107, 154, 161
Botha, L., Cmdt.-Gen., 92, 93, 99
Botha, P., Cmdt., 99
Bowman, J., Pte. (later L/Sgt.), 99, 164 (twice).
Boyes, J. E., Maj.-Gen., 77-79, 81, 82
Brabant, E. Y., Brig.-Gen., 81
Bright, R., Pte., 62
Briselden, C. G., Pte., 135
Brock, R. G. C., Lieut., 126
Brock, T. H., Lieut., 11; Maj., 18; Lieut.-Col., 47, 48, 57, 59, 163; Brev.-Col., 65, 153; Col., 110, 111, 113, 114, 124, 152
Brock-Hollinshead, L., Lieut., 157, 158; Maj., 76, 92-94, 97, 98, 104, 115, 159
Brooks, W., Pte., 78
Brown, E. W., Hon. Capt., 102, 161
Brown, D., Pte., 135
Browne, C. H., Lieut.-Col., 14; Col., 15, 153; C.B., 163
Browne-Clayton, W. C., Lieut., 61, 62, 144, 158
Buckland, H., Pte., 62

INDEX OF PERSONS 171

Buckle, M. P., Capt., 76, 78, 79, 82, 92, 159, 164; D.S.O., 164
Bucklow, W., L/Cpl., 91
Buller, Sir R. H., Maj.-Gen., V.C., 35, 36; Gen., 75
Bullock, E. J. A., Col.-Sgt., 81, 159, 164
Bunbury, V. T., Col., 139
Burbury, F. W., Lieut., 44, 51; Capt., 161
Burton, F., Hon. Gen., C.B., 43; K.C.B., 111, 113, 152, 165
Butler, W. F., Brig.-Gen., 39
Byng, G., Viscount Torrington, 16, 153

Cairns, R., Pte., 81
Cali, Professor, 117
Camber, W., Cpl., 32, 141
Cambridge, H.R.H. Duke of, Fd.-Marshal, 9, 13, 14, 46, 49, 53
Camden, Marchioness, 129, 136
Camden, Marquess, 129, 136, 139
Campbell, B. B. D., Maj.-Gen., 80, 81
Campbell, Sir C., Gen. (later Fd.-Marshal Lord Clyde), 4
Campbell, W. P., Maj.-Gen., 132
Canterbury, Archbishop of, 49
Canty, W., Sgt., 87, 145
Capper, T., Brig.-Gen., 132
Cardwell, Lord, 1
Carpenter, C., Pte., 25, 141
Carr, E. H., Capt., 24, 25, 27, 157, 162; Maj., 35, 36, 41, 141, 157
Cautley, J. C., Capt., 14, 157; Lieut.-Col., 51, 52, 153
Chads, W. J., Col., C.B., 12, 152
Chapman, T., Pte., 87
Childs, H., Sgt., 135
Clarence, Duke of (later King William IV), 3
Clarke, Sir C. M., Gen., 116, 117
Clarke, J., Pte., 87, 145
Clarke, Pte. (1st Bn.), 70
Clipsham, P., Pte., 62
Clive, Lord, 64
Colborne, The Hon. Sir F., Gen., K.C.B., 11, 152
Coleman, J., Sgt., V.C., 4
Collins, J., Pte., 25, 142
Congleton, H., Maj.-Gen. Lord, 106
Connaught, H.R.H. Prince Arthur, Duke of, Maj.-Gen. (later Fd.-Marshal), 13, 16, 21, 53, 105, 116, 122, 136, 153
Conway, C., Pte., 101, 146
Cook, Thomas and Son, 31, 32
Cornwall and York, H.R.H. Duke of, (later King George V), 52, 67, 68, 107, 127, 130, 131, 135
Corrick, G., L/Cpl., 107
Cotterell, M., Pte., 25, 142
Couch, J., Hon. Lieut. (later Hon. Capt.), 76, 94, 159, 164 (twice)
Cowlard, S., Pte., 107, 146
Cox and King, Agents, 14
Craig, S. E., Lieut., 86
Cranbrook, Earl of, 139

Creasey, H. E., Pte., 111, 146
Crisp, J., Pte., 81, 165
Crowther, J., Cmdt., 84
Cuthbert, G. J., Brig.-Gen., 132

Dalison, J. P., Lieut., 158; Capt., 76, 158, 159
Daniell, O. J., Lieut., 157; Maj., 104
Darley, R., Pte., 117; L/Cpl., 113, 118; Cpl., 128, 131; L/Sgt., 132
Davis, C., Pte., 25, 142
Davies, W. C., L/Cpl., 95
Dawson, W., Q-M.-Sgt., 21, 32
De la Rey, Cmdt., 100
De Lisle, H. de B., Lieut.-Col., 94
Dent, A., Mr., 167
De Villiers, A. J., Cmdt., 81
De Wet, Christian, Cmdt., 75, 83, 95, 96, 99, 101
Dickinson, Messrs., 43
Dix, D., Pte., 93
Doran, R. H. P., Lieut.-Col., 21, 23, 28-30, 157
Dorrell, T. C., Cpl. (later Sgt.), 81, 164; D.C.M., 164
Doyle, W. S., Lieut., 49
Dunne, J. H., Maj.-Gen., 48
Dyke, E. F., Rev., 18, 49

Eccles, R. H., Lieut., 15
Edward VII (see Albert, H.R.H. Prince of Wales)
Edwards, W., Pte., 62
Egerton, Col., 105
Elgin, Earl of, 48
Elles, E. R., Maj.-Gen., 48
Emmerson, T., Pte., 87
Evans, C. W. H., Lieut., 157; Capt., 35, 36, 39, 157; Maj., 57, 59, 60, 64, 158, 163; D.S.O., 163; Lieut.-Col., 65-67, 153
Eveleigh, E., Sgt., 111, 146

Fergusson, Sir C., Maj.-Gen., 132
Ferrier, J. A., Capt. (R.E.), 39
Fitton, H. G., Lieut.-Col., D.S.O., 121, 166; Brev.-Col., 122, 133, 153; C.B., 166; Brig.-Gen., 133
Frankfort de Montmorency, R. H., Maj.-Gen., Viscount, 52
French, J. D. P., Lieut.-Gen., 77
Furber, H. A. de F., Lieut., 136
Fushimi, Prince, 118
Fyler, A. E., Lieut.-Col., 9, 13, 14, 21, 22, 24, 29, 153, 162; Hon. Col., 30

Garrard, F. N., Capt., 138
Garratt, F. S., Col., 92-95
Gassner, G., Bandmaster, 14, 29
George, III, H.M. King, 2
George, IV, H.M. King, 4
George V, H.M. King (see Cornwall and York)
Gordon, C. G., Maj.-Gen., 30, 31, 34, 35
Graham, G., Maj.-Gen., V.C., 21, 22
Grant, A. K., 2/Lieut., 98, 99, 159, 161; Lieut., 97, 100, 165; Capt., 117

Grellier, B. H., Col.-Sgt., 87, 159, 164, 165; Sgt.-Maj., D.C.M., 136
Grenfell, F. W., Brig-Gen., 38; Lieut.-Gen. Sir F., 72, 106, 107
Greville, The Hon. S., 126
Grierson, J. M., Lieut.-Gen., 130
Griffith-Boscawen, A. S. T., Capt., 161; Sir A., Lieut.-Col., Knt., M.P., 136, 137, 154, 165
Grove, E. A. W. S., Capt., 14, 28, 162; Maj., 32; Lieut.-Col., 52, 76-80, 82-84, 159, 164; Brev.-Col., 85-88; C.B., 91, 153, 163; Col., 111

Hadgkiss, J., Arm.-Sgt., 51
Haldane, R. B., Mr. (later Viscount), 113, 118, 124
Hale, L., Pte., 18
Hallett, H. W., Lieut., 167
Hamilton, B. M., Maj.-Gen., 87, 88
Hamilton, G. H. C., Brig.-Gen., 92-94
Hamilton, Sir I. S. M., Lieut.-Gen., 79, 101
Hammersley, F., Maj.-Gen., 130
Hardcastle, E. H., Rev., 126, 137
Hardinge, The Hon. Sir A. E., Gen., 45
Hardinge, C. S., Col. Viscount, V.D., 7, 45, 134, 154 (twice)
Hardinge, C., Lord, of Penshurst, 134, 135
Hardy, A. E., 2/Lieut., 126
Harold, H. E., Pte., 93
Harridine, R., Pte., 39, 163
Harris, J., Pte., 135
Harrison, C. E. C. B., Lieut., 14, 28, 157; Maj., 67, 76, 78, 80, 159; Lieut.-Col., 68, 69, 72, 80, 82, 115, 116, 153, 165
Harvest, E. D., Maj.-Gen., 42
Hastings, P., Lieut., 69, 70, 158
Hayman, H., Hon. Lieut., 110
Haysmore, T., Sgt., 47
Hayward, G., Pte., 25, 142
Helmer, F. A., Pte., 109, 111, 146
Henderson, K. D., 2/Lieut., 90, 159
Henson, F. J., Lieut., 138
Heward, E. J., Lieut.-Col., V.D., 125, 155
Hewett, E. V. O., Lieut., 158; Capt., 57, 63, 158, 163
Hibbert, J. T., Cpl., 43
Hicks, W., Col., 30, 34
Hickson, L. H., 2/Lieut., 159; Lieut., 76, 165
Hildyard, R. J. T., Lieut., 76
Hill, C. W., Col., 107
Hills, A. E., Lieut., 138
Hipkins, T., Pte., 87
Hitchins, C. F., Capt., 104
Holcroft, C., Lieut., 92, 109, 160
Holding, A., Pte., 128
Hole, Dean, 112
Howard, G., Sgt., 24, 142
Hoy, G., Pte., 70, 144
Hoye, J., Pte., 81
Hubback, A. B., Brig.-Gen., C.M.G., D.S.O., 167

Hudson, E. J., 2/Lieut., 69, 70, 76
Humphreys, E. F., L/Cpl., 81, 164
Hunt, G., Cpl., 11
Hunt, J., L/Cpl., 101
Hunter, Sir A., Lieut.-Gen., 83, 84
Hutson, T. C., Pte., 62, 144

Ingham, A. E., Bandmaster, 53, 103
Inglis, B., Sgt.-Drm., 53
Isacke, H., Lieut., 59, 62, 92, 102, 103, 158, 159, 164; Capt., 164

Jackson, F. A., 2/Lieut., 61, 158, 163
James, C., Lieut.-Col., 110, 156
James, E. L. H., Lieut., 76, 165
Jameson, J. H., Maj., 18
Jasper, A., Sgt., 91
Jeffreys, P. D., Brig.-Gen., 59, 60
Jipps, J., Pte., 62
Johnson, E., Cpl., 18
Johnson, F. F., Lieut., 28, 162
Johnson, T., Pte., 78
Johnstone, B., 2/Lieut., 92, 160
Jones, G., Pte., 62, 144
Jones, J. W., Capt., 25, 35, 157 (twice)
Jones, W., Cpl., 51
Joslin, F. J., Lieut., 91, 159
Joy, P., Canon, 111
Jupp, F. W., Pte., 89

Keeble, W. H., Sgt., 128
Keenlyside, G. F. H., 2/Lieut., 69
Kelly, C. H., Brev.-Col., 104
Kennedy, J. H., Lieut., 158; Capt., 161
Kent-Lemon, A. L., 2/Lieut., 127
Kew, G., Pte., 78, 147
Kill, S. J., Sgt., 69
Kirkpatrick, Civ.-Surgeon, 88
Kitchener, H. H., Gen., Lord, 88, 92, 96-99
Kitson, C. E., Lieut., 87, 88, 92, 93, 160
Kruger, President, 75

Langley, F., Pte., 86
Larkin, J., Mr., 132
Latter, B. H., Capt., 90-92, 109, 160
Latter, H., Pte., 81
Lattimer, E., Capt., 138
Leach, E., Brev.-Lieut.-Col., 23, 157, 162; Col., 30, 32, 35-37, 157, 162; C.B., 41, 43, 50, 153; Maj.-Gen., 44, 113, 117; K.C.B., 126, 127, 152, 165
Legard, G. B., Lieut., 130
Leir, B. H. F., Lieut., 122
Lister, G. D., Lieut., 88, 159
Lock, A. C. K., Lieut.-Col., 11
Locks, W., Sgt.-Maj., 21, 32
Long, W. H. B., Lieut., 76, 119
Lowe, N. H. S., Capt., 76, 84, 92, 97, 158, 159; Maj., 114, 153; Lieut.-Col., 134, 135, 153
Luard, E. D., 2/Lieut., 98, 159; Lieut., 90, 92, 149
Lucock, A. F., Pte., 111, 147
Lumley, C. H., Capt., V.C., 4

INDEX OF PERSONS 173

Maitland, P. J., Brig.-Gen., 70
Mann, H., Lieut., 35, 158
Manners, R. A., Col., 43, 152
Mansfield, A. E., Hon. Capt., 48, 57, 59, 158
Mansfield, G. S., Capt. (R.A.M.C.), 88
Marchant, C. S., Lieut., 109, 160
Marsh, F. C., Lieut., 76, 166; Capt., 164, 165; Brev.-Maj., 149
Marshall, G., Lieut., 47; Capt., 149
Martyn, A., 2/Lieut., 49; Capt., 76, 88, 159, 164, 165; Maj., 153, 166; Lieut.-Col., 132, 153
Martyn, A. Wood, Lieut., 40, 158, 163; Capt., 103; Maj., 124
Mary, H. M. Queen, 127, 135
Maunsell, G. W., Lieut., 14, 18, 27, 28, 157, 162; Capt., 39, 158; Maj., 76, 80, 82, 88, 92, 94, 122, 159, 165; Lieut.-Col., 116-118, 153; Col., 153
Maurice, Sir J. F., Maj.-Gen., 110
McCarthy, E., Pte., 135
McCracken, P. J. F., Lieut., 90, 109
McGee, J., L/Cpl., 61, 163
McGregor, J., Cpl. (later Sgt.), 44, 51
McGregor, W., Pte., 44, 51
McKelvey, T., Bandmaster, 119
Meagher, A., Pte., 62
Meiklejohn, W. H., Brig.-Gen., 57-59, 62, 64
Mentz, F., Cmdt., 96
Miles, G., Cpl., 34, 142
Minchin, W. R., Lieut., 35, 157, 158
Minto, Earl of, 134
Mitchell, C. B., S-I-of-M., 82; Sgt.-Maj., 165
Money, G. L. C., Brig.-Gen., 119
Montague, W., Sgt., 87, 147
Montgomery-Campbell, A., Capt., 76 159, 166
Moody, H. L. C., Lieut., 49; Capt., 76, 90, 92-94, 159
Moore, Sir J., Gen., 3
Moore, T., Rev., 18
Morphew, G., Capt., 108, 109, 160
Morris, G. E. W., 2/Lieut., 104; Lieut., 147
Morris, W. G., Lieut., 108, 160
Morrison, A., Pte., 25, 142
Morse, A. T., Lieut., 157; Capt., 31, 34, 36
Mott, G., Pte., 95, 147
Muir, W., Cpl., 95
Mukbil, Mohammed, 68-70
Mulloy, C. C., Lieut., 147, 159
Munday, J., Pte., 87, 147
Murray, G., Pte., 25, 143
Murray, J. A., Lieut.-Col., 48, 153
Nathan, Sir M., 121
Napier, C., Maj. (later Gen. Sir Charles), 3
Napoleon, Emperor, 6
Neame, L., Lieut., 138
Neighbour, W., Pte., 34
Nelson, H., Capt. (later Admiral Lord), 2, 6

Neve, H., Capt., 107, 161; Maj., 114
Newton, W., 2/Lieut., 130
Nixon, Sir J. E., Lieut.-Gen., 135
Noller, W. H., Q-M.-Sgt., 57
Norman, E. H., 2/Lieut., 91, 92, 98, 104, 160, 161
Nugent, C. B. P., Brig.-Gen., 27
Nunn, T. H. C., Lieut., 102, 103, 159, 165; Capt., D.S.O., 164

O'Dowda, J. W., Lieut., 63, 158
Ott, A., Pte., 81
Ott, H., Pte., 135

Pack-Beresford, C. G., Lieut., 57, 158; Capt., 84, 91, 98, 100, 160, 165; Maj., 153
Palmer, W. V., 2/Lieut., 129, 130
Parsons, E. M. K., Capt., 110
Partridge, C. E., Lieut.-Col., 49, 153
Pearson, R., L/Cpl., 25, 143
Pedley, S. H., Lieut., 44; Capt., 158; Maj., 134; Lieut.-Col., 135, 153
Pepper, W., L/Sgt., 51
Perceval J. M., Gen., C.B., 11, 43, 152
Phillips, W. C. O., Lieut., 129
Pocock, C., Pte., 99
Pole-Carew, R., Maj.-Gen., 77, 78
Pond, B., Cpl., 44
Powell, J., Cpl., 128
Preston, W. R., Gen., 43, 152
Pretorious, Fd.-Cornet, 87
Prinsloo, M., Cmdt., 83, 84
Pullman, A. H., 2/Lieut., 92, 160, 161

Ralph, T., Pte., 39, 163
Regan, J., Sgt., 62
Richardson, T. S., Sgt., 11
Richardson, W., L/Cpl., 51
Riddle, E. V., Lieut., 104
Roberts, F. S., Fd.-Marshal Lord, V.C., 51, 65, 75, 78-82, 88, 112; Earl, 139
Roberts, Pte. (2nd. Bn.), 86
Robinson, E. J., Maj., 29, 32, 157, 143
Robinson, P. M., Lieut., 158; Capt., 166; Maj., 153, 166
Roche, R. J., Hon. Lieut., 21, 32, 35, 157, 158; Hon. Capt., 103
Roe, W., Pte., 25, 143
Rogers, H. G., Sgt.-Maj., 129
Romney, Lord, 6
Ross, Mr., 48
Ross, W. C., Lieut.-Col., 115
Rowe, W. E., Lieut., 39, 157, 158; Maj., 65, 67-69, 72, 115, 116, 120
Rundle, Sir H. M. L., Maj.-Gen., 53; Lieut.-Gen., 77-81, 83, 84
Russell, C., L/Cpl., 135

Saddler, M., Q-M.-Sgt., 25, 162
Safford, D. J. D., Lieut.-Col., 15, 48, 153; Col., 43, 152
Sangster, T. A. G., Lieut., 35, 157, 158
Sands, W., Pte., 95

Satterthwaite, E., Lieut.-Col.-Cmdt., V.D., 110, 155; Col., 124, 125, 139
Saunders, W., Cpl., 100
Sawers, J., Lieut., 109, 160
Scott, A. T., The Venerable, 136
Sellings, W., Pte., 87, 148
Sewell, D. C. C., Lieut., 137
Seymour, Sir B., Admiral, 20
Sharp, J., Sgt., 44, 51
Sheppard, H., Sgt., 165; Col.-Sgt., 163
Sheppard, J., Cpl., 128, 135
Simpkins, H., Pte., 39, 163
Smith, E., Pte., 107, 148
Smith, G., Pte., 25, 143
Smith, J., Pte., 81
Smith, J. Taylor, Rt. Rev., 111, 129, 136, 138
Smith, T. P. C., Lieut., 47, 158
Smith, W., Pte., 117, 128, 131
Smith-Dorrien, H. L., Maj.-Gen., 79
Smithers, L., Lieut., 138
Smuts, J. C., Asst.-Cmdt.-Gen., 100
Smyth, Sir H. A., Lieut.-Gen., 46
Smyth, The Hon. Sir. L., Gen., 49
Snelgrove, J. S. N., Lieut., 136
Snow, H. W., Lieut., 69
Spence, J., Col., 107
Spencer, C. H., Sgt., 95
Spooner, J., Cpl., 44, 51; Sgt.-Maj., 138
Stanhope, A. P., Earl, 55, 110, 111
Stanhope, The Hon. C. B., Maj., 3
Stephenson, Sir, F. C. A., Lieut.-Gen., 39, 40
Stevenson, G. E. de St .C., 2/Lieut., 160; Lieut., 126, 129
Stewart, Sir H., Brig-Gen., 34, 35
Steyn, President, 75, 83, 96
Stokes, F. S. F., Brig.-Gen., 117
Style, R. C., Lieut., 158; Capt., 61, 62, 158; Maj., 114, 153; Lieut.-Col., 118, 129-132, 153
Styles, G., Pte., 81, 165
Sullivan, D., Pte., 62
Swinbourne, S., Pte., 35, 143
Sydney, Lady, 5

Taylor, G., Sgt., 51
Taylor, W. H., Pte., 11
Tewfick, Khedive of Egypt, 20, 28, 29
Thompson, J., Maj.-Gen., 19
Thorne, A., Col.-Sgt., 148, 159, 165
Thwaites, Sir, W., Maj.-Gen., 167
Tollman, J., Sgt., 57, 144
Tucker, J., Pte., 95, 148
Tudway, R. J., Lieut.-Col., 76
Tugwell, W. B. P., 2/Lieut., 92, 160
Tulloch, R. M. G., Lieut., 90, 92, 159
Turner, A. C., Civ.-Surgeon, 81, 88
Turner, W. E., Sgt.-Maj., 76, 159
Turpin, H., Pte., 111, 148
Tweedie, J. L., Lieut.-Col., 32, 37, 38, 41, 157, 162; D.S.O., 45, 50, 153

Twisleton-Wykeham-Fiennes, J. T., 2/Lieut., 90, 92, 159; Capt., 127, 130

Umfreville, P., Capt., 103

Valder, H., Pte., 81
Venables, E. F., Capt., 102, 158, 160, 161
Victoria, H.M. Queen, 13, 14, 42, 48, 52, 53, 65, 103, 107, 130
Vile, T., Pte., 101

Walker, M., Maj.-Gen., V.C., 44
Walter, W., The Right Hon., 5th Earl of Dartmouth, 55
Ward, A., Cpl., 70
Ward, E. W. D., Mr., 128
Warner, C. E., Maj., 125
Warner, J., Sgt., 62, 144
Watney, C. N., Lieut. (Capt. in Vols.), 108 160; Lieut.-Col., T.D., 155
Weeks, H., Cpl., 43
Wellington, Duke of, 3
Western, W. G. B., Lieut., 158; Maj., 59, 61, 158, 163; 67, 84, 87, 88, 160, 164; Brev.-Lieut.-Col., 164; Lieut.-Col., 91, 97, 99-101, 163; C.B., 119, 166; Brev.-Col., 121, 153
White, E., L/Cpl., 111, 148
White, E., Pte., 78
Whitehouse, J. H., Lieut., 137
Wilhelm II (German Emperor), 130
Wilkie, Hales, Brev.-Col., 12, 152; Maj.,-Gen., 45, 46, 50
William IV, H.M. King (see Clarence, Duke of)
Williams, C. S., Lieut.-Col., V.D., 155; Col., 138, 154
Williams, E. C. I., Lieut.-Col. (The Buffs), 88, 89, 91, 98, 99
Williams, E. M., Lieut., 35-37, 143, 158
Willis, G. H. S., Lieut.-Gen., 21, 24, 25
Willis, W. J., Col.-Sgt., 61, 163
Wilson, A. E., Lieut.-Col., 95
Wilson, Sir C. W.. Col., 35
Wilson, Sir T. S., Lieut.-Gen., Bt., 2
Wilson, Sir S. M., Bt., 55
Wintour, F., Lieut., 32, 35, 36, 157, 158; Brev.-Maj., 162, 166; Maj., 76; Brev.-Lieut.-Col., 164
Wodehouse. J. H., Brig.-Gen., 65
Wolseley, Sir G. J., Gen. (later Fd.-Marshall Viscount), 21-27, 31, 33-37
Wolfe, J.. Gen., 139
Woulfe-Flanagan. R. J., Capt., 76, 88. 98. 159. 165
Wyllie. H.. Lieut., 109
Wynyard, M., Capt., 21, 157; Maj., 18

York. H.R.H., Duke of (see Cornwall and York)

www.ingramcontent.com/pod-product-compliance
Lightning Source LLC
Chambersburg PA
CBHW031142160426
43193CB00008B/228